CASTRATION

castration (kas•trā′shen), *n.* [from an Indo-European root meaning "cut" or "knife"] 1. agricultural technology—first developed in Stone Age Eurasia, but found later in many Old and New World civilizations—for improving selected domesticated animal and human males by removing their testicles 2. social practice (strongly associated with slavery) for preserving purity of breeds, races, and dynasties 3. legal or pseudo-legal punishment (usually for violations of local sexual customs) 4. contraceptive surgery, producing sexually active but infertile males 5. religious sacrifice (at first involving actual genital mutilation, later allegorized to mere celibacy) that seeks to approach the divine by transcending the biological imperatives of reproduction and the social constraints of lineage 6. censorship of printed texts by excision of offensive passages, thereby preventing the reproduction of heretical religious (later, sexual) ideas 7. psychoanalytic concept (developed by Sigmund Freud in the period 1908–1939) that posits that all human children believe that females are males who have had their genitalia completely cut off as a punishment for their perverse desires 8. any action or behavior that makes a male more like a female (physiologically or culturally) 9. manipulation of the human genome by artificial circumvention of heterosexual biological reproduction

CASTRATION

An Abbreviated History of Western Manhood

GARY TAYLOR

ROUTLEDGE
New York and London

Published in 2000 by
Routledge
29 West 35th Street
New York, NY 10001

Published in Great Britain by
Routledge
11 New Fetter Lane
London EC4P 4EE

Routledge is an imprint of the Taylor & Francis Group.

Printed in the United States of America on acid-free paper.

10 9 8 7 6 5 4 3 2 1

Library of Congress Cataloging-in-Publication Data

Taylor, Gary, 1953–
    Castration : An Abbreviated History of Western Manhood / Gary Taylor.
    p. cm.
Includes bibliographical references and index.
ISBN 0-415-92785-4
    1. Castration complex. 2. Masculinity. 3. Men—Psychology. I. Title.

BF175.5.C37 T39 2000
155.3'32—dc2   00-029105

in dedication to

Celia R. Daileader

for asking unaskable questions
for opening the locked ward door
for teaching me how not to drown

CONTENTS

Insets: Words *(12),* The Castration Plot in A Game at Chess *(25),*
Leave It to Beaver *(47),* Codpieces *(59),* Political Characters in
A Game at Chess *(74),* A Man's Purse *(106),* The Female
Eunuch: Aristotle *(114),* The Female Eunuch: Germaine Greer
(118), Beards *(150),* Circumcision and Anti-Semitism *(164),*
The End of Castration? *(214)*

TIMELINE

c. 20,000 B.C.E.	Finger sacrifice
c. 7500 B.C.E.	Domestication of sheep and goats
c. 6200 B.C.E.	Domestication of cattle
c. 4500 B.C.E.	Castrated cattle and sheep
c. 4000 B.C.E.	First castrated humans? Uruk?
c. 1848 B.C.E.	Mesopotamian deity Ishtar "makes eunuchs"
c. 1650 B.C.E.	Mythical eunuch rescues Ishtar from the under-world
c. 1200 B.C.E.	Assyrian law punishes sodomy with castration
c. 750 B.C.E.	Cybele cult already established in Phrygia
415 B.C.E.	Self-castrated priests documented in Cybele cult
c. 28–33	Ministry of Jesus
c. 85	The Gospel according to Matthew
c. 209	Origen of Alexandria castrates himself
c. 240	Valesius founds Christian sect of compulsory castration
313	Emperor Constantine legalizes Christianity
325	Council of Nicaea condemns self-castration
385	Pope Siricius condemns sexual intercourse of priests with their wives
399	First eunuch consul (Eutropius)
c. 403	First known castrated Christian chorister
410	Sack of Rome

413–427	Augustine of Hippo composes *The City of God*
552	Narses (Byzantine eunuch general) defeats Goths in Italy
c. 1106–1108	Theophylaktos composes his *Defence of Eunuchs*
c. 1109	Castration of Abelard in Paris
1139	Second Lateran Council abolishes clerical marriage
c. 1146–1187	Founding of society of eunuchs to guard Tomb of the Prophet Muhammad
1453	Byzantium falls to Ottoman armies
1492–1496	Europeans encounter Carib castration-cannibalism
1520	Luther compares clerical celibacy to self-castration of priests of Cybele
1599	First acknowledged castrati in Papal Choir
c. 1607	First Western eyewitness account of eunuchs in Ottoman seraglio
1624	Middleton's *A Game at Chess* written and performed
1721	Debut of most famous musical castrato, Farinelli
1772	First official notice of self-castrating Russian cult (Skoptsy)
1823	First animal vasectomy
1894	First human vasectomy
1908	Freud formulates *Kastrationskomplex*
1933	Nazi "Law for the Prevention of Genetically Diseased Offspring"
1952	First human sex-change operation
1978	Birth of first test-tube baby
1998	First cloned mammal (sheep)
2000	First complete draft of human genome
20??	First cloned human

What Does Manhood Mean?

It is somewhat difficult, I must confess, to talk of eunuchs, without saying something that may shock the modesty of the fair sex.

—*Charles Ancillon, 1707*

"*My* boyfriend's been fixed."

This defiant boast—spoken by a twenty-nine-year-old woman at a Christmas party in New York near the end of a millennium—equates a sterilized man with a castrated animal. In place of the intrusive and deliberately shocking "boyfriend," the noun we expect is "dog" or "cat." A household pet, loved, groomed, even spoiled, but also tamed, dependent, domesticated. Likewise, although the notorious refrain of a 1999 hit single by Christina Aguilera—

I'm a genie in a bottle
gotta rub me the right way

—never implies that the female singer wants to be fixed up with someone who's been "fixed," it does demand of a lover what it doesn't take a fully equipped *man* to supply. You don't need testicles to rub your woman the right way.

Of course, mainstream popular music generally does its best to suppress or ignore this awkward fact. In interviews, Aguilera tried to pretend that "rub me" just meant "treat me," without any specific physical referent at all. Genital stimulation by a man, manually, was admitted as a possibility, only in order to be explicitly banished—and lesbian lovemaking never dared to cross the MTV threshold. Long before Aguilera, the Pointer Sisters had yearned for "a lover with a slow hand," but although such hands come in both male and female flavors the song insisted on "a man." Likewise, in their 1992 mock-gospel "Sex Is Strong So Believe in It," the hiphop group Snap brags, "I'm clever with my tongue," but any cunnilingual ambiguity is immediately foreclosed by the deep male voice singing the lyrics.

What is implicit in the Pointer Sisters, or Snap, or the singsong heteroteen Christina, the thirty-something bisexual Tori Amos shakes in your face.

> if you want inside her
>> well,
> boy you better make her raspberry swirl

That "boy" is as taunting as it used to be when employed as a racial epithet, but the target is no longer racial. White men are boys, too; every man is just a boy; the only man here is the female writer/singer ("I'm her man"). In a VH1 interview, she looks straight at the camera and tells her male rivals that this song is "going to kick your ass." Tori Amos challenges any male, any "boy," to compete with her for the female sex object they both desire. Hey, it doesn't take testicles, or a penis, to swirl a woman's "raspberry." And when it gets down to hand-to-hand erotic combat, who could compete with an oral and digital virtuoso like Tori Amos? "Things are getting des-desperate"—she rocks, backed by her male band, hammering her grand piano, or sitting between piano and electric harpsichord, facing the audience, legs apart, simultaneously fingering both instruments— "when all the boys can't be men." (This is a preacher's daughter from North Carolina.) Describing her performances, a male graduate student concluded, "She's a bit too much woman for me." Yessir. Which is why, although Tori Amos is arguably the sexiest woman on the planet, most of the fans who show up to see her in the flesh ("star-fuckers," as she puts it) are female. Men, in general, don't have the balls.

"What does woman want?" Sigmund Freud wondered.

(Well, obviously, dummy, it varies from woman to woman, and within the same woman from hour to hour, just as with men; but if we are going to generalize about "woman" not as multinational CEO or soccer mom but about "woman" qua ovulating human in sexual mode, then:)

What does woman want?

A eunuch.

Not the way you think, not the way Freud meant. Women do not want to "castrate" men, in the classic psychoanalytic sense; in my experience most of them do not want to *be* men, and in my experience most of them do not *hate* men, either. (Ex-wives excepted.) And although a tongue or a finger can give the clitoris a mighty fine time, most women still seek men as sexual partners, presumably because their biological wiring inclines them to accept Germaine Greer's assessment that "a clitoral orgasm with a full cunt is nicer than a clitoral orgasm with an empty one."

No, when I say that woman-qua-sexual-being wants a eunuch for a lover, I mean *eunuch* absolutely precisely: She wants a sterile human being with a penis. A sterile human being with a penis needn't be "impotent" in either a sexual or a social sense. Indeed, the boyfriend of my opening anecdote, the one who had been "fixed," was neither sexually dysfunctional nor socially disempowered; otherwise, he would never have been trumpeted in competitive party-talk. Few women would envy another woman for having an *impotent* boyfriend. But in New York in the late twentieth century, a young professional woman could count on other young professional women to envy her for having a *sterile* boyfriend. The logic of this party exchange presumes that desire is mimetic, that women want "what other women challenge and possess." At the junction of millennia, what some other women have is a eunuch in the bedroom. Increasingly, the most attractive and ambitious women in our culture suffer not from penis envy, not even from pregnancy envy, but from eunuch envy: They envy other women whose boyfriends are sterile.

Why sterile? Because one orgasm per baby is not a pleasure/reproduction ratio that appeals even to women who do want children—and an increasing minority of women don't want children at all. (And for the planet's sake we should all get down on our knees and thank them for their voluntarily vacant wombs.) Do you think it's an accident that the campaign for birth control was fought by women?—publicly by propagandists like Marie Stopes and Margaret Sanger, privately by innumerable wives in boudoir bickering with their husbands. Most of the time, most women want sex without reproductive consequences. Pregnancies disrupt a woman's life far more than they disrupt a man's. Historically, and still, most contraceptives are unreliable, and/or intrusive, and/or a woman's burden and responsibility. So, from a sexual woman's point of view, most or all of the time, "nothing could be finer than a baby-free vagina."

All that has always been true. What has changed is the sexual balance of power, expressed in Christina's lyric imperative ("*gotta* rub me") and in Tori's taunting threat ("boy *you better* make her raspberry swirl"). These women are demanding. Why shouldn't they be? In the aftermath of what I will call in this book "the fall of the scrotum"—an event far more momentous than the fall of the Berlin Wall—the whole logic of sexual relations is changing. The old psychosociosexual system was geared to reproduction, to the union of testicles and ovaries; the goal of intercourse was a shared product, a child with two parents, and a woman could earn respect and affection and even a measure of power for her fertility. Fertility no longer yields such reliable dividends. In 1990, for the first time, American households without children outnumbered households with them; 20 percent of the baby boomer generation remains childless; by 2010, the number of married couples without children is expected to increase by another 50 percent. What most men want, nowadays anyway, most of the time, is their own personal sexual pleasure. And if that is what a man expects, then a woman has every right to expect the same. If not a child for both, then pleasure for both. If the old alliance of testicles and ovaries no longer holds, then the clitoris demands equal rights with the penis.

These clitoral women can afford to be demanding because they are protected by the law, by their own educations, by their economic independence (in some countries, at least). So Alanis Morissette can scorn a man who imagines he will play literal "meal ticket" to her "puppet," who "took me out to wine dine 69 me but didn't hear a damn word I said"; such men are anachronisms, they never expected a doll to become "a zillionaire," they weren't prepared for a mere girl, "a child," to "come back with my army and this ammunition on my back." Indeed, in her second album, anyone who dines with Morissette had better appreciate that she "could buy and sell this" restaurant. By 1999 she was literally playing God.

As long as men monopolized the meal tickets, they were pretty much guaranteed admission to the bedroom. No matter how ugly, boring, crass, or cruel, a man could count on getting his piece of the great pussy pie—because every woman needed a man to support her, and there were only so many men to go around. But, as the Elizabethans loved to say, "It is not now as when Andrea lived." Today, most American women can buy their own meals; more and more can buy their own bedrooms, and the homes to go with them, too. Such women can shop for men. And when a woman is doing the sexual shopping, a man had better package himself well, or he ain't gonna get bought.

Or stay bought. A lot of men, lately, get returned to the store. For instance, among the healthy divorce statistics in the last year of the millennium is the case of a well-educated, good-looking, ambitious young woman in Texas who left her husband. He was your classic corporate asshole who made more money than she did and kept nagging her to give up her piddling academic career. Within months of the divorce she got a tenure-track job and a "boy toy" (her phrase), a graduate student several years younger than herself. She now finds herself just staring at his body as he discourses about his latest cogitations; on one of these occasions, he stopped in mid-sentence and said, "You haven't heard a word I said, have you?" I don't think he realized he was quoting Alanis Morissette.

Early feminist theorists—particularly Lacanian feminist film critics—spoke of "the male gaze" as though only men had optical equipment. Women have eyes, too, and in cultures where they are allowed and empowered to use them, gals can survey the goods on display, just as guys do. Men now find themselves, increasingly, the objectified object of the appraising female gaze. Teenage males already know this. My three sons and their friends tell me all about it. They've heard girls in the high school cafeteria rating various guys on their butts, pecs, hair, clothes, moves. Among adults, as more women enter the workplace, more men have to regard the office as a fashion runway, where how they strut their stuff will determine whether they take off (sexually or professionally). Men constitute an increasing fraction of the patients who entrust their fates and faces to the cosmetic surgery industry. In some recent Hollywood films, naked male chests and naked male buttocks are more lovingly foregrounded than their female counterparts. The meat market is now a free market.

And eunuchs are a hot commodity. Not just because they are sterile. In 1972, in *The Persian Boy,* Mary Renault made a sensitive eunuch the protagonist of a historical fiction (still in print) that became a cult classic; in 1982, the hero of *Cry to Heaven*— by another popular novelist, Anne Rice—was a castrated bisexual; a gorgeous hetero castrato dominates the eye-catching ear-thrilling award-winning film *Farinelli* (1994). During the eighties, led by Calvin Klein, the advertising industry began to market male beauty with images drawn from America's gay subculture. Those images are, as often as not, languidly beautiful, silken, androgynous. Insofar as they define a new male ideal, they do so in terms that, like the eunuch, deliberately blur gender boundaries. Straight mainstream men pierce their ears; some even wear nail polish (two body modifications hysterically reviled in earlier periods). Even among athletes, jungle-thick chest hair has become unfashionable. Stud lifeguards secretly rub baby oil on their thighs to keep the skin soft. An emotional openness once gendered feminine is demanded of husbands and boyfriends—who are trashed if they fail the sensitivity test. Increasingly, the male of the female erotic gaze resembles a eunuch: a beautiful hairless permanent boy. Lots of women prefer the adolescent vulnerability of Leonardo DiCaprio or Brad Pitt to a testosterone-fest like Arnold Schwarzenegger.

So do many men. Because, of course, the erotic gaze need not be heterosexual. The centuries-slow ebb of the reproductive imperative has licensed a panoply of heteromarital "perversions" once condemned by church and state: vaginal intercourse during pregnancy, vaginal intercourse during menstruation, the rhythm method, various prosthetic forms of birth control (like the vasectomy by which a boyfriend is "fixed"). All these practices seek, and validate, sterile sex, and do so in a manner specifically heterosexual. But other practices that guarantee sex without pregnancy—mutual manual masturbation, fellatio, cunnilingus, anal intercourse—are not anatomically restricted to couples composed of one he and one she; they can be performed, just as easily and just as pleasingly, by he-pairs or she-pairs. A lot of the sexual activities enacted, on any given night, by couples we call "heterosexual" are also being performed that night by couples we call "homosexual." (They might be better described, using a less loaded term common in scientific descriptions of other species, as "isosexual"). Whole genres of "straight" porn specialize in these nonvaginal variations, and every new sex survey demonstrates the spread of such pleasures, the delta of Venus widening outward toward the open sea of unboundaried eroticism. Indeed, the most famous, best-documented, and historically significant sexual activities of the 1990s—the carnal encounters of Bill Clinton with Monica Lewinsky—never included vaginal congress. To the extent that such nonreproductive sex acts become commonplace, legitimate, even normative, the boundaries between heterosexuality and isosexuality shift, wobble, evaporate. The AIDS epidemic has only intensified this meltdown: By making dangerous the very exchange of bodily fluids upon which reproduction depends, it has increased the demand for semen-free sex. Likewise, by hyping the hymen, fundamentalist chastity movements in effect license everything that leaves it intact. Hence the rise of the "virgin slut" (male or female), who will try anything except vaginal intercourse. What was once the only sinless form of sex has become the only sexual sin.

Nonreproductive genital stimulation is older than our species; other primates practice it. But Michel Foucault seems right to detect a critical transformation, since the Renaissance, in the social character of such practices. By the middle of the eighteenth century, male sodomites ("unsexed male-misses") were being reviled in terms that no longer distinguished between penetrator and penetratee. What was once a miscellany of condemned practices had begun to become an identifiable "species" of person, an identity, one created not by involuntary physical marking (like the eunuch) but by cultural self-signing ("their manners, airs, lisp, skuttle, and, in general, all their little modes of affectation"). Although not literally castrated, the isosexual nevertheless practices, by choice, systematically, what the *ancien régime* of reproduction would categorize as "unsexed" sex.

By the late twentieth century, such castrated sensualities had come to seem, to some, not deviant but foundational. Eve Sedgwick reconceptualizes heterosexuality as a subsidiary formation, governed by the dominant homosocial and homoerotic relationships between men; Marjorie Garber, endorsing Freud's description of the "polymorphous perversity" of the infant, insists upon "the universal bisexuality of human beings"; Lee Edelman criticizes Freud's interpretation of a crucial episode in the Wolf Man case (where the child had seen the father penetrating the mother from behind, and therefore perhaps anally), but he accepts Freud's assertion that a child sees the mother as a castrated man, and thereby concludes that the "primal scene" establishes and presupposes "the imaginative priority of a sort of proto-homosexuality," with heterosexuality a "later" "compromise." Like Foucault's own *History of Sexuality*, these theories, all published in the last fifteen years of the millennium, challenge the "natural" primacy of male-female intercourse: Hetero-sexuality becomes just one late and suspect item on the bedroom menu. Whether or not this new queer essentialism is any more accurate, as a description of the world, than the heteronorm it aspires to displace, the mere promulgation of such theories among intellectual elites indicates how low the scrotum has fallen. In the new sex order, not only do full testicles confer no evident erotic advantage; they have actually become a suspect handicap. A castrated male, or another woman, may make a woman's raspberry swirl more ecstatically.

This is a specter that has haunted men for centuries: the fear that manhood will become, or has already become, obsolete, superfluous, ridiculous, at best quaint, at worst disgusting. Nowadays, you can buy a vibrating dildo (discreetly labeled a "muscle massager") in a novelty shop in your local mall. After the invention of the portable electric penis—even before the coming of the clone—who needs men anymore?

American males who insist on calling themselves "real men" acknowledge and defy this threat. Susan Faludi, reporting on self-help meetings for wife beaters, summarizes their worldview in one sentence: "Men cannot be men, only eunuchs, if they are not in control." Real men, an embattled minority, emphatically distinguish themselves from the millions of fake men or half-men who have been "castrated" by so-called feminazis. Tori Amos epitomizes the women such men revile: powerful, talented, pan-sexual, unsubmissive—and is probably most famous for an autobiographical song about being raped ("me and a gun and a man on my back"). Rape, of course, like domestic violence, is a form of terrorism, intended to empower the perpetrator and humiliate the victim. Some men feel so unmanned by women like Tori Amos that they can only preserve their fragile masculinity by means of a prosthetic penis-pistol. But by singing her rape song, the invaded survivor refuses to shut up, refuses to be per-manently terrorized; she unrapes herself, and others. The rapist can prevent such a reversal only by killing his victim. But he can't kill *all* the women on the planet, after all, and nothing short of gynocide could free him from his impotence. If women survive and refuse to be silenced, then the rapist's artifically inflated manhood lasts only as long as it takes to inject his pathetic milliliter of sperm into an unwelcoming orifice. If that's masculinity, then vibrators are a definite improvement.

But why should men be threatened by plastic penises? As Germaine Greer insisted, "A man is more than a dildo." Every man is more than his genitalia. Most animals retract the penis into the body when it isn't in use; they become, as it were, part-time eunuchs. Unfortunately, we haven't learned to do that yet. But when a man is not actually having sex, psychologically and socially he should (and can) tuck his unemployed cock in his pocket, reverting to the status of a neuter human, relating to other neuter humans in sexually neutral terms. When he wants to be sexual, of course, he can take it back out. But, even then, it serves its sexual function whether it's loaded with spermatozoa or not. And it's never the only tool in his box. A eunuch has, in addition to that sterile dildo-dick, two hands and a mouth, muscles and skin, eyes, tears, laughter, a voice, a mind. The measure of sexual manhood is the ability to deploy those varied assets to make yourself more attractive than a vibrator, more attractive than all the other erotic options available to any desirable sexual partner. A penis-being who has freed himself from the biological demands of his testicles, who no longer limits his sexual identity or imagination to sperm delivery, can create and sustain spirals of excitement, vortices of reciprocal engagement. That is not impotence, but power.

In declaring this, I mark myself as one of those fake men so despised by the real ones. Few readers will be surprised to discover that I am the "boyfriend" fixed in my opening anecdote. In 1980, after the birth of my second child, I got a vasectomy. Since then I have adopted two more children, but I have stopped siring offspring of my own. I have not stopped having sex. But to me it seemed then, and still seems now, immoral to overreproduce; other methods of birth control interfere with sexual spontaneity and pleasure or require much more intrusive and dangerous interventions in the female reproductive system. So, two decades ago, I let a surgeon take a knife to my testicles, in order to ensure that I could no longer impregnate anyone. For two decades, I have lived the life of a eunuch, an artificially sterile male. I am today a happily manufactured man. Contented castrated.

I do not intend to ignore the technical distinctions between vasectomy and other forms of castration, but for most men those distinctions don't matter. Hence their unpersuadable irrational resistance to a cheap outpatient operation that guarantees ever-ready contraception (and lets you indulge your most sensitive and eager member without having to wrap it in plastic). You aren't going to get many men to volunteer for a vasectomy if they equate it with radical genital amputation. Whatever its form, self-castration remains, for the male majority, simply incomprehensible. As the rhetoric of "real men" demonstrates, the uncastrated do not even know what to call a castrated human being. He resists definition. Is he still male? Is it still human?

That bewilderment did not originate in the 1990s; it has a long, loud, angry history. One of the first literary descriptions of the castrated—in a Mesopotamian myth between three thousand and four thousand years old—culminates in a curse.

> I shall curse you with a mighty curse!
> I shall decree for you a fate never to be forgotten.
> The scrapings of the city's ploughs shall be your food,
> The city drains your only drinking place,
> The shadow of a wall your only standing place,
> The threshold steps your only sitting place!
> Drunkard and thirsty both shall smite your cheek!

Real men have been raging against unreal men for millennia.

How can we possibly overcome the rage, confusion, or depression of contemporary men without understanding that history? Such emotions—like the overpowering suicidal panic that landed me in a locked psychiatric ward three years ago—originate in the perceived gap between actions and definitions.

How can a man know how he should *act* without knowing what he should *be*? And how can anyone "be a man" without knowing what the word *man* means? To begin with, does it mean

Words

According to *The Oxford English Dictionary*, the verb *castrate* is first recorded in English in 1613, though the noun *castration* dates from at least the early fifteenth century; both originate in the Latin verb *castrare*. That Latin verb is itself presumably related to the Hebrew word *sārîs*, meaning "eunuch," and to the Sanskrit word *nirasta* or *asri*, meaning "knife"; these different words in different languages almost certainly derive, independently, from the same ancient Indo-European word. Likewise, the old Germanic English word *carve* originally meant "cut"; its specific technical meanings in the sixteenth and seventeenth centuries included "circumcise" and "castrate." *Emasculation* and related forms—from Latin *emasculare*, derived from the noun for "diminutive male"—are later transfers into English, first recorded with the meaning "gelding of a man" in 1623. The commonest English word, until the twentieth century, would have been *geld* (from a Saxon root that also appears in Old Norse, Dutch, and German dialect); this appears in English by 1300 and supplies the verb in Wyclif's fifteenth-century translation of Matthew 19:12. The verb *unman*, in the medical sense "castrate," is first recorded in the 1610 translation of Augustine's *Of the City of God*, but the related Latin *evirate* and *eviration* came into English in 1603. (Shakespeare never uses *castrate* or *castration* or *emasculate* or *evirate* at all and never uses *unman* or *carve* in the relevant senses, but *geld* and its derivatives appear thirteen times in his works.)

"male" or "human"? In either case, it does not seem to mean anymore what it once meant. In 1942, a character in Albert Camus' *The Stranger* could declare that "everyone knows what it means" to be "a man." But even in 1942, that was probably ironic: When someone asks you, "What does that mean?" you cannot logically answer, "Everyone knows," because the questioner obviously does not know. Certainly, six decades later, most men's experiences do not fit the definition of *man* we have inherited. Is that because something has gone wrong with the world or because something was always wrong with the word? Every man's self-assurance, his sense of ethical and practical direction, depends upon a definition, a point of orientation outside himself—whether he identifies that personal North Pole as the tradition of a people or the biology of a species or the commandment of a god. Consequently, whenever we lose our way we retrace our steps until we can realign ourselves in relation to that magnetic point of orientation.

I have written this book in an effort to reorient myself (and other men, including my sons) by retracing the steps that have led us to this mess. Because actions depend upon definitions, this is a book about meanings. It is organized conceptually (like a dictionary, in which one definition follows another). In order to answer the question "What does it mean to be a man?" I am asking, "What does it mean to be castrated?" That may seem like an odd way to proceed, but it has a distinguished philosophical history. In one of Plato's earliest dialogues, Socrates is reported to have said, "What I mean I may explain by an illustration of what I do *not* mean."

The nature and culture of maleness is, after all, a dauntingly large territory to map. Who could possibly, in one lifetime, master the whole history of every word (in every language) or every social practice (in every civilization) relevant to a definition of manhood? Obviously, I must cut the subject down to a manageable size. "Man" is a large category; "eunuch" is, by comparison, a small one. Fortunately, the small category implies the larger one. By helping us to identify what a man is *not*, the eunuch clarifies what a man *is*.

So, what does it mean to be castrated? For one thing, it means—in our culture—not being a Christian. My voluntary vasectomy automatically excommunicated me from the Roman Catholic church in which I had been raised. Castration has in fact been deeply entangled in the central beliefs and practices of Christianity for two thousand years. And that makes sense, because any attempt to understand the relationship between God and man must assume or construct a definition of *man*.

What then doth all that which remained of him after his gelding signify? Whither is that referred? The meaning of that now?

Saint Augustine—the most influential of all Christian theologians—asked these outraged, uncomprehending questions almost sixteen centuries ago, in the twilight of the Roman Empire. He was describing the pagan Roman "massacre of manhood" associated with the earth goddess Cybele, the "Great Mother"; her male devotees, "unmanning of themselves," made themselves "barren by their own hands." The resulting "gelded person" (who was "left neither man nor woman") is what Augustine did not know how to name, define, or explain.

Gods and goddesses come and go, but the eunuch remains. The goddess Cybele, for whom men once castrated themselves, has shrunk to the status of a footnote in a college textbook. Augustine's God, by contrast, is all around us. And his preoccupation with the meaning of castration originated in a text still familiar to hundreds of millions of readers who have never heard of Cybele, or even Augustine. In the twelfth verse of the nineteenth chapter of the first book of the New Testament, the Gospel according to Matthew, Jesus tells his disciples:

there are some eunuchs, which were so born from their mother's womb: and there are some eunuchs, which were made eunuchs of men: and there be eunuchs, which have made themselves eunuchs for the kingdom of heaven's sake.

Augustine himself, recounting in his *Confessions* the story of his own journey toward God, quoted this enigmatic passage twice. In the first centuries of Christianity, the meaning of Christ's words about eunuchs fascinated and divided devotees of the new faith. The word *eunuch* appears more than five hundred times in the surviving works of the early Church fathers. Even now, the debates about clerical celibacy that sunder Christian denominations derive in large part from different interpretations of "made themselves eunuchs for the kingdom of heaven's sake."

At the beginning of the third century the first great Christian polemicist, Tertullian, citing that passage, declared that the followers of Jesus had been "trained by God" in order to "emasculate the world." Nietzsche, at the end of the nineteenth century, agreed:

> The Church combats the passions with excision in every sense of the word: its practice, its "cure" is *castration* . . . it has at all times laid the emphasis of its discipline on extirpation (of sensuality, of pride, of lust for power, of avarice, of revengefulness.)—But to attack the passions at their roots means to attack life at its roots: the practice of the Church is *hostile to life*.

How often does "being a man" coincide with the imitation of Christ? Almost never, in my experience. Do I have to cut myself, literally or psychologically, to enter the kingdom of heaven? Some members of the Heaven's Gate cult did just that; police examining the bodies discovered that several of the men had been castrated. Whither is that referred? The meaning of that now?

Castration is bigger than Christianity, of course, or any other religion. Its most famous modern theorist, Sigmund Freud, attributed to it a meaning both secular and universal—and readers who are expecting psychoanalysis to loom large in this book will not be disappointed. Freud was entirely right when he realized that castration is fundamental to what makes us human. If you think this is a book about "other people" and about the comfortably distant past, you are wrong; this is a book about all of us (male and female, castrated or not), about the human past and present, about the posthuman future.

But castration is bigger than Freud, too. Indeed, psychoanalysis is, for me, not a solution but another problem: Why was Freud's castration theory, so obviously mistaken about both history and anatomy, nevertheless so widely accepted and influential in the twentieth century? Why, for the first time in human history, did so many people *then* want castration to mean *that*?

And Freud is not the only person to have misinterpreted castration. The eunuch attracts myths as fruit does flies. Consequently, many of my conclusions are bound to seem counterintuitive or paradoxical. Eunuchs are in fact not impotent, but powerful; they are often sexually active, and capable of erections; castration does not so much suppress eros as redirect and in some ways liberate it; castration need have nothing to do with the penis; Jesus did not mean what all modern commentaries say he meant; texts were originally "castrated" in order to regulate religion, not obscenity; women are not castrated and do not aspire to castrate men; the relationship between castration and racism is not accidental or anecdotal or limited to the American South, but fundamental and structural; circumcision is more ancient than castration; castration is not an obsolete and degrading savagery, but a humane corollary of civilization and a first, prescient technology for transcending our genetic limitations; castration, by treating people as livestock, distinguishes humans from animals.

The evidence for these propositions lies in the physiology of puberty and the history of agriculture, in censorship and cannibalism and cancer treatments, in Nazi eugenics and the mapping of the human genome, in Islamic harems and papal choirs, in nigger-lynching and bitch-hating and fag-bashing, in the operations performed on John Wayne Bobbitt and in the meat you buy at your local grocery store, in novels by Hemingway and Faulkner, Rabelais and the Marquis de Sade, in London plays, Italian operas, American science fictions, Latin satires, Greek historians, Dead Sea scrolls, paleolithic art. The answers, in other words, lie outside of any single academic discipline or any single Dewey decimal category, in what I call a "federal" intellectual space, linking different territories of knowledge into what sociobiologist Edward O. Wilson calls "consilience."

Why do we need all that, just to answer one simple question? Because the eunuch defies inherited categories and cannot be defined by any inquiry that respects them. To understand castration we need to situate each conceptual site where it occurs (Christianity, for instance) in relationship to every other conceptual site where it occurs (psychoanalysis, for instance)—and to relate such diverse sites to one another, we have to construct a multidisciplinary historical topography of male sexuality. After all, since eunuchs are created by surgically altering male genitals, "What is a eunuch?" cannot be answered without asking "What is the relationship between male genitals and male identity?"

Freud treats *Kastration* as a synonym for *Entmannung* (unmanning); for Augustine, the eunuch amputates *virilitas* (manhood) and no longer remains *vir* (a man); for both, and for our civilization as a whole, castration produces a "not-man," a marked category that assumes and requires an already existing, widely accepted, seemingly unremarkable, genitally specific definition of "man." For an anomaly cannot be understood except in relationship to the unspoken norm. The eunuch, the castrated male, has always been understood in opposition to the uncastrated male. But at the same time, the anomaly of the eunuch shadows and challenges the sexual norms of manhood. The eunuch circles the uncastrated man like a scarred satellite, eternally exiled and intimately distant, its faithful circuit illuminating and enabling us to locate that center of gravity outside itself.

The unmanned man, the eunuch, gives us a fulcrum and a focal point (and a future). But even the history of the eunuch is a dauntingly large domain. It would be easy to get lost. To keep from getting lost, I have tried to follow an injunction articulated in a Greek treatise on eunuchs, written early in the twelfth century by a bishop in the Byzantine Christian church:

> Even if some of the laws and the canons
> interdict the removing of the testicle-twins,
>   home in on the mind of the inscriptions,
> and the epoch of those laws examine,
>   and the whole expanse of circumstance behold,
> confident in the laws of rhetoric.

Like Theophylaktos, nine centuries ago, this book tries to "home in"—the Greek word can be used for a ship coming into harbor or a servant's intimate attendance on a master—and the master/home I am seeking is the meaning of these texts, "the mind of the inscriptions." And so, although every text I quote will be translated into English, I do occasionally have to call attention to the strangenesses of languages we no longer speak, the unfamiliar letters left by alien meaning-minds.

Meanings evolve, from one "epoch" to another, one "expanse of circumstance" to another. In the pursuit of meaning, we cannot ignore the history of words or the history of social worlds to which those words refer. Nevertheless, "the laws of rhetoric" compel me to organize these vast masses of disparate material into an intelligible narrative. And so, in order not to be overwhelmed by the number of epochs and circumstances pertinent to this abbreviated inquiry into abbreviated maleness, I will keep returning to three authors who wrote in three European languages: Latin Augustine (as a representative of the branch of Christianity dominant in Western Europe and the Americas), German Freud (as a representative of psychoanalysis), and an underappreciated playwright of the English Renaissance/Reformation, Thomas Middleton* (as a representative of literature). The divine, the self, and the social. Behind these three authors, uniting these three categories, is a fourth author in a fourth language: Saint Matthew and his Greek memory of Jesus.

---

* What follows does not presume any prior knowledge of Thomas Middleton or his play *A Game at Chess*. More information about both—including a plot summary of the play—can be found in the appendix (pp. 235–43).

Theophylaktos himself, who enjoins us to study the history of castration, was writing to defend one interpretation of it against others. Like Theophylaktos, both Augustine and Freud were polemical writers. (*Polemical* comes from the Greek word for "war.") That is not a coincidence. As I have argued elsewhere, human civilizations are dynamic nonlinear systems, and culture is always contested. Some feminists and pacifists might dismiss that very concept—culture as an unending series of pissing contests—as "typically male." Maybe it is. Long before the Sylvester Stallone films, my grandfather nicknamed me "Rocky" (after the then World Heavyweight champion Rocky Marciano) because, when he dandled me as an infant on his knee, I used to punch with my little fist at the massive palm of his hand. So maybe my intellect was molded by a hard-drinking truck-driving Kansan. But is a "typically male" theory of culture inappropriate to the analysis of maleness? Even if you do not accept my personal polemical theory of cultural selection, you surely have to agree that men do fight other men over the meaning of manhood. Sometimes they fight with their hands; sometimes they fight with things their hands have made. Defending their manhood, men throw at other men weapons and texts. And sometimes the losers get castrated.

Christianity, Freudianity, Humanism

> By *what authority dost thou these
> things? and who gave thee this
> authority?*
> —*Matthew 21:23*

What exactly does castration mean?
  Different things to different people.
  And the same thing to everyone.

The most famous answer to the questions posed by Augustine of
Hippo came from Freud of Vienna, fifteen centuries later. Freud
of course was not a Christian or a doctor of theology, but a
Jewish medical doctor, and in the psychoanalytic Gospel according to Dr. Freud castration has a secular meaning, a meaning not
confined to one sect or another of a Mediterranean religion, but
as universal as the difference between a penis and a vagina.
Young children will eventually notice the difference between
their own genitals and those of the other sex. To these two unde-
niable observations—the anatomical fact of genital difference
and the social fact that the difference gets noticed, usually in
childhood—Freud appends a hypothesis about how that differ-

ence, when noticed, is interpreted. Both male and female children, Freud contends, sooner or later ask themselves a question very like Augustine's: What does the girl's "lack of a penis" *mean*? And they answer that the girl's lack is "a result of castration." The female child believes that she *has been* castrated; the male child believes that he *may be* castrated. And just as the child in Freud's text asks a question that echoes Augustine's, so the emotions recorded by Freud echo the emotions recorded by Augustine. For Augustine, horror and disgust were the appropriate reactions to a castrated half-man (*quasi hominem*); for Freud, every woman's genitalia could be "regarded as a mutilated organ," with the result that they arouse "a feeling of disgust" or "horror instead of pleasure."

This childish error—the horrified conclusion that the female genitalia are just the residue left over after someone has been castrated—may later be corrected in the conscious mind, but it remains locked into the very structure of the unconscious. Freud did not formulate or articulate this "castration complex" until 1908, but it subsequently became central to his understanding of infantile sexuality, the dissolution of the Oedipus complex, the formation of the superego, the logic of fetishism, the nature of male and female sexuality, and the origins of civilization. Every significant psychoanalyst of the twentieth century, orthodox or heretical, has repeated, developed, or reinterpreted Freud's theory of castration. In America at the beginning of the twenty-first century, millions of people who have never read a word of Freud know something about the psychoanalytic emphasis on castration.

Augustine himself was an astute and unsentimental observer of childhood; the first book of his *Confessions* is our earliest surviving memoir of the pain, rage, jealousy, and raw desire of an infant. But Augustine the heretic-thumper would not have been impressed by Freud's secular answers to the riddle of castration. Psychoanalysts, in turn, are prone to interpret Christianity itself as little more than a symptom: Augustine's love of God becomes simply one particular sublimation of genital excitations that are primary and universal. Christianity and Freudianity offer us two

competing, apparently incompatible, interpretations of castration, each bound up with a theory about the origin of human
sexuality. But how can that origin be determined? How could
Aurelius Augustinus, bishop of Hippo, writing *The City of God*
between 413 and 427, know what Jesus of Nazareth had said or
meant four hundred years before? How could Freud know what
his adult patients had really been thinking and feeling years
before, when they were children? How could either man know
what castration meant?

Augustine may have been separated from Jesus by hundreds
of miles and years, but he had directly experienced eunuchs. The
"Ganymedes that were consecrated unto the said Great
Mother," who so disturbed him, "with anointed heads, painted
faces, loose bodies and lascivious paces, went even until yester-
day up and down the streets of Carthage, basely begging off the
people wherewithal to sustain themselves." Followers of Cybele
were less common on the streets of Freud's Vienna. Of course,
eunuchs can still allegedly be found in the brothels of Bombay
and the harems of Morocco; as late as 1971, boys were being
castrated and sold as slaves in Afghanistan. Only a few hundred
miles from Freud, unemployed Ottoman eunuchs were still
meeting on the streets of Istanbul in 1931 to reminisce about the
good old days, and Leninists were suppressing an old Russian
religious cult of self-castrators. Indeed, in 1908, the very year
that Freud in Vienna formulated and first published his castration theory, in Paris another medical doctor, Richard Millant,
published a description of "eunuchs through the ages" (volume
thirteen of a series called "Sexual Perversions"), citing examples
from many countries and centuries. I will be looking at such
social worlds, at societies in which castration is a routine practice, later in this book; but those worlds were as foreign to Freud
as fifth-century Carthage. Freud was no ethnologist.

How then could he uncover the meaning of castration?
Freud's method resembled Augustine's. Augustine had been
trained as a teacher of rhetoric, what we would now call a professor of English, a literary critic, someone paid to teach others
how to interpret admired texts; the text he read, intensely and

profoundly, was the Christian Bible (in Latin translation). Freud, too, was primarily a lifelong interpreter of other people's texts: the narratives recounted by his patients and the canonical narratives of Western civilization. Christianity and Freudianity do not much differ in their method (allegorical reading), but they do differ profoundly in the hierarchy of texts to which that method is applied. For the definition of man, which texts are most important? Augustine's texts, or Freud's? the visions of prophets, or the dreams of patients?

Of course, Freud did not depend entirely upon the confessions of patients. Since those were confidential, and in any case came from neurotic or psychotic witnesses, theories based upon them might not be believed. Freud therefore turned to literary texts displaying similar symbolic structures in a more public form. He articulated the Oedipus complex through interpretation of a single exemplary dramatic text, *Oedipus the Tyrant*. Unfortunately, the literary sources on which Freud regularly depended did little to substantiate his castration complex. The only mythological example he could cite was the castration of Uranos by Kronos, but this myth—in which a son mutilates his father—says more about Freud's hostility to his own parent than about the parental mutilation of a child described in the castration complex. In fact, the Greek story itself derives from an old succession myth that occurs in Hittite, Hurrian, and Phoenician forms, dating back to the second millennium B.C.E.; in all its versions, the son castrates the father, not vice versa. The mechanisms of hermeneutic substitution enable psychoanalytic devotees to detect castration anxiety and castration symbolism everywhere—Freud himself, for instance, claimed that both blinding and decapitation were metaphors for castration—but in his usual literary sources Freud had trouble finding castrations as literal as the incest in *Oedipus the Tyrant*.

Freud apparently never read an exemplary dramatic text in which an actual castration is both narratively central and symbolically resonant: Thomas Middleton's allegorical play *A Game at Chess*, written and first performed in 1624. In the story Middleton tells, the White Bishop's Pawn is castrated by the

Black Knight's Pawn, his rival for the affections of the White Queen's Pawn; that castration prevents the marriage of the White Bishop's Pawn and the White Queen's Pawn, and thereby makes her susceptible to the advances of the Black Bishop's Pawn. The

The Castration Plot in *A Game at Chess*

WHITE QUEEN'S PAWN: An English virgin, and lady-in-waiting to the White Queen; literate, young, fair-skinned, blonde, and beautiful; formerly betrothed to the White Bishop's Pawn before he was castrated; ardently religous, but doctrinally uncertain, and susceptible to the advances of the Black Bishop's Pawn.

WHITE BISHOP'S PAWN: An English Puritan minister; formerly betrothed to the White Queen's Pawn, before he was castrated by his romantic rival (the Black Knight's Pawn); seeks to protect her from the Black Bishop's Pawn.

BLACK KNIGHT'S PAWN: An illiterate servant of the Black Knight; unsuccessful suitor, in love with the White Queen's Pawn; responsible for castrating his romantic rival (the White Bishop's Pawn); seeking absolution for his crime.

BLACK BISHOP'S PAWN: A Jesuit priest; confessor to the Black Knight's Pawn, White Queen's Pawn, and Black Queen's Pawn; refuses to absolve the Black Knight's Pawn for having castrated his rival; attempts to seduce, or rape, the White Queen's Pawn.

BLACK QUEEN'S PAWN: A member of the society of female Jesuits founded by the English Catholic Mary Ward; formerly seduced by the Black Bishop's Pawn, she begins the play helping him to convert the White Queen's Pawn, but later frustrates his attempted seduction and rape.

meaning of that act of "unmanning" (1.1.164) is thus central to any interpretation of the allegorical identities and relationships of those four characters. A castration sets in motion the play's entire pawn plot, which is—in a reversal of social hierarchies characteristic of Middleton—not the subplot but the main plot. So the play as a whole cannot be understood unless we understand castration.

Moreover, A Game at Chess sets castration within a frame that both Augustine and Freud would immediately have appreciated. In Middleton's play, as in The City of God, the practice of castration differentiates one religious culture from another: The Black House castrates, and the White House gets castrated. (The racial overtones of these terms are not accidental or anachronistic.) And the bulk of the play consists of the re-presentation of "a dream" (Ind. 49). For Middleton as for Augustine, dreams may afford us "a vision" of realities normally invisible to human eyes. For Middleton as for Freud, a dream can say and show things that would elsewhere be repressed; the dream is a means of evading censorship. It is also a form that must be interpreted allegorically.

A Game at Chess was the most remarkable play written by a most remarkable writer. Thomas Middleton (1580–1627) is the only contemporary of Shakespeare who created acknowledged masterpieces of both comedy (The Roaring Girl, A Chaste Maid in Cheapside) and tragedy (The Revenger's Tragedy, Women Beware Women, The Changeling), in addition to the unique history play A Game at Chess. His range extends beyond these traditional genres to tragicomedies, masques, pageants, pamphlets, epigrams, and biblical and political commentaries. Favorably compared by critics to Shakespeare and Sophocles, Jean Racine and Henrik Ibsen, he has influenced writers as diverse as Aphra Behn and T. S. Eliot. He is, in my own estimation, at least the second greatest dramatist in English. Like the author of Oedipus the Tyrant, the author of A Game at Chess produced a body of work that deserves and rewards the attention of anyone seriously interested in the Western literary imagination.

In particular, Middleton rewards the attention of anyone interested in sex. In his oeuvre, as in Freud's, castration takes its place in an ambitiously global account of human sexuality. In 1963, celebrating Middleton's return to the London stage, the theater critic Kenneth Tynan remarked that "where sexual vagaries are concerned there is more authentic reportage in *The Changeling* and *Women Beware Women* than in the whole of the [Shakespeare] First Folio." In 1990, the religious historian John Stachniewski claimed that Middleton's plays embody "the Calvinist idea of the unconscious"—an idea that is itself "the main cultural origin of what eventuated in Freudian depth-psychology." Although neither Tynan nor Stachniewski mentioned *A Game at Chess*, either could have quoted from it the following proto-Freudian defence of an attention to polymorphous perversity:

> All actions
> Clad in their proper language, though most sordid,
> My ear is bound by duty to let in
> And lock up everlastingly.
>
> (1.1.147–150)

Middleton sexed language, and languaged sex, better than any other writer in English. Ordinary heterosexual intercourse, licit and illicit, pops up everywhere in his language; his plots feature the usual parade of frustrated young lovers, casual copulators, unwed mothers, jealous husbands, adulterers, whores and whoremongers and whore managers. But he did not limit himself to the standard sexual situations. He dramatized literal incest in *The Revenger's Tragedy* and *Women Beware Women*, an adult son's obsession with his mother's sexuality in *A Fair Quarrel*, a young man's oedipal desire for the wife of his father's old friend in *The Widow*, a mother's attempt to prostitute her daughter in *The Revenger's Tragedy*, a father's pimping in *The Lady's Tragedy*. A husband literally sells his wife in *The Phoenix*; another husband has his wife abducted and blindfolded so that he can sadistically rape her in *Hengist, King of Kent*; a third husband not only acquiesces in his wife's adultery, but abets and celebrates it in *A Chaste Maid in Cheapside*. In *Your Five Gallants*, a wealthy woman regularly visits the brothel, combining voyeurism with the pleasure of occasionally letting herself be taken for a prostitute. Middleton explores the sexual fascination aroused by a male transvestite in *Microcynicon* and by a female transvestite in *The Roaring Girl*, rape in *Women Beware Women* and *The Ghost of Lucrece*, stalking and sexual blackmail in *The Changeling*; male impotence in *The Witch*, masochism in *The Nice Valour*, necrophilia in *The Lady's Tragedy*, pedophilia in *Anything for a Quiet Life*, a woman forced to eat the corpse of her adulterous lover in *The Bloody Banquet*. He created worlds wholly dominated by homosocial and homoerotic male relationships in *Michaelmas Term* and *Timon of Athens* (which he co-wrote with Shakespeare), but he also refers to explicitly heterosexual sodomy more often than any of his contemporaries. He repeatedly inventively circumvents the prohibition on performing live sex acts in the theater. In *A Mad World, My Masters* we hear a couple copulating just offstage; in *The Roaring Girl*, a woman character places a musical instrument between her legs and fingers it, in a manner that clearly mimics masturbation; in *No Wit, No Help like a Woman's*, a woman character disguised as a man exits to consummate her newly solemnized marriage with another woman character, in a manner that clearly encourages an audience to imagine lesbian sex taking place just offstage during the intermission between the acts. Such moments invite our fantasies to paint the explicit visual image that his stage could not; not surprisingly, he was also interested in the varied psychological and physiological effects of actual "dirty pictures," which he dramatized in both *Women Beware Women* and *A Game at Chess*. In Middleton's writing, sexuality saturates humanity. His no-holes-barred sexual imagination was at least as comprehensive as Freud's—and more varied tonally than the repetititive mathematical porn of writers like de Sade.

At the very end of his career, in his most popular and scandalous play, this brilliant sexual observer and theorist concentrated his attention on the mutilation of male genitals. But *A Game at Chess* does more than represent the meaning of castration for a single gifted writer. It epitomizes a period—that pivotal moment variously characterized as "the Renaissance" (for those focusing on the arts) or "the Reformation" (for those focusing on religion) or "the scientific revolution" (for those focusing on empirical exploration and discovery) or "the early modern" (for those focusing on political and social history). I prefer to unite these elements under the category "humanism." All these cultural transformations, separated by modern institutions, were fused in the life-work of Middleton and his contemporaries, educated by humanist teachers in Protestant schools, writing for an unprecedented secular entertainment industry in an emergent capitalist marketplace. *A Game at Chess* begins with a speech by the ghost of Ignatius Loyola and dramatizes the Reformation as a struggle between black and white chess pieces; it draws upon key figures of the European Renaissance, from Rabelais and Aretine to the great humanist scholar Julius Caesar Scaliger. Middleton's stepfather participated in the first English effort to colonize North America, and *A Game at Chess* critiques the first European imperial power (Spain) for its treatment of New World natives; in its incredulity about magic and miracle, in its invisible God who may or may not be manipulating the pieces on a visible chessboard, it reflects the pragmatic English gentry skepticism that helped Francis Bacon and William Harvey—in the years just before and after 1624—lay the foundations of modern science. *A Game at Chess* also made a larger profit in a shorter time than any other play of its era; written during and about the outset of the Thirty Years' War, the play represents, and contributed to, the fundamental shift from a feudal politics of faction and familial alliance to a modern politics of ideologically defined parties. In a single text, *A Game at Chess* brings together most of the elements—in religion, literature, art, philosophy, politics, economics—that transformed medieval Christendom into the modern world order.

Its treatment of male sexuality also epitomizes an era. In the thirteenth and fourteenth centuries, the Church had mobilized all its resources against the Cathar heresy, which regarded the human body—and the genitals especially—as a creation of Satan, not God; Cathars denied the corporeality of Jesus. In

reaction, the Church began systematically stressing and celebrating the incarnation of a Christ fully enfleshed, from toenails
to testicles. Painting and sculpture from the fourteenth to the
sixteenth centuries pay extraordinary tribute (documented by
art historian Leo Steinberg) to the genitals of Jesus.
Michelangelo's *Risen Christ*, for instance, stands completely,
full-frontally, unashamedly nude. But with the Counter-
Reformation shame triumphed; by order of Pope Paul IV, "many
beautiful and antique statues" in Rome were—as Montaigne
reports—"castrated."

Castrations of one sort or another particularly fascinated
humanist Europe. The noun *eunuch(s)* appears at least 240 times
in at least seventy-eight different English plays written between
1580 and the closing of the theaters in 1642; early modern synonyms for the verb *castrate* appear more than 150 times in the
plays of those decades. Actual eunuchs step in front of an audience as speaking characters in twenty-five dramatic texts written
between 1600 and 1640. From the end of the fifteenth century
to the beginning of the seventeenth, European humanists
encountered, firsthand, eunuchs in African and Asian kingdoms,
Caribbean castration rituals, and Ottoman harems. At the same
time, the enthusiasm for antiquity combined with the printing
press to ensure that most of the classical and early Christian
texts on eunuchs that I cite in this book were circulating in
humanist Europe in Middleton's lifetime. The first European histories of castration were written, in Latin, in the seventeenth
century. And many of Middleton's own ideas about castration
also surface in other English writers of his time (although only
in *A Game at Chess* do they all congregate).

None of this would matter if the meaning of castration had
always stayed the same. According to psychoanalysis, it has: The
castration complex shapes the psychological biography of every
individual, in 24 B.C.E. in Palestine or 424 C.E. in North Africa
or 1624 C.E. in England or 1924 C.E. in Austria. For Sigmund
Freud as for his contemporary Henry Ford, "History is bunk."
If Freud is right, there is no real reason to read a text about castration from 1624, because any text about castration, or any

other aspect of human sexuality, should be telling the same story. For some readers—the Harold Blooms and Camille Paglias of this world—that conviction is comforting. It assures us that we can read a text from any period, any place, and immediately understand it, without knowing anything specific about that time or that place; castration anxiety and castration symbolism pervade all texts because they pervade all minds.

A Game at Chess will not let its readers so easily escape from the intransigent grit of history. Notoriously, much of the play's plot allegorically enfigures the domestic politics and international rivalries of the early 1620s; at times, the actors impersonated actual historical individuals. Such an insistently particularized context forces us out of the perpetual present tense of psychoanalysis. What did castration mean in England in 1624? Why, there and then, did it mean so excessively much?

The uncompromisingly specific question Middleton compels us to ask—"What does castration mean *in England in 1624?*"—points us toward, and in part helps to answer, another question: What happened to male sexuality, and its representation, in the centuries between Augustine and Middleton? Those twelve centuries were the very period Michel Foucault did not live to describe in his projected five-volume *History of Sexuality*. And Foucault, like Freud, seems never to have read *A Game at Chess*. Freud and Foucault—the two most influential theorists of sexuality in the twentieth century—cannot answer these questions for us. Middleton can. Middleton can, in part, because he is literally the man in the middle, the writer at the juncture where the ancient Christian world ordained by Augustine begins morphing into the modern secular world described by Freud (and Tori Amos).

A Game at Chess should be as central to theories of castration as *Oedipus the Tyrant* has been for theories of incest. This is a claim that will, I suspect, surprise every reader of this book. Even readers who recognize the historical importance of the humanist transition would expect me to focus on Shakespeare, not Middleton. (If Shakespeare had anything to teach us about castration, we would already have learned it.) But even if you are willing to entertain my high assessment of Middleton's genius, you might reasonably object that I am attempting to do too much: to change the place of *A Game at Chess* and of Middleton in our literary and cultural canon, in the course of changing the literal and symbolic place of castration in our models of sexuality and humanness. How can one book revise, not only our models of the history of psychosexual hierarchies, but our history of literary hierarchies, too?

But how can we revise one without revising the other? *Oedipus the Tyrant* was less familiar than Sophocles' *Antigone* when Freud developed his theory of incest; the "Oedipal complex" itself accounts, in large part, for the contemporary canonicity of *Oedipus the Tyrant*. The truth is, I know of no literary work more familiar than *A Game at Chess* that encapsulates the meaning of castration as succinctly and comprehensively as it does; its text is the only possible site for the kind of excavation I am undertaking here. It is, for the history of castration, the equivalent of the Rosetta Stone: an absolutely indispensable key. In recovering and elevating this text, I am restoring to our collective memory a complex and forgotten history of sexuality—a history that would not have been forgotten if it had been preserved in one of the texts we all read in school. Indeed, one hypothesis of this book is that the two histories and hierarchies—psychosexual and cultural—are knotted together. To separate them is to tear them, and ourselves.

Three writers, three languages, three competing views of castration: the Christian theologian Augustine, the humanist playwright Middleton, the modern psychoanalyst Freud. Behind them all, chronologically and conceptually, looms Jesus of Nazareth. Augustine and Middleton were Christians; Freud (like Jesus himself) was a circumcised Jew, living (like Augustine and Middleton) in a predominantly Christian society. The Gospel according to Matthew reports that Jesus spoke of three kinds of eunuchs. Doing so, Jesus—or the evangelist who translated his sayings into Greek—used a word that existed hundreds of years before Jesus was born.

Contest of Males
The Power of Eunuchs

Blessed are they which are persecuted.
—*Matthew 5:10*

The English word *eunuch* derives from the ancient Greek word εὐνοῦχος, which is a compound of εὐνή (meaning "bed," especially "marriage bed") and ἔχω (to hold, keep, guard). Eunuchs were guardians of the marriage bed. They were qualified for that social function by being disqualified from a biological one. Aristotle, the Greek zoological philosopher, wrote a treatise on animal reproduction in the fourth century B.C.E. (which remained the best analysis of embryology until the seventeenth century); in it, he noted that "the castrated do not have the power to breed."

The power to breed—as Aristotle did not know—is what drives evolutionary change. Only those animals that reproduce pass their genes to the next generation, and populations evolve as some genes prove more successful than others in producing animals that reproduce successfully. The Darwinian struggle for survival is best understood as a struggle to breed, which—

among other things—generates sexual rivalry between males of the same species. The exact nature of that sexual rivalry is shaped by the biological, social, and environmental particulars of breeding in any given species. In mammals, where fertilization takes place within the female body, males cannot be confident of their paternity of the offspring that eventually emerge from a particular female. This epistemological problem generated one of the favorite castration jokes of the humanist Renaissance. Question: How can you know for sure that your wife is faithful? Answer: Castrate yourself. (Then if she gets pregnant, you know she's cheating on you.)

This solution, understandably, has never been popular among humans or other animals. Usually, male mammals try to solve the problem by preventing other males from gaining sexual access to a female. Hence the harem, exemplified in primates like gorillas: One dominant male monopolizes a group of females and fights off any other males who attempt to approach one of "his" females when she is in estrus (and thus impregnable). In this way the dominant male ensures that all the offspring of all "his" females carry his genes. The Swedish biologists Birgitta Sillén-Tullberg and Anders Møller have convincingly argued that the "missing-link" primate progenitor of modern gorillas, chimpanzees, and humans, nine million years ago, regulated reproduction within just such a harem system.

But the harem system did not work well for early humans, whose sexual biology differs from that of all other primates (and all other mammals). In particular, human females can and will have sex at any time during their menstrual cycle, and their ovulation is invisible to males (and, for the most part, themselves); in combination, these traits make it impossible for a male to know when his female is in estrus, and it is therefore impossible for him to guarantee his own paternity of her offspring unless he can personally guard *every* female in his harem *continuously*, day and night, every day, every night. No male in the wild could manage that. While he is busy fighting off one male from one of "his" females, behind his back another intruder male could be busily impregnating another of "his" females. Hence the human evolution of a basically monogamous mating system, which is still normative in most societies (and which includes a limited allowance for infidelity). Monogamy gives each male only a single female to guard, and thereby increases his confidence in *his* paternity of *her* children; strong emotional pair-bonds reduce the temptation to cheat and increase the incentives for shared child rearing.

But the invention of the eunuch allowed some human males to reintroduce the harem system in a new form. Because he is physiologically incapable of inseminating a female, a eunuch can be employed by one man to prevent other men from impregnating "his" women. By multiplying the number of eunuchs under his command, a dominant male can multiply the number of females he can effectively guard against impregnation by other males, and thus can increase the number of offspring that perpetuate his own genes. Having created such a genetic monopoly—a large female harem, guarded by a corps of eunuchs, and sexually accessible to him alone—a man like Morocco's emperor Mawlāy Ismāil could sire more than seven hundred sons who survived infancy (not to mention uncounted daughters, many strangled at birth); the birth of forty sons was recorded in one three-month period in 1704. Ismāil may not fit modern definitions of a good husband or a good father, but in biological and evolutionary terms he was a great gene spreader.

Such sexual monopolies could only be created and sustained through the use of human eunuchs as "guardians of the marriage bed." The eunuch was a prosthesis, a weapon used by one male in his sexual rivalry with other males: more eyes, more minds and hands, guarding all those precious uteruses. Eunuchs served that function in the ancient civilizations of both eastern and western Eurasia. They are unequivocally identified in Western legal records as early as 1305 B.C.E., and they remained prominent in the courts of eastern Mediterranean kingdoms for millennia. Within those societies, castrated males regulated reproduction by policing female sexuality. That role could not be securely entrusted to uncastrated males (who might be sexually tempted themselves) or to other women (who might be more loyal to a fellow female than to a male master). Only the eunuch makes the human harem biologically practicable.

But why could the harem be entrusted to a eunuch? The eunuch might not be able to impregnate any of the women himself, but he could certainly betray his master and allow a rival male intruder into the harem. Why should a eunuch remain loyal to the dominant male whose sexual and genetic interests he served?

Eunuch loyalty was secured by two social mechanisms. First, the eunuch's master was almost never the man responsible for cutting him. The earliest account of castration commerce, by the Greek historian Herodotus (c. 484–425 B.C.E.), described the lucrative activities of Panonius of Chios, who "would procure beautiful boys and castrate and take them to Sardis and Ephesus, where he sold them for a great price." Unfortunately, those he sold hated him for having made them "to be no man, but a thing of nought"; one of them, Hermotimus, lures Panonius into a trap and gets revenge by making the castrator castrate his own sons, who are then forced to castrate their father. Noticeably, Herotimus remains faithful to his master; his rage is safely focused on someone else.

Like the Persians, both the Romans and the Ottomans used large numbers of eunuchs for centuries, but in both these later empires castration of human males was a crime subject to severe legal penalties; as a result, the eunuchs were generally imported, having been enslaved and mutilated in "savage" societies on the periphery of "civilization." Moreover, importation made each new eunuch a vulnerable stranger in a strange land, utterly dependent on the master who fed, clothed, and educated him. Eunuch resentment was systematically separated from eunuch gratitude.

Second, the eunuch was richly rewarded for his loyalty. Only socially dominant males could afford to buy and maintain eunuchs, and within such powerful households the eunuch performed an especially intimate function. In any pyramidal social structure, power is defined in large part by access to the apex, and eunuchs served as the guardians of access, not only permitted but required to remain in close proximity to the innermost sanctum sanctorum of dominance.

Thus, although they might lack "the power to breed," eunuchs were not impotent in any other sense. Castrated human males could be exceptionally powerful. In a Sumerian myth inscribed eighteen centuries before the birth of Jesus (and probably circulated orally for generations before it was written down), the goddess Inanna was rescued from the underworld by two creatures "neither male nor female"—presumably the eunuchs with whom she is so strongly associated in all later accounts. In the world of history rather than mythology, in the Assyrian empire the chief eunuch was also commander of the royal army; two of the most successful and renowned Byzantine generals (Narses in the sixth century, Nicephorus Uranus in the tenth) were eunuchs; so was Eustathius Cymineanus, the great eleventh-century admiral. Another admiral, the Chinese eunuch Cheng-ho, led fleets carrying more than 27,000 sailors into Sri Lanka, India, Arabia, and Africa between 1405 and 1422. In the later Roman Empire—especially but not only in its Eastern half—"the real power" often lay, or was at least often thought to lie, "in the hands not of the emperor nor of his aristocrats, but of his chief eunuch." And this was not an accident of individual personalities; as the modern historian Keith Hopkins concludes, "The most significant aspect of the power held by eunuchs is its consistency, its repetitiveness from the middle of the fourth century onwards." This pattern has been repeated in other societies. In the African state of Oyo, the grand eunuch controlled access to the palace and administered justice in the king's name; the second eunuch impersonated the king at religious rituals; the third eunuch received notables in his place and impersonated him at public ceremonies; eunuchs also decided which of the king's children became his successor. The first Western eyewitness account of the sultan's seraglio in Istanbul notes that in the Ottoman state "all things, in a manner, are swayed by the discretion of the eunuch." In Persia, the palace eunuchs contrived the succession of a new shah in 1667 and effectively seized control of the state, which they governed under a string of figurehead monarchs until the fall of the Safawid dynasty.

(Hence another humanist castration joke: An early modern hick from the boondocks is so impressed by his first encounter

with Islamic civilization that—unaware of what the job entails—
he labors assiduously to get promoted to the rank of a great and
powerful . . . eunuch.)

Although the power of eunuchs began in the bedchamber, it
soon extended to the rest of the palace, and then the rest of the
empire. The Greek historian Xenophon noted that the Persian
king and conqueror Cyrus (sixth century B.C.E.) "appointed all
the guard of his person to be of gelded men," and explained the
general usefulness of eunuchs:

> It might be thought that they be weak and effeminate,
> whereas the truth is not so; for by example of other beasts,
> as horses, fierce and untractable, being gelded, leave their
> wildness, and yet be meet for the war. . . . Men likewise,
> in this case, though they be bereft of voluptuous instinct,
> yet they be not the less meet to serve, in riding, in shoring,
> in obeying, in diligent doing of their duty, and no men
> more desirous of honor than they, as appeareth in war,
> and warlike chases.

For certain specialized purposes, the eunuch was not a defective man but an improved one. Indeed, Herodotus noted that the
Persians valued castrates "more than testicled men, by reason of
the full trust they have in them."

If castrated males were for such reasons "much esteemed" in
the courts and households of the classical world, they were
equally admired for musical reasons in the Mediterranean
Christian world. When a boy is castrated before puberty,
his voice never "breaks," or deepens the usual octave.
Physiologically, such eunuchs don't develop the Adam's apple
typical of adult males; the position, form, and plasticity of the
larynx remain the same as a boy's, but the rib cage dispropor-
tionately expands, and in combination these two physical features produce a unique vocal register. The early Arab writer al-
Djāḥiẓ noted that the peculiarity of eunuch voices was recognizable by everyone. The musical potential of that peculiarity was
realized by a female contemporary of Saint Augustine: the
entourage of Eudoxia, the scheming wife of the emperor

Arcadius (395–408), included the first known Christian eunuch chorister. The social world of Eudoxia was already well supplied, for quite other reasons, with castrated males; the eunuch choir was an unanticipated useful by-product of an operation that had, for centuries, been manufacturing sexual guardians. But once recognized, the by-product became an end in itself. For a millennium, eunuch choirs remained traditional in the Byzantine Church. Medieval Christianity in Western Europe stopped producing household eunuchs, but castrati appeared in Roman Catholic choirs perhaps as early as the twelfth century, and certainly by the 1550s in Italy. Eunuchs sang better than other men.

Although such eunuchs sang Christian music, the function they performed was not intrinsically Christian, or even intrinsically religious; they were simply human musical instruments whose altered physiology made them capable of creating vocal sounds that could not be duplicated by children, women, or uncastrated men. Indeed, their musical function was eventually secularized, as castrati moved out of papal choirs and into Italian opera houses.

But castration could also sometimes serve an explicitly spiritual purpose. Christianity, a religion founded upon a wounded god, particularly valorized wounded bodies. "The root perception," as Stephen Greenblatt argues, "is that there is a link between mutilation, as a universal emblem of corporeal vulnerability and abjection, and holiness." Certainly, many early Christian martyrs were physically tortured by their persecutors; sometimes such mutilation included castration. But a number of early Christian martyrs were already eunuchs before they became Christians. Indeed, a eunuch, having already suffered a genital wound, could, by dying for his faith, redouble his claim to holiness. Finally, some Christians voluntarily "made themselves eunuchs for the kingdom of heaven's sake." The early Alexandrian theologian Origen was the most famous, but not the only, early Christian who allegedly castrated himself.

But eunuchs were not only exemplary martyrs; they were also exemplary readers. As palace functionaries, eunuchs as a class were probably more literate than the overwhelming mass of the population in ancient civilizations. A Chinese eunuch, Tsai Lun, invented the first usable writing paper. And the first gentile converted to Christianity was "an eunuch of great authority" from the kingdom of Ethiopia, which the apostle Philip converted by interpreting for him a passage from the text of Isaiah that the eunuch was reading (Acts 8:26-40). The early Church fathers repeatedly emphasized the significance of that eunuch conversion. Chrysostom and Theodoret contrasted the faith and humility of the earnestly reading eunuch with the apathy and pride of later Christians, deaf to gospels and preachers; Athanasius contrasted the eunuch's correct reading with the ignorance of Jews and false reading of heretics; Jerome saw in him a fulfillment of the prophecies of Isaiah. In the fourteenth century, the English bishop Richard of Bury recommended, as an exemplary reader, that first "all-powerful eunuch" whose "love of his book" earned him salvation.

Within this religious tradition, it is hardly surprising that the eleventh-century French philosopher Peter Abelard believed that the mutilation of his own genitals had been ordained by God and that castration had made him a better theologian: "The hand of the Lord had touched me for the express purpose of freeing me from the temptations of the flesh and the distractions of the world so that I could devote myself to learning, and thereby prove myself a true philosopher not of the world but of God." Thereafter, Abelard adopted as his personal model "the greatest of the Christian philosophers, Origen."

But unlike Origen, and unlike the worshipers of Cybele described by Augustine, Abelard had not castrated himself. Although he may have reaped spiritual rewards for his condition, he did not seek it. In this as in other respects, Abelard resembles the White Bishop's Pawn in Middleton's *A Game at Chess*. Like Abelard, the White Bishop's Pawn is apparently a member of the clerisy; like Abelard, he is regarded by his enemies as "An heretic" (1.1.155), and he is castrated in an act of "revenge." Like Abelard, the White Bishop's Pawn is ambushed and castrated by another man, who wants to stop his sexual liaison with a young woman they both love. The young woman, as a result of that castration of the man she loves, withdraws from the heterosexual economy: Abelard's lover, Heloise, became a nun, and in *A Game at Chess* the White Queen's Pawn declares, "I'll never know man further than by name" (5.2.118). In both stories, castration takes place in an explicitly religious context, structured by doctrinal and sexual rivalry.

The Latin texts of Abelard's *Historia calamitatum* and of the letters he and Heloise exchanged first appeared in print in 1616, in two different editions. No plausible source for the pawn plot in *A Game at Chess* has been identified, and I think it is likely that Middleton was influenced by the story of Abelard and Heloise, printed only eight years before. But determining Middleton's "source" is less important here than recognizing that these two closely related stories of castration both draw upon a historical tradition, a collective memory once widely shared, which Freud and most other twentieth-century interpreters of castration ignore.

All these roles of the eunuch—the harem guardian, the gifted singer, the trusted servant of emperors, the exemplary Christian—were familiar in humanist England. Take Shakespeare: In *A Midsummer Night's Dream*, singing to a harp accompaniment is a role fit for "an Athenian eunuch," and in *Twelfth Night* a modern eunuch is expected to "sing, And speak . . . in many sorts of music"; *The Two Noble Kinsmen* is even more specific, recognizing that "at ten years old"—that is, before puberty—"They must be all gelt for musicians." Shakespeare also associated eunuchs with a very specific kind of "voice" in *Coriolanus* and *Cymbeline*. But such knowledge was not restricted to Shakespeare. In 1595 Sir Richard Champernowne of Devon was accused of being "a gelder of boys for preserving their voices." In 1598, the poet Francis Rous took it for granted that a eunuch "sweetly sings"; in the same year, the playwright Ben Jonson expected his audience to know that being castrated would qualify someone to "sing ballads" for the rest of his life. John Marston and Edward Sharpham recognized castration as a way "to preserve" a "high-stretched minikin voice"; John Webster knew it produced "squeaking"; Henry Glapthorne claimed that being turned into a eunuch might earn you "A petty canon's place in some blind chantry."

(Fictional) eunuchs were expected to sing in Robert Greene's *Selimus*, Ben Jonson's *Volpone*, and Philip Massinger's *Duke of Milan*.

Castrated singers were still a feature of European life in the seventeenth century, but English writers also knew quite a bit about the other uses of castration. Christopher Marlowe translated Ovid's complaint, "Ay me! an eunuch keeps my mistress chaste"; William Shakespeare described a woman so lecherous that she would "do the deed Though Argus were her eunuch and her guard"; John Donne, satirizing an ugly woman, explained that she "needs no spies, nor eunuchs" to protect her sexual fidelity. Another Elizabethan satirist, Joseph Hall, recognized that some early Christians "held it good service unto God to geld both themselves and strangers." Thomas Heywood, in a poem of 1609, even referred to the Byzantine general "Narses the eunuch, a right valiant knight."

The significance of the eunuchs in the New Testament was even more widely appreciated. A sermon preached at Paul's Cross in 1617—noting that the "blessed eunuch" from Ethiopia "did . . . more esteem the favor of God than he feared the malice or disgrace of men"—urged Londoners to read the Bible "with the like mind with which this noble eunuch read it." And John Donne, having turned from poetry to preaching, reminded his congregation that "the first of the Gentiles, which was converted to Christianity, was that eunuch, which was Treasurer to the Queen of Ethiopia"; that eunuch exemplifies Donne's thesis that "the first persons that are recorded to have applied themselves to the profession of the Christian religion were rulers, persons of place, and quality." In another sermon, Donne turned to Matthew 19:12, where Jesus, having referred to those who "have made themselves eunuchs for the kingdom of heaven's sake," followed that enigmatic pronouncement with the injunction "Let him, that is able to receive it, receive it." Quoting the Latin Vulgate translation, Donne turns "*Possum capere*" into a refrain: "I shall have power to receive the gift of continency, against all temptations of that kind." The condition of being a eunuch thus paradoxically produces, according to Donne, "an extension of power. . . . This that seems to have a name of impotence, *Non possum*, I cannot, is the fullest omnipotence of all, I cannot sin."

Contemplating eunuchhood, Donne says, "Power accrues and grows unto me." That is not how psychoanalysis talks about castration. Freud ignored what castration had meant for millennia and substituted a radical new meaning of his own. In twentieth-century psychoanalysis, castration means loss, unequivocal loss, the epitome of loss. In the world before Freud, castration could produce a powerful voice, a powerful general, a powerful intimate of women and emperors, a powerful spirituality. The eunuch could only serve the purposes for which he was created by being in some way powerful.

The power is there in *A Game at Chess*. Although the White Bishop's Pawn has been sexually incapacitated, he has not in other respects been rendered any less potent. Like the eunuch who guards a harem, the White Bishop's Pawn protects the virtue of a desirable woman from the sexual assaults of a would-be seducer, the Black Bishop's Pawn. In 2.1, the Black Bishop's Pawn is interrupted, in his attempt to rape the White Queen's Pawn, by an offstage noise, which he assumes comes from the White Bishop's Pawn; in 3.1, the White Bishop's Pawn brings information that releases the White Queen's Pawn from the clutches of the Black House; finally, in 5.2, the White Bishop's Pawn captures and incarcerates the Black Bishop's Pawn, thereby permanently removing the sexual and religious threat to the White Queen's Pawn.

You might object that the White Bishop's Pawn could have performed all these functions without being castrated; he is powerful not *because* he is a eunuch, but *despite* it. But that is not how the play sees it. The man who castrated him, the Black Knight's Pawn, retrospectively recognizes that—ironically—the castration has actually helped his rival:

The Bishop's White Pawn undertook the journey—
Who, as they say, discharged it like a flight.
I made him for the business fit and light.

(3.1.149–151)

The two most recent editors of *A Game at Chess*—living, as they do, in a mental world shaped by Freud—regard the final sentence here as nonsensical: "I made him for the business fit and light." *Why* would a Black Pawn do anything to make his White rival better able to frustrate the plans of the Black House, and how could castration have improved the White Pawn's abilities? Moreover, one of the physiological effects of castration is a tendency toward obesity—an obesity noted by some seventeenth-century English writers. Castration might have made the White Bishop's Pawn fat; how could it have made him "fit and light"?

The first clue to an answer is given by the preceding phrase: "discharged it like a flight." A "flight" is not only a volley of arrows; it is also a "flock," particularly an angelic flock, as in Hamlet's "flights of angels sing thee to thy rest." The castrated White Bishop's Pawn, moving with great speed to save vulnerable virtue, is being compared to a messenger of God. The comparison would not have been surprising. Basil of Ancyra, Jerome, and Augustine had all compared human celibates to angels. And Christian images of angels were modeled upon the eunuchs who attended Roman and Byzantine emperors: beautiful beardless asexual beings with sublime voices who attend upon a supreme ruler. Castration makes a man more like an angel.

But Middleton also had a very particular reason for believing that castration might make men "light." The same male gift for sexual hyperbole that extended the *length* of a penis by calling it a "yard" magnified the *mass* of a testicle by calling it a "stone." This idiom creates the possibility for a pun on "testicle" (= stone) and "measure of weight" (= stone). For instance, in Edward Sharpham's popular comedy *Cupid's Whirligig*, Sir Timothy Troublesome resolves to "geld" himself, and sends for "the stone-cutter" to perform the operation; the first thing he says upon reentering is, "How many pounds go to a stone of beef?" His servant answers, "Eight, sir"—and the newly gelded eunuch concludes, "Then I am lighter by sixteen pound now than I was; I may now lie with any lady in Europe for any hurt I can do her." In Philip Massinger's *The Renegado*, a eunuch says, "I was made lighter By two stone weight at least to be fit to serve you." Likewise, in Richard Brome's *The Court Beggar*, a "gelder" tells his prospective victim, "you look heavily methinks; You shall be lighter by two stone presently."

By relieving the White Bishop's Pawn of his load of stones, the Black Knight's Pawn may have disqualified him for (sexual) "business," but he has also inadvertently made him "light," and so, like an angel, capable of "flight," able to move faster, and thereby—ironically—"fit," able to frustrate the sexual and political "business" of the Black House. Moreover, as humanist agricultural treatises observed, their "seed and stones" make stallions "very fierce, truculent, and unruly," creating often "an intolerable rage . . . towards their colleagues and guides." By contrast, gelded horses are more "serviceable and quiet" and so better able to live together in "one herd." What is biologically true of animals is psychologically true of the characters in Middleton's play. The headstrong lust of the Black Bishop's Pawn is typical of the unruliness of the whole Black House; as Loyola says, "I would rule myself, not observe rule . . . I would do anything to rule alone" (Ind. 71, 73). In Act Three, the Black House is exposed and embarrassed by the cooperation of the White Knight and White Duke with a gelded (quiet, serviceable) angelic messenger, the White Bishop's Pawn. Castration, in *A Game at Chess*, actually makes a man better able to protect, against the depredations of rival males, the woman—and the religion—he loves.

More is at stake here than understanding one line, or one character, in an old play. According to psychoanalysis, castration designates loss and impotence—archetypally, paradigmatically, and always. By contrast, in Middleton's text, and in the premodern Western civilization Middleton represents, it does not. Castration instead results in the first place from rivalry between males, and the males consequently castrated may then be employed to give one uncastrated male an advantage in his rivalry with other uncastrated males; to give one male such an advantage over another—by guarding a woman or an emperor, or providing a more impressive choir than anyone else's, or getting to heaven—the eunuch must have some desirable attributes and powers. In Middleton's world, castrated males sometimes had powers that uncastrated males lack.

Castration was not, accordingly, the worst loss that men could imagine. Although Freud considers beheading a symbolic substitute for castration, most men do not regard them as interchangeable; after all, the only really powerless man is a dead one. As the eunuch in Thomas Heywood's *Fair Maid of the West* exclaims, "Die? 'Sfoot, this is worse than being made an eunuch as I was"; in James Shirley's *Hyde Park* a man volunteers, "I'll geld myself: 'Tis something less than hanging." In contemporary America, men suffering from testicular cancer often undergo orchiectomy; there are undoubtedly more castrated men in New York City at the beginning of the twenty-first century than in the whole of Elizabethan England. But it's not only the loss of life that has seemed to most men worse than surgery on the scrotum. In early modern France, castration was the normal medical treatment for hernias. For Origen and many other Christians, actual castration now was infinitely preferable to possible damnation later. In Jonson's play *The Devil Is an Ass*, the devil Pug worries, "Sure he will geld me if I stay—or worse, Pluck out my tongue." Pug would rather lose his fertility than his power of speech. Maybe that only proves he's an ass, but it certainly does nothing to prove Freud's thesis. Would Pavarotti rather lose his tongue or his testicles? Which would Yo-Yo Ma give up first, his fingers or his family jewels?

Of course, these would be terrible and tragic choices. Few men relish castration. The notion of "castration anxiety" therefore seems, at first blush, obvious enough. But Freud's "castration complex" means something much more specific and much more ambitious. And that meaning cannot be found in Middleton's play.

Which text is right? Middleton's or Freud's? Is psychoanalysis a fruitful intellectual tool—or a blinkered twentieth-century sexual mythology?

But the question is larger than that, because each of these two writers epitomizes an entire cultural tradition. The two opposed texts represent two rival systems of theories, experiences, and memories about what castration means. And those complex rival systems turn upon opposed evaluations of the significance of different parts of the male anatomy. Which is more important in the hierarchy of manhood: whether a man carries a big stick, or whether he has balls?

Leave It to Beaver

"That a beaver, to escape the hunter, bites off his testicles or stones, is a tenet very ancient." So begins Sir Thomas Browne's chapter "Of the Beaver" in his *Pseudodoxia Epidemica; or, Enquiries into very many received tenets and commonly presumed truths* (1646). He traces the opinion back to Egyptian hieroglyphics and records its reappearance in Aristotle's *Ethics*, Aesop's fables, the Roman naturalist Pliny, the satirist Juvenal, and other classical and medieval authorities. He might also have mentioned more recent writers, like the French Protestant poet Sieur du Bartas, whose *Divine Weeks* (1578–1584) was considered a modern classic: "The wise beaver who, pursued by foes, Tears off his codlings, and among them throws" (I.vi.139–140). As Don Quixote explains to Sancho, the beaver, "seeing himself hotly pursued by the hunters . . . tears and cuts away that with his teeth, for which he knows by natural instinct he is followed" (Part One, III, 7). The Latin word for "beaver" was *castor*, and what the hunters were seeking was castor oil. Browne debunks the whole story: Experimental vivisection has demonstrated that the "cod or visible bag about the groin" does not contain the beaver's testicles "or any spermatical part," and there is no reliable evidence of beavers in the wild biting it off. But although the story is bad science, it is good morality: "We may hereby apprehend a real and useful truth" in this parable of one "who, to escape with his life, contemneth the loss of his genitals," thereby reminding us that "in case of extremity" we should "not strictly endeavor the preservation of all, but to sit down in the enjoyment of the greater good, though with the detriment and hazard of the lesser."

Genital Plural

We have many members in one body, and all members have not the same office.

—Romans 12:4

The ultimate male "hard body" is Michelangelo's marble *David*, sculpted in the first years of the sixteenth century and now displayed in the Galleria dell'Accademia di Belle Arti in Florence. But if, like most American men, you prefer casinos to museums and Las Vegas to Tuscany, you can see a full-size reproduction of *David* (and a lot of other familiar statues) in Caesar's Palace. In fact, in one respect the Nevada copy is larger than the Italian original. Fearing the notorious puritanism of postwar Americans, the management at first had placed a fig leaf over *David*'s crotch; but when highbrow purists and prurients looked up and were robbed of the expected sight of those famous male genitalia, they complained about the censorship of Michelangelo's masterpiece. Realizing that people willing to play slot machines and watch scantily clad dancers might be less inhibited than other Americans, management had the offending fig leaf removed. However, some customers then began to giggle, because the leafless *David*'s *cazzo* was obviously, by modern American standards, a little . . . well, little. Underendowed. The customer is always right. So the statue was taken away again, and *David* was given a couple of extra inches where it counts.

Was the original artist making some ironic or symbolic comment on the Hebrew hero? No. The penis of Michelangelo's *The Risen Christ* is no bigger than *David*'s. How are we to explain this discrepancy between our expectations and the actual measurements of Western art's most admired males? How could Michelangelo—not only a master of proportion, but also, as a homosexual, particularly interested in male equipment—have made such an elementary miscalculation? Obviously, the answer to such questions cannot be found in the statuesque modified males that festoon a modern desert pleasure palace. But for anyone who visits Florence and pays attention to the handsome collection of sculpted male genitalia on display in the Piazza della Signoria, the riddle is quickly solved—or multiplied. *David* and *The Risen Christ* are not anomalous but typical. In Renaissance art, testicles loom larger than penises.

Another sixteenth-century masterpiece, in another medium and from another country, displays the same puzzling proportions. François Rabelais' *Gargantua and Pantagruel* went through ninety-three editions between 1531/2 and 1626; it was one of the most popular books produced in humanist Europe— and, incidentally, one of Middleton's sources for *A Game at Chess*. In the very first chapter of the first published volume of his French classic, Rabelais describes people with various gigantic body parts, including "*merveilleusement long*" penises and testicles "*enormement*" large. But in Book Three Rabelais abandons this initial equal treatment, devoting two chapters to praise and dispraise of the testicles, in the form of contrasting adjectival lists that repeat the word 303 times; in another chapter, the testicles are interpreted as the "stones" with which Deucalion repopulated the earth after the mythical flood. Altogether, Rabelais names the penis (*couille, membre*) 45 times, but the testicles (*couillon, couillons*) a whopping 336 times.

These proportions are more than reversed in the works of Sigmund Freud. Like Rabelais a medical doctor famous for his frankness about sexual matters, Freud refers to the testicles or scrotum (*Testikel, testis,* or *Hodensack*) only 12 times—against 468 references to the penis (*penis, phallus, männliches Gleid*). Rabelais, like Michelangelo, found the testicles more important than the penis; Freud, like the punters at Caesar's Palace, has lost interest in the testicles almost completely.

It is hard to believe that in only a few hundred years, the bodies of Western European men changed as radically as these opposed representations would suggest. Biological evolution cannot account for the difference between the sixteenth-century emphasis on bowling balls and the twentieth-century emphasis on bowling pins. Our physical measurements remain the same, but we have changed our minds. Psychoanalysis reflects, and may even have helped cause, that change. Did Freud overcome a massive regime of psychic censorship that had for centuries concealed the real importance of the penis—an importance that could only be acknowledged by the unconscious? Or did Freud merely reflect, and institutionalize, changing Western perceptions of the male anatomy? And, in either case, whose perceptions were changing? Men's? Women's? Everybody's? Who was giggling in Caesar's Palace?

For Freud, castration is a genital loss that all women believe they have suffered and all men fear to suffer; it organizes the human sexual imaginary. For Freud's most influential and controversial disciple, the postmodern French analyst Jacques Lacan, castration is an even more fundamental loss, afflicting the entire symbolic realm. In Lacan, both sexes are castrated. Where Freud referred to the "penis" (originally a Latin word, which entered English in 1676, and has become the normal medical term for the male sexual organ), Lacan instead refers to the "phallus" (originally a Greek word, first recorded in English in 1924, in a psychoanalytic context, and normally used to distinguish "the erect male organ in action"). But Lacan uses *phallus* in an even more specifically psychoanalytic sense. Lacan insists that "the institution of the subject" results from "a relation of the subject to the phallus that is established without regard to the anatomical difference of the sexes." No one has "the phallus," in part because "the phallus" is no longer a mere physical "organ" but instead a transcendental "signifier."

For feminists, Lacan's pancastration might seem preferable to Freud's gynecastration. That *everyone*, "regardless of his or her organs, is 'castrated'" represents, for women, "not a loss but a gain"; in 1985 Jane Gallop characterized Lacan's project as "profoundly feminist" because it called into question "the phallic illusions of authority." But even in Lacan, "The phallus is the privileged signifier." Why should it be? Lacanians insist on a distinction between physical penis and psychical phallus; but, as Gallop herself later objected, that distinction cannot be maintained. Phallus "also *always* refers to *penis*." Dympna Callaghan is surely right to protest the Lacanian privileging of the penis. Biologically, the maternal womb or breast have stronger claims to signify what is always lost, perpetually sought, and never regained. Why should we ask, "What does castration mean?" when we could be asking, "What does hysterectomy mean? What does mastectomy mean? What does weaning mean?" Lacan reinscribes the primacy of male anatomy.

These objections to psychoanalysis might be dismissed as "politically correct" whining. After all, the fact that some people do not *like* certain aspects of Freud's or Lacan's picture of the human psyche does not mean that the unpleasant picture is necessarily inaccurate. Ugliness is. (Look around you.) The truth-claims of psychoanalysis have always depended, to some extent, upon its very unpalatability. "I will not flatter you," the analyst proclaims; "I will help you see yourself as you really are. Look!"

But when we really do look, when we look carefully, we discover something embarrassing. The psychoanalytic reading of castration keeps insisting that we stare at the penis. But castration need have nothing to do with the penis. Freud's theory (which Lacan recapitulates) would have us read "the lack of a penis" as a consequence of "castration." But *castration does not necessarily or even normally remove the penis*. Castration— what medical dictionaries more precisely define as "bilateral orchiectomy"—is the removal of the testicles, not the penis. The earliest extant medical description of the operation, by the seventh-century Byzantine physician Paul of Aegina, makes this absolutely clear: Both techniques (compression and excision) target the testicles only.

Poets and playwrights and philosophers knew this as well as physicians. In a play written and performed in 1607, a character determined to geld himself speaks of "cutting off the traitors that makes the flesh rebel." The plural suggests he is thinking of testicles, and John Day, in a play of 1606, makes the plural even more specific: "Cut them off both, sir, and make . . . an eunuch." What two things do you cut off to make a man into a eunuch? If you're having doubts, William Rowley should resolve them for you: "I will see your mill gelded, and his stones fried in steaks." Here we have, again, a pun on *stones*, this time conflating testicles and millstones. The same pun occurs in the anonymous *Merry Devil of Edmonton*, where a miller says, "I would to God my mill were an eunuch, and wanted [= lacked] her stones." In Middleton, the millstone becomes a grindstone: Ricardo threatens to "immediately geld" another man "and grind his face upon one o'th' stones." When Shakespeare refers to "the voice of unpaved eunuch," the seemingly bizarre adjective *unpaved* refers to paving stones (the only method of paving, before modern asphalt); testicles are like paving stones, and therefore a castrated man is "unpaved." In Heywood's *Fair Maid of the West* those same scrotal stones are punningly transformed into jewels: A man "gelded" in order to become "chief eunuch" explains that he "sold certain precious stones to purchase the place." If such jokes seem frivolous, they are no worse than the puns so important to Freud. And Freud was not alone. The commentary on Augustine's *City of God* written by the great Spanish humanist scholar Juan Luis de Vives traces the pun back to Plato, who in a riddle in *The Republic* defined a eunuch holding a rock as "a man and no man" with "a stone and no stone."

The popularity of such puns in early texts reflects a biological and social reality. The gelding of human males is simply a subset of a larger class of operations routinely performed on other animals. In any agricultural society gelding and its effects would have been familiar because of the routine castrations of livestock. In early modern Europe, such animals were more numerous, relative to the human population, than they are today, and they were also less segregated from humans, even in urban environments: "Animals were everywhere." As the French historian Emmanuel Le Roy Ladurie demonstrated in a classic study, the superstitious rituals of "magical castration" in the French countryside in the late sixteenth and early seventeenth centuries applied symbolically to humans a practice applied literally to domesticated animals. Across the Channel, in Middleton's London, the testicles of castrated lambs, fried with parsley, were considered a delicacy, and an aphrodisiac; the capon, a gelded rooster, was a regular part of the early modern diet; Edward Topsell's *History of Four-Footed Beasts* (1607) cites various authorities on the best times and means for gelding bulls, horses, pigs, and sheep.

When humanist writers described castrated men, they routinely compared them to castrated animals. One of Shakespeare's frustrated men exclaims, "Let me be gelded like a spaniel." A man in George Chapman's *Humorous Day's Mirth*, infuriated by a sexual rival, threatens to "geld the adulterous goat." A Marston character speaks of being "gelded like a capon"; one of Fletcher's angry queens threatens to have her entire entourage "cut . . . like colts." For the humanist mind, a man resembles a dog, goat, chicken, or horse, in that he is a castratable animal. In each case, it is perfectly clear that *gelding*— or any of its synonyms—means "removing the testicles." As Robert Burton says, "Peter Abelard lost his testicles for his Heloise."

Like the literary genre of pastoral, Freud's theory of castration is an urban myth, plausible only among populations physically and imaginatively distant from agricultural practices. It has never been taken too seriously by farmers. A friend of mine, who grew up on a family farm in western Ohio in the fifties and sixties, still remembers the rhythm of the annual assembly line for castrating young male pigs:

slash—
snip snip—
squeal squeal—
staple staple—
swish swish—
slash . . .

Or, more prosaically: While your partner holds the little pig's back legs apart, you slash open the scrotum with a knife, then with your scissors snip out the two testicles which lie inside the scrotum; the pig squeals as its loses each testicle; you promptly staple the wound closed, and brush it with antibiotic to prevent infection. Then you start on another pig. If you do this enough times—or perhaps, if you do it even once—you are not likely to follow Freud when he treats castration as an operation that removes the penis.

But unlike my female friend from Ohio, I spent my own 1960s adolescence in air-conditioned libraries, reading books by people like Freud. I have always lived in cities. And so have most people alive today. When we go shopping, we do not realize that most of the supermarket's neatly packaged cuts of meat come from castrated male animals. If we want to find out how many tens of millions of veterinary castrations are performed every year in the United States, we visit an Internet website, not a farm. City dwellers like us have few personal experiences to set against Freud's theories. Neither did Freud, or most of his con-temporaries. As an urban European born in the middle of the nineteenth century, Freud belonged to the first generation of the first human civilization that was not primarily agricultural.

Agriculturally, farmers have excellent reasons to remove the testicles of young male animals; it allows them to control breed-ing, and it produces less aggressive males who are accordingly easier to manage. But farmers have no reason to remove the penises of domesticated animals. Likewise, most civilizations have, for a variety of different reasons, de-testicled some men; the operation is as simple, and safe, for humans as for other ani-mals. By contrast, there is no obvious need to remove a penis, and for most of human history few people survived such amputations. Why bother?

One good reason is given in a scene of Middleton and Webster's play *Anything for a Quiet Life* (1621), where a young male apprentice visits a London barber-surgeon (2.4). The surgeon has been led to believe that the apprentice has contracted a venereal disease (or "*morbus Gallicus,* or *Neapolitanus,*" as he prefers to call it). Preparing for the impending operation, the surgeon calls for his "dismembering instrument," a "cauterizing iron red-hot" (to prevent infection), and "bolsters and pledgets" (different sizes of plug used to keep the urethra open after penis amputation, to enable urination). He begins by assuring the patient that "if *praeputium* be not too much perished, you shall lose but little by it"; if the disease has only begun to destroy the foreskin, the surgery will amount to little more than circumcision. However, he has to admit that "if there be exulceration between *praeputium* and *glans,* by my faith, the whole *penis* may be endangered as far as *os pubis*"—that is, if damage has already spread to the shaft, he may have to cut the whole thing off, all the way down to the pubic bone—because "If they be gangrened once, *testiculi, vesica* and all may run to mortification." The surgeon here describes a spectrum of infection, from mildest to worst, and of amputations, from foreskin to penis to testicles and bladder. In these circumstances, as he wisely recognizes, "Better a member cut off than endanger the whole microcosm."

What is happening in this remarkable scene—the first of its kind, to my knowledge—clearly differs from all the gelding plots, gelding allusions, and gelded characters in early modern drama. Words like *geld* and *eunuch* and *stones* never appear; instead we get *penis* (a Latin word, still, italicized, like all the technical medical terms) and *member* and *yard*. Instead of puns on *stones* we get puns on *yard* (the patient is a tailor's apprentice). Middleton and Webster make it absolutely clear that we are dealing not with the familiar and traditional operation of gelding or castration, but with something different, novel, and technical: potential amputation of the penis itself.

Surgery had for millennia been the disreputable strong arm of medicine, left to mere manual laborers (like barbers) who used cutting instruments too coarse for the university-educated "doctors" qualified to write prescriptions. The epidemic of syphilis that infected Europe at the very end of the fifteenth century helped alter the balance of medical power, as sixteenth-century surgeons like the Italian Giovanni de Vigo and the French Ambroise Paré advocated cauterization and surgical excision of chancres. By the seventeenth century, surgical operations on diseased or injured penises became more common and more often successful. Of course, such operations on the penis were undertaken as a last resort to save the patient from worse amputations or death: "Better a member cut off than endanger the whole microcosm." In general, although few men want to lose any of their sexual equipment, most prefer life without any genitals to no life at all.

But in the humanist world, some men weren't given that choice. A convicted traitor—like those condemned for the 1605 Gunpowder Plot to blow up the English king and Parliament—was publicly disemboweled and dismembered; before his heart was plucked out, his genitals were chopped off and burned before his face to demonstrate (as Francis Bacon said) that he was "unworthily begotten" and unfit "to leave any generation after him." Similar rituals were observed in violent riots. In the Saint Bartholomew's Day Massacre (1572), after the Protestant leader Coligni was murdered his head was sent to the Pope, and "Others cut off his hands, and others his secret parts." Likewise, in 1617, after the assassination of Concini, the Parisian crowd that dug up his body amputated his upper and lower lips, tongue, ears, "shameful parts," and then fingers, joint by joint. Such ritual mutilation of the dead was intended—as Montaigne recognized, when discussing similar practices among cannibals—"to represent an extreme, and inexpiable revenge."

By the seventeenth century, Europeans knew about medical amputation of part or all of the penis (designed to sacrifice one part of the body to preserve the rest), and they knew about disciplinary dismemberment of all the genitalia (designed to humiliate a criminal, spectacularly and fatally); but they also knew, had known for millennia, about transformative mutilation of the scrotum (designed to adapt a living body for a specialized function). They knew the differences between these actions and outcomes, and in particular they paid attention to the difference between penis and testicles. Freud disregarded that difference.

Recent apologists for psychoanalysis have also disregarded it. Consider, for instance, Freud's description of the origins of "envy for the penis": A little girl notices "the penis" of a little boy, "strikingly visible and of large proportions," and contrasts it with her own "small and inconspicuous organ." Many women found this claim anatomically and psychologically ridiculous:

> The first step in the sexual development of little girls begins with a momentous discovery. They notice the penis of a brother or playmate and respond with explosive fits of laughter, so amused are they by the absurd appearance of this flaccid, vulnerable, and apparently useless extra appendage. Invariably the girl questions the deformed child as to the purpose of this strange member, and he, being too young to have discovered its role in reproduction, is at a loss to respond. From that time forward the girl falls victim to *disdain for the penis*. At the same time, fear of female scorn, shame of his vulnerable genitals, and above all resentment toward the entire female sex become central to male identity.

But in 1974 Juliet Mitchell's extraordinarily influential book, *Psychoanalysis and Feminism*, rebuked such feminist objections, arguing that Freud did not condone patriarchy, but simply *described* it. When the little girl sees the penis, what she really sees, and envies, is the social and political power given to penis-people by the social world she inhabits. As Carol Smart says, early feminists had "buried Freud . . . but Mitchell resurrected him." Perhaps it would be more accurate to say that what Mitchell resurrected was the "strikingly visible" penis. Although Freud's biological claim ("anatomical difference") became in

Codpieces

Ask people to describe what men wore in the days of
Shakespeare, and the first article of clothing that usually
comes to mind is the codpiece. The codpiece is also what
apparently came first to Shakespeare's own mind. In *The
Two Gentleman of Verona* (probably the first play he
wrote), Julia decides to disguise herself as a man; her maid
immediately reminds her that cross-dressing will require "a
codpiece" (2.7.53). Likewise, Middleton's famously cross-
dressed *Roaring Girl* is a paradoxical "codpiece daughter,"
and John Marston satirizes men that "wear a codpiece,
Thereby to disclose what sex they are"—as though the article of clothing was the only detectable distinction. All trans-
vestism depends on the fact that, ever since humans began
clothing themselves, we have relied on conventions of dress
to advertise (and magnify) sexual difference. Hence, mere
"apparel oft proclaims the man" (*Hamlet* 1.3.72).

Originally Swiss, codpieces became popular in England
in the fifteenth century; over the decades of their use, they
went through numerous transformations in shape, fabric,
color, decoration—and size. Men were often accused of
stuffing them to exaggerate the amplitude of their genitals:
Shakespeare satirizes a codpiece "as massy as" Hercules'
club (*Much Ado* 3.3.132), and Middleton mocks "the great
codpiece with nothing in't" (*Your Five Gallants* 2.3.305).

Although occasionally in circulation until the early eighteenth century (at least in literature), codpieces had become
passé by the 1590s, and in 1612 Samuel Rowlands claimed
that "no tailor" knows anything about them, unless he con-
sults an "old painted cloth." The fashionable classes had
given them up. "Of all fond fashions that were worn by
men, These two" (Robert Hayman hoped, in 1628) "will
ne'er be worn again: great codpieced doublets and great
codpieced britches." Blatant display of the male crotch had

become a "filthy" habit; indeed, by 1652 even the word *codpiece* was "uncouth." The offending article continued to be worn only as hand-me-downs (in a society where clothes were too precious to be thrown away), descending down the social and moral scale until it disappeared altogether.

What the codpiece emphasized, as the banner of masculinity, was the scrotum. *Cod* means "bag," hence "scrotum" (and eventually, by transference from the bag to what the bag contains, "testicle"). In *A Game at Chess*, after the Black Bishop's Pawn (a Jesuit priest) has been caught attempting to rape a woman in his congregation, the Black Knight complains that what he has "seven years labored to accomplish" politically is undone in a minute by "some codpiece college" (2.1.166–167); that metaphor characterizes the educational institutions founded by Jesuits as male schools dedicated to testicles and to immoral exaggerated crotch display. The Black Bishop's Pawn defends himself by observing that he is not "alone" in this fault: "The Black House yields me partners"—and the Black Knight agrees. The sign of the Black House is the codpiece, epitomized by the Black Bishop's Pawn; the White Bishop's Pawn, in contrast, has been castrated—he doesn't need a codpiece because he has no cods.

Mitchell's reinterpretation sociological ("patriarchy"), it was still founded and focused upon a contrast between "possessing the penis" (males) and "castrated" (females). But Middleton's world, and Augustine's, had been patriarchal, too—and *their* notion of castration had nothing to do with penises. Freud's theories about castration anxiety and the penis envy of castrated females can hardly be an accurate description of "patriarchy," because they misrepresent almost the entire history of castration and almost the entire history of patriarchy.

Anachronistically, Freud reduced castration to a single meaning and reduced sexuality to a single organ. As anthropologist

Gayle Rubin complains, "Much of the psychoanalytic approach to sexual variation" is "incredibly reductionist and over-simplified" and "prone to impoverish the rich complexity of erotic meaning and conduct." It doesn't take an intellectual magician to pull the rabbit "castration" out of a hat, any hat; but we are not in Wonderland, and the white rabbit has nothing to tell us. Exclaiming "Eureka! castration!" implies that we have thought about a problem in some profound way, when in fact we have simply muttered an incantation. And a compulsory incantation at that; in certain intellectual circles, any scholarly investigation of sexuality that does *not* make the expected ritual obeisance to Freud will not be taken seriously. But what does Freud illuminate? "For example," Rubin says, "to look at something like fetishism and say it has to do with castration and the lack, or maybe it's the knowledge of castration, or maybe it is the foreclosure of the knowledge of, or the displacement of the knowledge . . . well, it says very little to me about fetishism." It also says very little about genital mutilation or about men's or women's attitudes toward castration (of themselves or others).

To conceptualize "the anatomical difference between the sexes" in terms of castration, Freud silently redefined "castration" as an operation that removed the entire male genital apparatus. As a medical doctor, Freud must have been aware of the distinction between (common, ancient) removal of the testicles and (uncommon, historically recent) removal of the penis. But then, Freud also knew that female nerve endings were clustered in the clitoris, not the vagina; this did not prevent him from creating the myth that "normal" or "mature" female sexuality was characterized by vaginal orgasm. In both cases, Freud repressed his own knowledge of the body to erect a penis-shaped model of the mind.

But—and I hope men will forgive me for betraying this secret—*the penis isn't everything.*

It isn't the only thing in a man's crotch. Even when fully inflated, it isn't a man's largest erogenous organ. (What is? His epidermis.) "The penis"—as novelist John Varley says—"is just skin covering two blood-filled chambers." It isn't a god.

Or is it? The sexually insatiable would-be seducer and rapist in *A Game at Chess* (the Black Bishop's Pawn) is compared to "Priapus, guardian of the cherry gardens, Bacchus' and Venus' chit" (1.1.269–270). Priapus was the Roman deity of the erect penis, the son of Dionysus (god of uninhibited ecstatic abandon, including drunkenness and violence) and Aphrodite (goddess of sex); he was always envisaged with a phallus of anatomically impossible enormitude, and statues of him were often stationed in gardens to ward off intruders. In *The City of God*—in the only passage in his works ever cited by Freud—Augustine indignantly described a Roman ritual that required brides to sit atop the "huge and beastly member" of a statue of Priapus.

A woman I know was raised in a devout Catholic family with six older brothers; one day, when she was six years old, an appalling thought popped into her head: "Jesus had a penis!" She was sure she would be damned for even thinking such an irreverent thought. By contrast with the gods ancient Romans adored, the God modern Roman Catholics worship is not usually pictured publicly displaying his penis, which is instead scrupulously kept out of sight and, whenever possible, out of mind. But that does not mean the genitals of Jesus are unimportant; indeed, their invisibility may be an index of their supreme significance. When Tori Amos asks Lucifer, "How's your Jesus Christ been hanging?" the image of a well-hung Jesus (crucified, big-genitaled) is outrageously blasphemous, but the equation of male sex organs with an object of (Satanic) religious devotion is immediately comprehensible.

Obviously, for Augustine and Middleton and Freud and any good Christian girl, the worship of Priapus and the worship of Jesus are incompatible. So how do we decide what to worship? Which deity is the most powerful? And what have genitals got to do with it?

Contest of Gods
Dream Divination

The letter killeth, but the spirit giveth life.

—2 Corinthians 3:6

Before we can encounter the Most High, we have to pass through the Valley of the Shadow of Interpretation.

When we ask if a man's penis "stands," the question has a physical answer. But when we ask what a man's penis "stands for," the question has to be answered allegorically. Manhood is always allegorical, from the Gospel according to John to *Iron John*.

But why are we driven to allegorize an erection—or anything else for that matter? When is literalism not enough? How do we know when to resort to allegory in interpreting a text or a body part?

We resort to allegory when we find the thing itself inadequate in some way. In particular, we allegorize whenever something seems significant, but unsatisfactory in its current or apparent form. Allegory solves a hermeneutic problem by resolving a conflict between the thing itself and our expectations of that thing.

Our species has learned to allegorize from dreams. All humans dream; dreaming is an inevitable consequence of the neurochemistry of sleep. But the world of our dreams, insofar as we remember it when we wake, differs dramatically from the world perceived by our conscious senses. Dreams illogically connect and combine; they represent actions and entities apparently impossible, or at the very least never before encountered, in the waking world (like the castration of a chess piece). Yet in other respects they uncannily duplicate details of the dreamer's own life (just as some characters in *A Game at Chess* mimicked living persons well known to its first audiences). The dream therefore poses a problem: What is the relationship between these familiar and sensible elements and their apparently nonsensical co-components? Answering this question seems important to us for at least three reasons. First, humans are hermeneutic animals; we are hard-wired to solve interpretative problems and to seek significance in representations. Second, dreams often generate unusually strong and disturbing emotions in the dreamer (just as *A Game at Chess* affected its audiences); that affective force persuades us that something important has happened—because if the dream were trivial, why should it so extravagantly have frightened or delighted us? Finally, dreaming does not seem to be in the dreamer's own volitional control; our consciousness feels like a passive recipient of representations that come to us from somewhere else. But where else could they be coming from? Who or what that we cannot see has the power to get inside our heads while we are helplessly sleeping? Anyone or anything who can do that to us must be powerful and must have reasons for making us dream these dreams. Dreaming is therefore naturally perceived as a communicative signal of some sort—a signal simultaneously important and confusing. Consequently, as anthropologists have discovered, all human cultures engage in dream interpretation; that is, all human cultures allegorize their dreams. Therefore, when he claims, in its first scene, that *A Game at Chess* is "a dream, A vision," Middleton is telling us that his play—including its narrative of castration—can only be understood allegorically.

Freud also understood dreams allegorically; for him, their source was the dreamer's own unconscious. Therefore, if properly interpreted, dreams were the "royal road to a knowledge of the unconscious," a way into the undiscovered dark substrata of the human psyche. Freud repeatedly saw evidence for his castration complex in dreams. "To represent castration symbolically, the dream-work makes use of baldness, hair-cutting, falling out of teeth and decapitation. If one of the ordinary symbols for a penis occurs in a dream doubled or multiplied, it is to be regarded as a warding-off of castration." Or castration may be enfigured by a child ("the little one") being run over by a train.

But these allegorical interpretations do not substantiate a universal castration complex. They depend upon Freud's theory of the mechanisms that generate human dreaming—a theory that has been decisively refuted, in the century since he formulated it, by a scientific revolution in studies of the brain. The discovery of REM sleep, PGO waves, acetylcholine nerve cells, norepinephrine, serotonin, and geniculate nuclei in the thalamus does not mean that dream interpretation has stopped being necessary or useful. The most important sleep researcher of our time, J. Allan Hobson of Harvard Medical School, acknowledges that in at least one sense "Freud was right: Dreams are trying to tell us something important about our instincts (sex, aggression), our feelings (fear, anger, affection), and our lives (places, persons, and times)," and that dreams accordingly impose an "interpretive obligation." The god of medical science has not, as professors of literature might fear, driven the god of hermeneutics out of the temple: Aesculapius has simply given Hermes more sophisticated tools. Hobson complains, rightly, that psychoanalysts "became so caught up in the analysis of the *content* of particular dreams that they lost sight of the *form* of all dreaming." Any adequate interpretation must attend to both content and form; thus, the medical doctor Hobson is a better literary critic than the medical doctor Freud.

Moreover, neurochemistry in this instance supports the postmodernist consensus that "human nature" is in many ways not fixed and eternal, but variable and artificial, constructed differently by different societies. It is Freud who insists that the dreams of an Austrian boy in the twentieth century deploy the same symbolism as the dreams of Leonardo da Vinci and can be interpreted in the same way. Hobson would not agree. Neither would Artemidorus of Daldis, who—in the middle of the second century in what is now western Turkey—wrote a Greek treatise entitled *Oneirokritika* ("Dream-Criticism"); Artemidorus concluded that "the interpretation of dreams is nothing other than the juxtaposition of similarities." Dreams work in part by processes of association; therefore dream symbolism depends on which associations are likely for a given person in a given culture; those probabilities will be determined by the historical particularities of language, social practice, and personal experience.

The male genitals, in the particular social world of Artemidorus, were full of an equally particular dream significance. Although the psychoanalytic word *phallos* comes from ancient Greek, and although English translations of Artemidorus (and Foucault) specify *penis*, Artemidorus himself is anatomically unspecific: the word he uses (αἰδοῖον), like English "private parts," refers to the whole genital ensemble, in either a man or woman, and derives from the word for reverence, awe, and shame (αἰδώς). Because the genitalia "contain the seed" (or "spermatic principle"), in a dream they stand for your parents or children or any blood relative; because they are used for "Aphrodite things," they may represent your sexual partners; because they all (penis, scrotum, vagina, clitoris) both stretch and contract, they resemble personal wealth, which may increase or diminish. These ungendered allegories depend upon biological facts relevant to all societies. But when Artemidorus refers to the slang expression "the manhood" for the genitalia, does he mean that manhood, normally small and limp, is only occasionally and briefly roused to effort? Probably not. And what does it mean that in Greek the word *manhood* could be used of women? (As in "that bitch has balls"?) Dream-genitals might also, for Artemidorus, allude to education, speech, poverty, necessity, slavery, bonds, and personal names.

The differences between these second-century allegories and those that twentieth-century psychoanalysis might assign to the

phallus demonstrate that the social significance of the male genitalia changes historically—and therefore, presumably, the significance of cutting off those genitalia changes, too. But the allegorical *form* changes, as well as its *content*. Artemidorus sees the
genitals as a symbol of innumerable other things; Freud sees
innumerable other things as a symbol of the penis. In Freud,
therefore, the penis remains constant, the still center of the turning world, the key to interpretation. Likewise, Freud postulates
the significance of castration, and then interprets various other
words or actions as symbols that "stand for" castration. But for
Augustine and Middleton the allegorical point of view—what
Hobson calls "orientation"—is completely reversed. In
Augustine and Middleton, we begin with a castration and have
to ask what that castration "stands for."

The castration Augustine must interpret is the one described
by Jesus himself: "There are some eunuchs, which were so born
from their mother's womb: and there are some eunuchs, which
were made eunuchs of men: and there be eunuchs, which have
made themselves eunuchs for the kingdom of heaven's sake"
(Matthew 19:12). Quoting this passage, Augustine exclaims,
"What truer, what clearer word could have been spoken? Christ,
the Truth, the Wisdom and the Power of God proclaims that
they who, by a holy resolve, have restrained from taking a wife
make themselves eunuchs for the sake of the kingdom of heav-
en's sake." This parenthetical paraphrase ("they who, by a holy
resolve, have restrained from taking a wife") is, of course, not
exactly what Jesus is reported to have said. The word *eunuchs*
does not literally mean "men who have chosen not to marry a
wife."

The normal literal meaning of the word is acknowledged by
Augustine elsewhere:

> Jesus, the Master Himself, and the source of all sanc-
> tity . . . when specifying in the Gospel three kinds of
> eunuchs, natural, artificial, and voluntary, gives the palm
> to those who have *made themselves eunuchs for the king-
> dom of heaven*, meaning the youths of both sexes who
> have extirpated from their hearts the desire of marriage,

and who in the Church act as eunuchs of the King's
palace."

By comparing the Gospel eunuchs to palace eunuchs, Augustine
explicitly defines the words of Jesus by reference to the castrated males who served Roman emperors. But he still insists that,
when Jesus said "eunuchs," he did not mean that; he meant persons "who have extirpated from their hearts the desire of marriage," rather than males who have extirpated their testicles.

Obviously, the words of Jesus are not as self-evidently clear
as Augustine wanted to insist. To make his allegorical interpretation of the New Testament plausible, Augustine contended
that the same spiritual meaning informs the Old Testament,
where the eunuchs in Isaiah 56:4–5 are actually to be understood as persons who "abstain from all carnal relations." But
there is no more linguistic evidence for Augustine's interpretation of the Hebrew scriptures than for his interpretation of the
Greek Gospel. To equate "made himself a eunuch for the kingdom of heaven's sake" with "embraced a life of celibacy,"
Augustine had to interpret *eunuch* allegorically.

This allegory did not originate with Augustine. It can be
found as early as Clement of Alexandria (Origen's teacher):
"The true eunuch is not he who is unable, but he who is unwilling, to gratify his passions." Saint Ambrose was also adamantly
allegorical: "It is the will, not incapacity, which makes a man
continent." Indeed, this interpretation—that literal castration is
here merely a metaphor for celibacy—has always been orthodox
in the Christian theological establishment.

Whether Jesus was really speaking allegorically may be
debated; I will return to that question later in this book. But the
more immediate question is: *Why* did orthodox Christians so
vehemently insist upon allegorizing this passage? After all, what
Jesus said makes literal sense; metaphor is possible, but hardly
necessary. And Christian interpreters pay a price for resorting to
allegory. Augustine's figurative reading brought him dangerously close to the reasoning of the heresy that "contends that the
commands given in Scripture . . . are not to be taken literally, but

figuratively"—especially when he was allegorically interpreting Matthew 19:12 in the same sentence where he attacked those other (heretical) allegorizers. Riding a metaphor is no safer than riding a tiger; once you mount, it's difficult to dismount.

So, why allegorize Matthew 19:12? We allegorize whenever something seems significant but unsatisfactory in its literal form. Anything Christ said is, by definition, significant to a Christian; so, something about the literal sense of Matthew 19:12 must have seemed unsatisfactory. Allegory solves a hermeneutic problem by resolving a conflict between the thing itself and our expectations of it. In this case, allegorizing *eunuch* to mean "celibate" resolves a conflict between the value Christians give to Jesus and the value they give to a sexually intact male body. As Ambrose decorously put it, "It is seemly to preserve the gift of divine working whole." But more is at stake than seemliness; at stake is a contest of texts.

The words of Jesus here appear to contradict the words of Saint Paul. Paul's missionary success depended upon rejection of the Jewish ritual of circumcision; you can cut the penises of infants without their permission, but it's harder to persuade adult males to suffer the same mutilation voluntarily. Circumcision was a serious obstacle to converting male gentiles. Paul's "gospel of uncircumcision" (Galatians 2:7) allegorized the ritual, substituting an invisible circumcision "of the heart, in the spirit" (Romans 2:29), "made without hands" (Colossians 2:11), for manual surgery on physical penises. Under Paul's leadership, as Tertullian put it, "the faith . . . turned away from circumcision back to the integrity of the flesh." Thus, literal castration not only threatened the integrity of male flesh; it threatened the integrity of the Jesus-Paul union, the integrity of the New Testament itself.

Jesus therefore *must* have been speaking allegorically because Jesus *could not possibly* have praised or encouraged literal castrations; that would have contradicted Paul, and Jesus *could not possibly* have contradicted Paul.

Moreover, if Jesus had been speaking literally, then the Christians' god might have seemed no better than the pagan

gods they were laboring to replace. Christian polemicists—
Tertullian, Origen, Theophilus of Antioch, and Athenagoras, as
well as Augustine—regularly condemned the pagan pantheon
for the castrations mythologically attributed to it. The same
Clement of Alexandria who insisted that Jesus was *not* encour-
aging men to castrate themselves "for the kingdom of heaven's
sake" elsewhere attacked the pagan gods precisely because they
were worshiped by castrated priests: "Let any of you look at
those who minister before the idols . . . many of them castrated,
who show the idol's temples to be in reality graves or prisons."
Saint Jerome was equally outraged that "the high-priests of
Athens to this day emasculate themselves . . . and once they have
been drawn in to the pontificate, cease to be men." Such emas-
culations, according to Minucius Felix, "are not sacred rites, but
tortures"; the gods ("of the greatest ferocity and fable-renowned
cruelty") who demand such castrations are, according to
Augustine, "tyrants"—and "gods who wish to be worshiped in
this fashion should be worshiped in none."

Middleton, like Augustine and the other Church fathers,
found castration appalling. He describes the amputation suffered by the White Bishop's Pawn as "a villainy" (1.1.159), a
"crime" (1.1.163), a "foul offence" (5.2.115) of "base treachery
and ignoble violence" (1.1.155–156), which defines its perpetrator as an "ignoble villain" (220) and "son of offence" (228)
who commits "violence That shames creation, deeds would
make night blush" (223–224). The Black Knight's Pawn himself
describes the castration as "inhuman violence" (2.1.228) of
"such base malice that my very conscience Shakes at the memory
of" it (1.1.214–215).

But, in Middleton as in Augustine, this arguably exaggerated
appraisal of the male genitalia exists only to justify an even higher appraisal of something else. The rhetorical function of the
amputated flesh becomes clear when we move from the act to its
agent. Who is responsible for the alleged atrocity?

Augustine had blamed not the individuals who castrated
themselves, but the goddess who incited them to do so: the Great
Mother (*Magna Mater*)—or, in Augustine's formulation, the
"harlot goddess" (*dea meretrix*) who had castrated Attis. This is

the context in which Augustine asked the questions I quoted at the beginning of this book.

> *Quid ergo ipse reliquus, & quid remansit absciso, quid eo significari dicitur? Quo refertur? Quae interpretatio inde profertur?*

> What then doth all that which remained of him after his gelding signify? Whither is that referred? The meaning of that now?

What remains of a male after he has been gelded is a eunuch. So what does a eunuch signify? Significance, for Augustine, is teleological: *Meaning* refers to "purpose." Most eunuchs at least served a social purpose: Involuntarily castrated, thereafter they protected the imperial marriage bed and in return were supported by their patrons. But the devotees of Cybele, who gelded themselves, had to beg in the streets for their maintenance. Because they castrated themselves for a deity who did not exist, and because they also lacked any secular function, such eunuchs could not reward interpretation, social or symbolic. What significance does a eunuch have? None. What does castration signify? Nothing.

Of course, this denial of meaning had itself a meaning: It characterized a rival religion, one much older than Christianity. The fourth century was as decisive for the conflicts between Christian and pagan as the sixteenth century would be for conflicts within Christianity itself. By the late fourth century, when Augustine converted, a newly hegemonic Christianity was refusing to grant its defeated rivals even the tolerance of religious difference that it had once begged from them. Although later translations tend to call it only *The City of God* (which sounds saintly enough), the fuller ancient title of Augustine's work was *Dei Civitate Contra Paganos*. Augustine, a rhetorician before he was a saint, defined/defended Big Brother Christianity *against* the residual paganism that he defined by maligning—maligned, in fact, by the very word *paganos* (peasants, hicks) set in opposition to an elite urbane city of Christians.

Moreover, although most of the quotations he quotes to refute come from a work four and a half centuries old (Varro's *Antiquitates Rerum Divinarum*), Augustine was actually targeting intellectual opponents much closer to home. In the first place, a particular Christian heresy had collapsed the distinction between Jesus and Attis by interpreting the castration of Attis allegorically. The Naassene heretics believed that "Attis has been emasculated, that is, he has passed over from the earthly parts of the nether world to the everlasting substance above, where . . . there is neither female or male, but a new creature, a new man, which is hermaphrodite." Montanus, who circa 156 founded a Christian sect that persisted into the ninth century, is said to have been a self-castrated priest of Cybele who converted to Christianity. On the other side of the doctrinal divide, in the fifty years before Augustine began *The City of God*, the castration of Attis had been allegorically interpreted by Sallustius, Macrobius, and the emperor Julian the Apostate. Similarities between Attis and Christ had become increasingly prominent in the ritual celebrations of Attis in Rome and elsewhere: The "Hilaria" turned his humiliated suffering into an occasion of joy, celebrants were "redeemed by the blood" of a sacrificial victim, and the promise of resurrection was held out to believers.

Such developments obviously made orthodox Christians uncomfortable, and Augustine was not the only Christian writer intent upon differentiating Christ from Attis, a crucifixion that meant something from a castration that meant nothing. In his description of the devotees of Cybele, Augustine carefully avoided the common word *eunuch*: The priests are *castratos* or *abscissorum* or *mollibus* or *Galli* or *reliquus* or *quasi hominem* or *homine castrato*, but never *eunuchus*. Augustine's contemporary and fellow eunuch hater, Claudian Claudianus, gleefully and frequently used *eunuchus*, but Augustine avoided it—because Augustine, unlike the pagan Claudian, had to prevent his readers from associating the castrated priests of Cybele with the "eunuchs" that Jesus praised in Matthew 19:12. After all, Augustine knew that his questions about "the meaning" and "the referent" of the castrated Attis could just as easily be asked—and had been asked—about men "who made themselves eunuchs for the kingdom of heaven."

And such self-castrations seem to have been fairly widespread in the fourth century among people calling themselves Christian. In a popular treatise on virginity, Basil of Ancyra (c. 336–358) attacked the "many" self-made eunuchs who had grown prominent in Christian churches, claiming that they imitated the *galli*; in 377, Epiphanius reported that "not a few" Egyptian monks had "eunuchized themselves"; in about 380, the *Apostolic Constitutions* described anyone who mutilated himself as "an enemy of God's creation"; in 389, Arians were condemned as "eunuchs"; in 390, John Chrysostom accused self-castrating Christians of being Manichaean heretics who "scorn God's creation"; in 395, Pope Leon I by papal decree forbade voluntary emasculation. Augustine—here as always—was establishing the orthodoxy of his own opinions by branding all variant interpretations and practices as heretical. And how do you prove that an opinion held by other Christians is heretical? By showing that it resembles the opinions of pagans. Self-castration could not be Christian because it was practiced by pagans.

In Middleton, too, castration is meant to characterize a rival, rejected religious ideology. About that much, every interpreter of *A Game at Chess* has agreed; but there has been no agreement about the exact meaning of Middleton's castrated pawn. In earlier chapters, I have treated the castration in the play as though it happened to a real person, or at least to a character in a "realistic" text. But we must attend to the form as well as content of Middleton's dream play. Seven characters of the aristocratic subplot were identified, by Middleton's contemporaries, as impersonations of living European politicians, but no contemporary linked any of the characters of the castration plot to living individuals. Clearly, the (main) pawn plot obeys different protocols than the aristocratic (sub)plot; it does not deal in hyperspecific individuality, but in generic human commonalities of some sort. If the aristocratic plot is a roman à clef, the pawn plot is a morality play. And it must be allegorical.

After all, chess pieces do not have penises, and castration is

---

Political Characters in *A Game at Chess*

WHITE KING: King James I of Great Britain

WHITE DUKE: George Villiers, duke of Buckingham (court favorite of King James I)

WHITE KNIGHT: Prince Charles (the future Charles I)

BLACK KING: King Philip IV of Spain

BLACK DUKE: Conde-Duke Olivares (court favorite of Philip IV)

BLACK KNIGHT: Conde Gondomar (Spanish ambassador to Great Britain)

FAT BISHOP: Marc'antonio De Dominis (formerly the Catholic bishop of Spalatro; then Protestant dean of Windsor, before returning to Rome)

---

not a move permissible or useful within the rules of the game of chess; when, in someone's recounting of a dream of chess, we hear of a castrated pawn, the conspicuous irrationality of the narrative forces us to seek an allegorical referent. Any actor or spectator, reader or editor, censor or critic confronted by Middleton's fan dance of allegorical desire is compelled to ask, "What does that castration mean?"

According to E. C. Morris (1907), the castration plot alludes to the struggle for the Palatinate, which precipitated the Thirty Years' War; in particular, the gelding of the White Bishop's Pawn represents "the loss of Bohemia." According to Jane Sherman (1977), "The unfortunate loss of the White Bishop's Pawn" indicates that the English clergy "is powerless to assist or warn [the

White Queen's Pawn], since all preaching against Spain, against Papism, and against the [Spanish] Match, ha[d] been banned at the instigation of Gondomar [the Black Knight]."

Both these allegorical interpretations are complicated and obscure. They are also coy. Both rewrite the gelding of the White Bishop's Pawn as no more than an allegorical "loss." Morris does not actually say this, but the logic of his allegory forces us to deduce that the White Bishop's Pawn's balls are Bohemia, which has been cut off from the Palatinate. Sherman does not actually say this, but the logic of her allegory confuses the White Bishop's Pawn's testicles with his tongue.

Sherman at least recognizes (as Morris does not) the importance of chess categories. Bishops, obviously, belong to the clergy; one would therefore expect a bishop's pawn to be a lower-ranking churchman, and that expectation is confirmed by the Black Bishop's Pawn, a Jesuit. Since the Black Bishop's Pawn is a Catholic priest, it seems reasonable to assume that his opposite number, the White Bishop's Pawn, was represented onstage as an English Protestant minister. The English clergy did feel embattled in the early 1620s, as official royal policy became more tolerant of Catholics in anticipation of a dynastic alliance between the Protestant Prince of Wales and the Catholic Infanta of Spain; as that marriage loomed closer, Protestants became more frustrated, and Catholics more exuberant, even arrogant. In September 1623 (nine months before Middleton finished his play), at the height of Catholic confidence, one fervent Protestant wrote to another, complaining, "The Papists here everywhere assault and insult upon our poor brethren in the ministry."

Physical assaults on English clergy were at least imaginable, perhaps experienced, in the 1620s; but anything as spectacular as genital amputation would surely have been recorded somewhere among the burgeoning gossip and propaganda of those years. It isn't, and we must assume that the castration of the White Bishop's Pawn had no literal historical referent. Middleton invented it. Why? The allegories of Morris and Sherman, like those of Freud and Lacan, fail to satisfy precisely because they refuse to focus—as Middleton insistently does—upon the disturbingly insistent particularity of the act of castration. All twentieth-century rereadings of Middleton make sense of castration by allegorizing it as "loss"—a loss that, in its ungendered generality, could be suffered by any female or any male.

Morris and Sherman seek a historical *signified* (in European politics of the 1620s) without attending to the history of the *signifier* (castration, as a word or a practice, a practice that produces a signed body, an embodied sign). Just as we can learn something about individuals by analyzing the associations they assign to the arbitrary signs used in a Rorschach test, we can learn something about cultures by analyzing the associations they assign to the physical signs created by a body modification. In humanist Europe, body modifications produced a strong and complex set of associations.

Gelded human males were not common in England. So, when eunuchs appear as characters in English plays they serve primarily as an exotic signifier, the theatrical sign of a social world conspicuously alien. For instance, the household of Ben Jonson's Venetian magnifico, Volpone, features a dwarf, a hermaphrodite, and a eunuch—a gratuitous baroque zoo kept for the entertainment of their master. Jonson's disciple, the playwright Richard Brome, also locates Venice under the sexual sign of the eunuch; in his play *The Novella*, an Ethiopian maid turns out to be—in the final scene's final revelation—an Ethiopian boy eunuch in disguise. In both plays, from the perspective of plot the eunuch is as gratuitous as the dwarf or the Ethiopian; rather, he functions metonymically as a symptom of Italian sexual depravity. Eunuchs similarly characterize the Egyptian court as dramatized by Shakespeare (*Antony and Cleopatra*), Fletcher (*The False One*), and May (*Cleopatra*); the Persian court as dramatized by Alexander (*Darius*); the Byzantine courts of Fletcher (*Valentinian*) and Massinger (*The Emperor of the East*); the Jewish court of Markham and Sampson (*Herod and Antipater*); and Islamic courts dramatized by Heywood (*The Fair Maid of the West*), Mason (*The Turk*), Daborne (*A Christian Turned Turk*), Massinger (*The Renegado*), Glapthorne

(*Revenge for Honor*), Carlell (*Osmond the Great Turk*), and Davenant (*The Siege of Rhodes*). Likewise, Robert Burton's compendium of melancholy miscellanea recorded the use of eunuchs by "the Grand Seignior among the Turks, the Sophies of Persia, those Tartarian Mogors, and Kings of China" and the "Xeriffes of Barbary." In all these humanist texts, eunuchs belong to an "Eastern" rather than "Western" culture; they are associated—in one of the recurring tropes of orientalism—with absolutist and despotic forms of government.

Both the eunuchs of Asiatic courts and the castrati of papal choirs were, like domestic livestock, gelded before puberty; none of these categories provides an exact parallel for the White Bishop's Pawn, who—like Abelard—was the adult victim of an *ad hoc ad hominem* castration. Nevertheless, all these circumstances share one attribute: a politics of slavery. Aristotle had distinguished the power of a "master" over his slaves from the legitimately political powers of an official, king, father, or husband; but Aristotle also acknowledged that in "barbarian" Asiatic regimes all forms of power, within the family and the state, tended to emulate the slave-master (*despotikon*). Two millennia after Aristotle formulated these distinctions, in 1453, Byzantium fell to an expansionist Ottoman Empire, and Western Europeans faced a serious military threat from what Aristotle would have characterized as a despotic barbarian regime—alien not only in its religion but also in its forms of political and social organization. That alien despotism fascinated English playwrights, from *Tamburlaine* on; indeed, they may first have encountered living eunuchs when a sixteen-man ambassadorial mission from Barbary visited London for six months in 1600. Certainly, eunuchs seem not to have appeared on the English stage as speaking characters before 1600, but they do appear frequently thereafter, and verbal allusions to eunuchs most often associate them with Islam.

But by the seventeenth century the stark binary opposition between Islamic despotism (East) and Christian kingship (West) had been complicated by ideological schism within the West itself. In 1520, Martin Luther attacked the canons of clerical

celibacy. His argument depended in part upon a legal distinction: The Church did not have the authority to pass such legislation. The New Testament itself made clear that several of the
apostles had wives; not until Augustine's lifetime (in 385) did
Pope Siricius make it a sin for priests to continue having sexual
relations with their wives after ordination. This papal insistence
on priestly celibacy had contributed to the schism between the
Roman and the Byzantine Churches, thus dividing Christendom
and demonstrating that the rule was arbitrary; and although
celibacy was expected, until the Second Lateran Council (in
1139) marriage and the priesthood remained compatible. The
prohibition therefore had resulted from a series of gradual
usurpations, as the papacy over the course of centuries
encroached upon and finally overturned the authority of
Scripture. The divine law (of an ancient written code) had been
displaced by the purely personal and arbitrary despotism of individuals sitting in the Chair of Peter.

Such usurpations were characteristic of what Luther called
"the *Babylonian* Captivity of the Church"; by forbidding priests
to marry the Popes had "acted like anti-Christian, *tyrannical*,
unholy scoundrels" (my italics). Luther characterized the papal
demand that priests make themselves eunuchs for the kingdom
of heaven's sake as an Asiatic despotism; Calvin, too, repeatedly condemned "the tyrannical law of celibacy." This tyranny was
epitomized by the "cruelty" that would "strangle millions of
souls by the cruel cords of a wicked and diabolical law." Calvin's
description of clerical celibacy recalls both the method of execu-
tion favored in Ottoman courts (strangulation) and a common
technique of castration (strangling the testicles). Like other
tyrants, the Popes had, according to Protestants, usurped a
power God had never given them, the power to desexualize
human beings, "to make a female creature out of a male"—that
is, to turn a man into a eunuch. "Like the Galli, who were the
priests of Cybele," Luther maintained, Roman Catholic priests
"unman themselves by assuming the burden of a very spurious
celibacy." And Calvin, too—in the midst of a diatribe that linked
the ceremonies, nuns, and saints of Catholicism to the rituals,

vestal virgins, and pantheon of paganism—made the same comparison. Augustine's attack on the *galli* had come full circle; it could now be used by "heretics" to attack the Christian ecclesiastical establishment.

The Roman Church responded to such criticisms by intensifying its public commitment to sexual abstinence. The Counter-Reformation Council of Trent decreed, "If anyone says that it is not better and more godly to live in virginity or in the unmarried state than to marry, let him be anathema." Celibacy distinguished the Catholic clergy from the laity; that distinction legitimated their power. By sacrificing his sexuality "for the kingdom of heaven's sake," the celibate priest acquired a special proximity to God, which enabled him to serve as an intermediary between ordinary people and the unapproachable divine monarch who controlled their destinies. Like palace eunuchs, priests were rewarded for their sexual deprivation with access to power. I will return in a later chapter to the problem of Catholic priests who violated their vows of celibacy; but certainly some, perhaps most, did indeed make themselves eunuchs for the kingdom of heaven's sake, and those who broke their vows recognized the moral superiority of those who kept them. Even sexually active priests could not contract legitimate marriages, could not father legitimate and acknowledged children, could not bequeath their possessions to a son. These were real sacrifices. Celibate or not, the Catholic clergy did not want to surrender to other men the prerogatives they had labored so long to acquire. And their public commitment to sexual sacrifice was one way to distinguish themselves from the heretics and to justify their continuing claim to special access to God.

The Reformation was fought, in part, over sex—over male sexuality, in particular. Luther, Calvin, Henry VIII, and the other Protestant leaders were all men, men who refused to become allegorical eunuchs, men who denied the supremacy of celibacy and demanded instead the right to marry women they wanted. In the rhetoric of northwestern European Protestantism, the Italian Church became an Asiatic castrating tyrant, and the Mediterranean was a sea of overlapping tropes of tyranny and sensuality. What better bride for the oversexed sultan than the Whore of Babylon?

But the Black House of *A Game at Chess* is not just the Vatican. It also—as the resident Spanish ambassador clearly saw—represents Spain, and particularly the combination of Roman Catholic ideology with Hapsburg political and military power. The Catholic Hapsburg dominions, run from Madrid, included all of Iberia, Austria, Belgium, much of what is now Italy and Germany, the New World, and colonial outposts around Africa and the Indian Ocean to Indonesia and the Philippines; it was the first truly global empire. What Catholic Spain hopes to impose upon the world is a "Universal Monarchy" (1.1.51, 243)—which is also an "absolute monarchy" (2.1.126). The Black House is also an "Inquisition house" (2.2.261) that imposes "slavery" upon its subjects (3.2.16). The genocidal colonization of the New World, the Inquisition, the suppression of the Dutch revolt, the sack of Amsterdam, the behavior of victorious imperial troops in the Palatinate and Bohemia—all had fed the "Black Legend," which stereotyped Spaniards as "lecherous, deceitful, and cruel." In England in the 1620s, castration of a sexual rival—that is, cruelty in the service of lecherous absolutism—plausibly epitomized Spanish ethics. And even more damning than the act itself is the Spanish attitude toward what the audience could be expected to regard as an appalling crime: The Black Knight dismisses it as a mere "suckling villainy" (4.2.11).

But if this attitude blackens the Black Knight, it intensifies interest in the Black Knight's Pawn, the man who actually committed the crime. In a house dedicated to revenge, his is the voice of remorse. The desires that motivated his gelding of the White Bishop's Pawn have already, by Act One of the play, been terminally frustrated. The elimination of his rival has not endeared him to his beloved; the woman he salutes as "Most noble virgin" answers by vilifying him as an impudent leper (1.1.219–227). He has begun "to be extremely burdened," and seeks a reconciliation with his victim (236–241). When he next appears, "The sting of conscience" has taken away his "joy" and "rest," and he is seeking absolution from his confessor (2.1.227–232); he continues seeking it throughout the play. The "absolute" power of the Black House (2.1.126) derives in large part from its promises of "absolution" for crimes committed in its name (1.1.162, 4.2.2, 132). But he who can forgive anything can also license anything; the "Absolute sir" (4.1.66) who holds the keys of absolution becomes "The absolut'st abuser of true sanctity" (2.2.112), whose promises of "absolution" turn out to be false (1.1.162, 4.1.27–28). The relationship between absolution and absolute power is not simply etymological, but causal.

For Middleton as for Augustine, the gelder is rhetorically more important than the gelded—because the gelder represents what's wrong with a rival religion. The gelded White Bishop's Pawn hardly speaks; he has endured physical "suff'rings" (1.1.199), but he is compensated by "religious joys" (1.1.203) and remains an effective champion of the White cause. By contrast, the Black Knight's Pawn is a major dramatic character; but, unmanned by his own "unmanliest" crime (1.1.158), he is so preoccupied by remorse that he never performs another exploit for the Black House. Nevertheless, despite his awareness of his own sin and his persistent search for salvation, in the end the Black Knight's Pawn is cast into the bag and damned. Like Augustine's *galli*, he zealously dedicates himself to a dead end.

A personal servant "brought up in blindness," the Black Knight's Pawn "scarce can read" (3.1.134); he may have come up from the country, for he speaks with sympathy of "the poor countryman" with "but one plot To keep a cow on, yet in law for that" (3.1.127–128). He epitomizes the Catholic layman, entirely dependent for his salvation on what his superiors tell him. They tell him that he cannot be absolved for gelding but can be absolved for murder, particularly if he murders a heretic. Innocently, he tries to do what he is told, and for his pains is consigned to the bag of hell. The story of the Black Knight's Pawn is the story of a Catholic layman who has committed a sin—it could be any sin—and seeks absolution for it in the wrong place.

But in fact the Black Knight's Pawn has committed a very particular sin, and that sin is itself associated with Catholicism. The English verb *castrate* derives from the Latin verb *castrare* (to

castrate, prune, expurgate, deprive of vigor). It is used figuratively as early as 1627 to describe the mutilation of a text by censorship: "An Oxford man . . . had his sermons perused and castrated." This obsolete textual sense is even earlier and common-
er for *geld* and its synonym *lib* in the sense "to mutilate (a book,
a quotation, etc.) by excising certain portions, esp. objectionable
or obscene passages; to expurgate." The Elizabethan Protestant
polemicist William Fulke used the idiom in at least three different anti-Catholic books published between 1577 and 1583 (and
reprinted in 1633). William Crashaw, documeing *Romish
Forgeries and Falsifications* (1606), showed that Catholics had
been "taking out words and whole sentences," and thereby leaving "a book so gelded" that the author would not acknowledge
it as his own. In John Donne's *Ignatius His Conclave* (1611),
Ignatius explains that various members of his order "did use to
geld poets and other authors." And John Gee, in a popular pamphlet of 1624, noted that the Jesuits "gelt . . . their writers, when
they meet with anything that makes not for their turn."

A modern mind has little difficulty understanding the censorship of obscenity as a kind of castration. But these images suggest that castration had, in humanist England, a more specific
textual and political meaning than our dictionaries recognize.
All these passages describe what English Protestants perceived as
the mutilation of texts by Counter-Reformation Catholics.
Catholicism is represented as a religion that can only be defended by dismembering textual authorities. Moreover, in England in
the early 1620s the suppression of true texts was epitomized by
the series of proclamations and directives by which King James
had outlawed and punished expressions of opposition to his
negotiations with Spain. In "castrating" the Protestant opposition, King James was widely perceived as a dupe or agent of
Spanish Catholics.

After the true texts have been castrated, the Jesuits can dis-
seminate their own false texts. The years that suffered the suppression of Protestant opposition also witnessed the proliferation of new Anglo-Spanish dictionaries and the release of
Catholics from English prisons. Gondomar/Black Knight boasts

both of his "politic restraint" of "all the barking tongue-men of the time" and of his having "made the jails fly open . . and let the locusts out" (3.1.89–90, 100–103). Accordingly, after the White Bishop's Pawn has been gelded, the Black Bishop's Pawn gives the White Queen's Pawn "a small tract of obedience" (1.1.190) and assures her that "that treatise will instruct you fully" (242); when we next see her, at the very beginning of Act Two, she enters "*with a book in her hand*," reading from it (2.1.1–3).

The book that the Black Bishop's Pawn gives to the White Queen's Pawn must be allegorical. Its title is not identified, and the book itself serves no necessary function in the plot; nevertheless, Middleton insists upon the book's emphatic theatrical presence, and upon her gesture, holding it, with a specificity rare in the stage directions of early modern plays. Why? What is symbolized, in the dreamwork of humanist Europe, by the small bilateral treasure that the White Queen's Pawn holds devotedly in her hand?

The scrotum, of course.

"Of course not!" you may retort. For most of my readers, the suggestion that a book is an allegorical scrotum will probably seem more far-fetched than any of Freud's by-now-familiar phallic symbols or castration allegories. Surely only an oversexed male author would *ever* think of that!

Exactly.

Contest of Reproductions
The Rise of the Penis,
the Fall of the Scrotum

The seed is the word of God.

(Luke 8:11)

Whatever the oversexed male author of *A Game at Chess* may have been thinking, to modern readers a book seems an improbable symbol for the scrotum. If we sexualize writing at all, we are more likely to think of phalluses than testicles. Of course, this penile preference reflects the historical shift in emphasis that I have already discussed, which makes us uncomfortable with the genital proportions assumed by Michelangelo and Rabelais. Most of us would accept Freud's insistence that maleness be symbolized by "long, stiff objects"; unlike the seventeenth-century French priest and influential skeptical philosopher Pierre Charron, when we think of "The body of man" few of us would begin by observing that it "consisteth of a number of parts inward and outward, which are all for the most part round and orbicular, or coming near unto that figure," and few of us would immediately go on to mention the "stones" (testicles) without ever even specifying the penis at all.

But in addition to our general collective focus upon the penis, we also have more particular reasons for associating the longer male member with literature. In a classic feminist text, *The Madwoman in the Attic*, Sandra M. Gilbert and Susan Gubar asked, "Is the pen a metaphorical penis?" Certainly, the two can easily be allegorically interchanged, and not just because the English *pen* sounds like the Latin *penis* (which educated Englishmen like Middleton would have learned in grammar school, where they went through puberty). Like the penis, the pen is a long cylindrical object, held in the hand, positioned above the passive white horizontal matter onto and into which it dispenses a precious fluid. And humanist writers did pun on the two words. Thus, when the Black Knight says that Italians "put their pens the Hebrew way" (1.1.305), he is literally saying that they write their secret messages backward, from right to left, like Hebrew; but he is also alluding to the alleged Italian fondness for sodomy, which involved putting a penis in "backward" (i.e., into the anus instead of the vagina). Elsewhere the comparison between pen and penis is simply implicit: When a boy passed through puberty, he was said to "write man," and when an adulterer seduced another man's wife, he "wrote him cuckold." In both cases, use of the erect penis so obviously resembled writing that the intermediate term of the equation wasn't even spoken.

Feminists object to this pen/penis metaphor for two reasons. First, it presumes that all authors are men; for three decades, much feminist scholarship has been dedicated to recovering unjustly neglected women writers. Second, if the pen is male, then the paper it writes upon is female; the metaphor consigns women to passivity, as the objects and instruments of male creative power. In the context of nineteenth-century literature (Gilbert and Gubar's specialty), these objections are legitimate enough. But in humanist Europe, most writers *were* men; as late as the early years of the seventeenth century, female authors accounted for only half of 1 percent of new books in England. Moreover, even a feminist like Germaine Greer concedes that the few women poets from the period were, mostly, not very good. And the pen/penis metaphor does not confine passivity to females; as the passages I have quoted from Middleton demonstrate, sodomites and adulterers use their penises to write on other men. Nor is the pen/penis the only writing instrument: Middleton can also describe a woman as "writing herself maid" or writing with her blood. The pen/penis metaphor is more complicated, and less sexist, than feminists sometimes assume.

And the textual economy could be sexualized and gendered by an alternative metaphor. In *A Game at Chess*, the origin of the book is male, but its destination is female: The Black Bishop's Pawn gives the book to the White Queen's Pawn. If he is the author (or publisher), she is unmistakably the reader; we actually see her, onstage, reading aloud from the book. And of course readers are not as passive as blank paper. Readers choose texts, actively interpret texts, and resist texts. Indeed, the White Queen's Pawn herself paradigmatically resists the efforts of the Black Bishop's Pawn to impose upon her his own sexual and ideological script.

Why is the play's emblematic reader *"a woman-pawn in white"* (1.1.0.2–3)? On the engraved title page of the 1611 edition of Richard Hooker's *Of the Laws of Ecclesiastical Polity*, the divine light radiating down from heaven falls upon the king, the Church, and a third, female figure apparently representing the individual soul. In traditional Christian exegesis, the individual soul is often female. God the Father and the Son of God are both male; in a heterosexual universe, the soul that a male godhead loves, and that in turn desires union with that male godhead, is naturally gendered female. Hence, the Church is the Bride of Christ, and the explicit and daring eroticism of *The Song of Songs*, which made celibate Christian theologians so uncomfortable, could be safely allegorized as a celebration of the purely spiritual union of a male God with a female spouse/ Church/soul.

Nevertheless, earlier (Catholic) morality plays had allegorized the spiritual temptation of Everyman; why does Middleton regender the allegory around Everywoman? Partly because Middleton was exceptionally dedicated to representing women;

he wrote more plays with female protagonists and female titles than did any of his contemporaries. But partly also because humanism had transformed the relationship between women and texts. All the most authoritative and religious texts of humanist Europe, and almost all its texts of any kind, were written by men, who were also responsible for commentary and censorship. Hence, the pen was still male, and the text produced by the pen was another male, the author's son. Cervantes described the text of *Don Quixote*, the most influential European novel of the seventeenth century, as his "son"; Sidney used the same metaphor to describe *Arcadia*, the most influential English prose fiction of the period. But although textual production remained virtually a male monopoly, the consumption of texts did not. Medieval women had had little opportunity, or reason, to learn to read. They seldom exercised political or judicial powers that would have required literacy, the clergy delivered Christianity to the laity orally and visually, and the educational system trained men for clerical careers closed to women. But sixteenth-century humanism, in emphasizing classical secular texts, also created a reading canon not tied to clerical careers; humanists advocated women's education and trained such remarkable intellectuals as Thomas More's daughter Margaret and Henry VIII's daughter Elizabeth. Moreover, the Reformation insistence on unmediated individual access to the Word of God made literacy obligatory for any serious Protestant. Although that obligation applied to both genders, women were far behind and thus had the most to gain. Accordingly, the rate of increase in literacy for women surpassed the rate of increase for men. And the novelty of female reading also probably made it more conspicuous, socially, than its familiar male counterpart.

Hence, although the text (and the clergy) remained male, the reader could now be female, literally and symbolically. The struggle between Catholic and Protestant Christianities, which shaped the ideological landscape of Europe, could therefore be imagined as a struggle between rival male writers, wooing female readers and essaying to inseminate their souls. Both the women in the White House are subject to attempted rape by the

Black House: the White Queen's Pawn by the Black Bishop's Pawn, and the White Queen herself by a Black Bishop. Both the would-be rapists are Catholic clergymen; both dispense books. The play's other major woman, the Black Queen's Pawn, has already been successfully seduced by the Black Bishop's Pawn, five years before, when she was "probationer at Brussels"; he has since "poisoned [her] with child twice," though he then refuses to acknowledge his "bastard" offspring (5.2.91–106). When initially stymied in his effort to seduce the White Queen's Pawn, he gives her a book to read, a tactic he calls "my old means" (1.1.190); so we know he has used this text-trick before, presumably on the Black Queen's Pawn. The two female pawns, white and black, thus represent two consequences of reading. One woman/soul resists black texts and remains spiritually intact; the other woman/soul succumbs to black texts, is impregnated by them, and gives poisoned birth. In contrast to her bastards, the only other child in the play is the White Knight, legitimate son and heir of the White Queen and White King. Chess pieces, of course, do not normally give birth (any more than they castrate), so these images of breeding must be interpreted allegorically, as the reproduction of white or black doctrines.

But why does the play contain no image of a female reading a white text? Because the white counterpart of the Black Bishop's Pawn has already been "gelded" before the play begins. Gelding, as I have said, removed the testicles, not the penis. In any case, cutting the penis hardly provides an appropriate image for censorship. If you want to use a quill pen, you have to cut the nib, repeatedly; cutting the pen therefore enables writing, rather than suppressing it. Moreover, since penises were only amputated as a punishment for treason or a treatment of disease, to compare texts censored by your adversary to amputated penises would imply that the suppressed texts were treasonous or sick. On the other hand, castration removed something that was itself intact and healthy, and did so for the sole purpose of preventing reproduction. Cutting testes therefore can easily stand for the cutting of texts.

The texts/testes metaphor assumes that texts have a particular shape, a shape that seemed natural to Middleton and his contemporaries, but that in fact arose at a particular historical moment. For most of classical antiquity, texts had been circulated in the form of papyrus rolls. The text was read by unrolling it and scrolling through it. Such texts may be mutilated at one end or the other, but they are difficult to mutilate anywhere in the middle because excision of material would cause a break in the roll. Mutilation of a text written on a papyrus roll is thus not easy to imagine in terms of castration, or bilateral orchiectomy. In fact, the cylindrical form of the roll made it a slang metaphor, not for testicles, but for the penis.

Beginning in the second century, the Christian codex replaced the papyrus roll. In the codex—a form familiar to us from our encounters with all modern books—pages of a certain size are bound together, and one reads a text by laying it on its back and opening it, then turning the pages. Unlike a roll, a codex is structurally bilateral: When we open a book, the opening displays two pages, symmetrically aligned. Moreover, a codex can be mutilated at any point by tearing out a page. And because a page is written on both sides, such mutilations always excise not one part of the text but two. In other words, mutilating a codex resembles mutilating a human male by removal of his two symmetrical bilateral testicles.

Middleton not only takes for granted the physical form of the codex; he also assumes that castration, as a social mechanism, is designed to regulate reproduction. Reproduction is controlled by controlling the originals that are to reproduce, the loins that become family lines. Animals (including humans) are gelded to prevent destructive male rivalries over the right to mate; castration enables selective breeding. Palace eunuchs could not father bastard children; castrated priests could not found a clerical dynasty. Fathers do not—as Freud imagined—regularly threaten to castrate their own sons; their "house" will survive only if those sons successfully breed. If anyone is castrated, it will be the young males of a rival house—as happens to the White Bishop's Pawn.

In humanist England, the expurgation of texts was described as castration or gelding not simply because it involved cutting something; after all, castration is a very particular form of dismemberment. To say that a text has been castrated is to imply that the text, in its natural original form, is a bilateral repository of male seed. Texts like those written by the Fat Bishop help "to propagate belief" (3.1.76). The parable of the sower figures the Gospels themselves as seed, and consequently in English *seed* has always been applied to religious teaching, described as "the sowing of the seeds of faith" or "a casting or sowing of such spiritual treasures and heavenly seed." The Reformation contended that the only legitimate Christianity was one originating in, fathered by, particular authoritative texts: the Bible in particular, but also the earliest Christian theologians, called "the fathers" of the Church or the "Apostolic Fathers." The resulting theological controversies were, in essence, disputes about textual paternity. Control of texts represented control of spiritual and intellectual fertility; textual castration was an attempt to cut off the life-giving seed, to prevent true texts from impregnating souls—and thereby to enable illegitimate suitors to father bastard doctrines. Castration, which had always been a mechanism for controlling biological reproduction, became a metaphor for mechanisms used to control textual reproduction.

That metaphor depended upon the fact that castration—in humanist Europe, as in previous human societies—attacked the scrotum. In twentieth-century psychoanalysis, by contrast, castration has been redefined as an attack on the penis. Within that new paradigm, the allegories of both human and linguistic reproduction, sexuality and textuality, changed, changed utterly. But why did those symbologies change? What happened, between the early seventeenth and the early twentieth centuries, to make that shift of genital attention not only possible, but plausible? If Freud's (re)definition of castration does not reflect a transhistorically constant human psyche, or even a necessary psychological concomitant of patriarchy, then where and how did it originate, and why did it so quickly saturate Western culture?

Any adequate answer to that question would require volumes; indeed, the transformations of European sexuality in those centuries have already produced a small library of scholarship. However, much of that work either accepts Freud's own claims about the universality of castration anxiety or does not directly address castration as a changing historical practice. Here I can do no more than sketch the outlines of a larger history of the transformations of the male genitalia in the centuries between Middleton and Freud. During those centuries, changes in contraception, surgery, theater, archaeology, anthropology, political theory, economics, and technology laid the foundations for the psychoanalytic redefinition of castration.

The Rise of the Penis

A new regime of contraception began early in the eighteenth century with the commercial manufacture and distribution of the condom. By the 1850s, the vulcanization of rubber made possible mass production of cheap, reliable condoms. Like castration, prosthetic contraception controlled male fertility, but it did so without surgically removing the scrotum. This technological provision for sex without procreation was complemented by technological provisions for procreation without sex: Lazzaro Spallanzani's successful experiments in the artificial insemination of animals and John Hill's satirical European best-seller, *Lucina sine concubitu* (1750), which imagined a machine capable of impregnating women without male intervention. In 1776, a Scottish surgeon oversaw the first known human pregnancy initiated by a syringe instead of a penis.

Moreover, while medical technology made removal of the scrotum increasingly unnecessary, it also made removal of the penis increasingly possible. By the middle of the seventeenth century, European surgeons were operating more often and more successfully on diseased or injured penises. And in the nineteenth and twentieth centuries, a rising proportion of military casualties were treated by battlefield surgeons, and survived, despite amputations of various kinds. The castrated narrator of Ernest Hemingway's enormously popular *The Sun Also Rises* (1926) was inspired by Hemingway's "personal experience" in a military hospital ward with other men suffering "genito urinary wounds," which made him wonder "what a man's life would have been like" if "his penis had been lost and his testicles and spermatic cord remained intact."

But the antecedents of Dr. Freud's redefinition of castration are not just medical. The pan-European rise of opera as a popular theatrical form moved musical castrati from a few papal chapels to the cosmopolitan public stage, where they became objects of urban adoration. In the eighteenth century, European women scandalously pursued operatic castrati, in part because they offered sexuality without semen, and so without pregnancy. One of the first histories of the social institutions of castration—Charles Ancillon's *Traité des Eunuques*, published in 1707—was written to warn women against the seductions of Italian castrati. A century later, Byron would confirm, by his "own knowledge," that "in Italy the women prefer" such castrati, because they offer sex "without the risk of pregnancy—or too rapid an emission."

In 1771, Tobias Smollett described one such castrato as "a thing from Italy"—thereby reducing an entire male body to a free-standing, untesticled penis. But other Englishmen were fascinated with a different collection of "things from Italy": ancient priapic objects unearthed in the archaeological excavations of Herculaneum and contemporary wax votive offerings in the form of male organs, still being purchased by women in the Italian village of Isernia in the 1780s. From these objects—literally, representations of male genitalia, amputated from their physical context—was born religious anthropology; its central thesis was "the existence of a universal phallic primitive religion." This thesis was first articulated in Richard P. Knight's *A Discourse on the Worship of Priapus*, published in London in 1786, translated into French in 1866, and appreciatively described by Freud in German in 1910.

These archaeological discourses ultimately originate, of course, in the Renaissance itself, and in the humanist program for recovering classical culture. But that recovery, and the coincident discoveries of non-European peoples, eventually threatened the intellectual primacy of Christianity, which became for the secular historian or anthropologist just one of a multitude of human religious beliefs. Thus, in the work of Freud's contemporary James Frazer, Christianity is not, as in Augustine, opposed to the worship of Attis and Cybele, but closely related to it. In *The Golden Bough* (1906–1915), after describing the worship of the Great Mother and "the emasculated priests of Attis," Frazer deplores "the spread of Oriental religions"—including Christianity, which began in the eastern Mediterranean and resembled in many ways the cult of Attis; these effete cults caused the decline of the Roman Empire, until "the tide of Oriental invasion" was turned by the "manlier views" of Western European humanism.

We do not have to accept Frazer's orientalist mythology here to recognize that the imperialist disciplines of anthropology threatened to make Christianity seem merely parochial. And Western Christianity has been much less tolerant of nonreproductive sex than other Mediterranean ideologies. Augustine himself enshrined the dogma that "a passion seeking no offspring," even within marriage, constituted "unlawful intercourse." Consequently, the increasing secularization of European culture between the sixteenth and twentieth centuries profoundly influenced attitudes toward the penis. That change did not happen suddenly. But Celia R. Daileader seems right to conclude that, in the London commercial theaters, sometime between 1590 and 1620 "sex replaced God as the supreme signified." During those same years events in Madrid and Paris confirm her thesis in a wider European context. In Madrid, in or soon after 1616, the first theatrical productions of *El Burlador de Sevilla* founded the legend of the great atheistic seducer Don Juan, while in Paris in 1616 the double entry into print of the letters of Abelard and Heloise produced another widely read and adapted story of sexual desire at odds with Christianity. By 1716, Pope's "Eloisa to Abelard" could sympathetically pit sex against God. In the contest of synecdoches in Pope's most popular poem, the male genitalia (sexual freedom) batter against the "Relentless walls" of a nunnery (incarcerating Christianity); in Eloisa's dreams, "Fancy restores what vengeance snatched away," and her lover's "image steals between my God and me." Pope's poem propagated a family of sequels and replies. In one of the first, Edward Jerningham's *Abelard to Eloisa* (1717), "the hallowed cross" has ceased to be "the saving all-atoning rood" and has become instead "The grisly symbol of" vengeful castration.

That opposition between God and sexual desire culminates in the political and sexual narratives of the Marquis de Sade. "It is erroneous that propagation is supposed to be one of nature's laws," de Sade argues in *Juliette;* "Nature permits propagation, but one must take care not to mistake her tolerance for an enjoinder." Instead, "the foremost of the laws Nature decrees *to me is to enjoy myself, no matter at whose expense.*" But this seeming anarchy in fact enables "the politicization of the sexual and the sexualization of the political," culminating in "the recreation of a social order and hierarchy, under a phallic, unifying economy." That phallic primacy is articulated most explicitly by Clairwil: "Pricks, aye, pricks, those are my gods, those are my kin, my boon companions, unto me they are everything, I live in the name of nothing but the penis sublime; and when it is not in my cunt, nor in my ass, it is so firmly anchored in my thoughts that the day they dissect me it will be found in my brain." And it is this same Clairwil who, having internalized the primacy of the phallus, externalizes the new form of castration: "When his prick had attained to full and towering erection, then my wicked friend . . . sliced that peerless member off with a razor, severing it close; later giving it to be prepared by a learned physician, she thus acquired herself the most extraordinary and I dare say the biggest dildo you have ever clapped eyes on." Clairwil's sexual surgery (which kills the male victim) has nothing to do with testicles or with "castration" in its traditional agricultural sense; instead, Clairwil literalizes the cultural transformation of penis into sexual prosthesis.

But of course de Sade, at the end of the eighteenth century, was transgressive and bizarre. By the end of the nineteenth century, most of the specific practices he celebrated remained illegal, but many of his assumptions were being normalized, in a process described and analyzed by J. N. Katz:

> In the United States, in the 1890s, the "sexual instinct" was generally identified as a procreative desire of men and women. But that reproductive ideal was beginning to be challenged, quietly but insistently, in practice and theory, by a new *different-sex pleasure* ethic. According to that radically new standard, the "sexual instinct" referred to men's and women's erotic desire for each other, *irrespective of its procreative potential.*

This transformation went through several stages. At first, "heterosexuality" described the sexual practices of people dedicated to lust for its own sake; this orientation was, in its first descriptions, regarded as a perversion, but by the 1920s heterosexuality had come to seem "normal." According to Katz, the key figure in this transformation was Freud.

All the foregoing developments contribute to what might be called "the rise of the penis." They make possible Freud's emphasis on penises in his theory of castration; that emphasis has seemed, for most of the twentieth century, not only plausible but "natural." For Katz, however, certain aspects of Freud's theories have themselves become strange. Katz takes his own intellectual protocols not from Freud's "Sexual Theories of Children" (1909), but from Michel Foucault's *History of Sexuality* (1976).

Although Foucault does not specifically historicize the meaning of castration, he does attend to the transformation of European sexual discourses between the age of Middleton and the age of Freud. In fact, he described his historical project as an attempt to provide "an archaeology of psychoanalysis." In the language of Foucault, "the deployment of sexuality" (what I would call the regime of the penis) is directly related to "the deployment of alliance," governed by imperatives of reproduction and kinship (what I would call the regime of the scrotum);

but the deployment of sexuality "has been expanding at an increasing rate since the seventeenth century; the arrangement that has sustained it is not governed by reproduction."

Clearly, at this point my account of historical shifts in the interpretation of castration meshes well enough with Foucault's influential account of the rise of "sexuality." But our agreement on the overall direction of this shift (from scrotum to penis, reproduction to pleasure) masks some important disagreements about castration in particular and the evolution of modern sexuality more generally.

To begin with the particulars: Foucault warns us not to imagine "the bourgeoisie symbolically *castrating* itself." What exactly does he mean by the verb I have italicized? He is referring here to the myth of "Victorian" sexual repression. According to that myth, the bourgeoisie—"believing itself obliged to amputate from its body a sex that was useless, expensive, and dangerous"—imposed upon itself an unnatural, restrictive sexual morality, from which we were freed by "the good genius of Freud." But Foucault denies that the bourgeoisie can be identified with "the repression of sexuality"; the philosophy of that class "is perhaps not as idealistic or as *castrating* as is commonly thought." As can be seen by these passages, Foucault equates "castration" with a myth of sexual "repression," what he calls "the repressive hypothesis." Furthermore, he repeatedly equates this mythical "repression" with "censorship" or "a massive censorship" or "the logic of censorship." Castration = repression = censorship.

We may seem here to have returned to the allegory of *A Game at Chess*: castration = censorship. But the intervention of the median term *repression* has utterly transformed this equation. In fact, although Foucault conceives and describes his project as a challenge to Freud, he here adopts from Freud a key element of his logic. In the first place, Foucault accepts Freud's redefinition of "castration": In Foucault as in Freud, it clearly removes not just the scrotum, but the entire male genital apparatus. Indeed, if anything, Foucault goes farther, making *castration* mean removal of the penis only—for in the mythology of repression the "Victorian bourgeoisie" somehow combines "amputation" and "castration" with "the serious function of reproduction" by "the legitimate and procreative couple." It is as though the bourgeoisie had managed entirely to dispense with the penis (and clitoris and vagina), allowing testicles to copulate with ovaries directly. As this anatomical fantasy demonstrates, for Foucault castration is a (sloppy) metaphor, always-already and only "symbolic." Clearly, then, in Foucault's post-Freudian definition, castration does not impair reproduction, indeed has nothing whatever to do with reproduction, and therefore cannot operate as it does in Middleton, as a precise metaphor for the-censorship-that-impairs-legitimate-reproduction.

Foucault thinks this way not only because he has internalized Freud's definition of castration, but because he has linked it to Freud's definition of repression. Repression is—like castration—a key concept in psychoanalysis. But Freud had described "repression" as "this process of censorship" as early as 1895 and 1896, more than a decade before he developed his theory of castration. In *The Interpretation of Dreams* (1900) and later works, he explicitly compared mechanisms of psychic "repression" to "the censorship of newspapers at the Russian frontier" or "press censorship" or "postal censorship." Thus, Freud compares psychic repression, including in particular the repression of libidinous impulses, to the censorship of texts; but he does not equate such "censorship" (which takes place *within* the individual) with "castration" (which for him is something the individual perceives in others and fears may be done to him by others—something, in other words, that comes from *outside*). Middleton used the physical act of castration as a metaphor for the social fact of censorship; Freud instead uses the social fact of censorship as a metaphor for an entirely psychological process.

And Foucault, in turn, conflates two separate strains of psychoanalytic thought ("censorship" and "castration") into the amalgamated myth he sets out to debunk, "the repression hypothesis." For Foucault, that allegedly massive repression simply did not happen—and, therefore, neither did castration—and, therefore, neither did censorship. For Middleton, censorship = castration = reality; for Foucault, censorship = repression = castration = myth.

How does Foucault know that repression is a myth? Instead of "censorship," he writes, "around and apropos of sex, one sees a veritable discursive explosion" and "a steady proliferation of discourses concerned with sex." He insists on the quantity and variety of texts about sexuality—a quantity and variety that did demonstrably increase steadily from the seventeenth through the nineteenth centuries, the very era of an allegedly deepening sexual repression: "Surely no other type of society has ever accumulated—and in such a relatively short span of time—a similar quantity of discourses concerned with sex." What we have all along interpreted as a "repression" of sexuality was in fact a "political, economic and technical incitement" to sexual discourse.

Foucault's critique of "the repressive hypothesis" has been enormously influential in literary and cultural studies, but as a historical explanation it suffers from disastrous weaknesses. First of all, one would have thought, after Derrida, that no intellectual would credit so simple a binary opposition. Incitement and repression can, after all, coexist, because no regime is homogenous. Foucault's binary logic blinds him to aspects of the historical record: The seventy-five men executed for sodomy in Holland between 1730 and 1732 would probably not share his indifference to the reality of sexual repression. But quite apart from this logical weakness and its consequences, Foucault's own evidence does not in any way support his historical conclusion. The number and variety of books about sexuality does increase, but that fact would be significant only if the number and variety of *other books* remained constant. Of course, as any historian of the book recognizes, those very centuries witnessed "a veritable discursive explosion" and "a steady proliferation of discourses" *of all kinds*, an exponential increase in the production and reproduction of texts, an expansion that necessarily entailed a corresponding ramification of systemic complexity, a rapid division and subdivision of the frenetically multiplying bacteriological culture into new modes, genres, disciplines, discourses. This explosion of textual matter resulted in part from revolutions in the technologies and economies of textual reproduction: the invention of the printing press in the fifteenth century, the capitalization and rapid geographical expansion of print-based and print-related businesses throughout Europe, the institutionalization of print-based literacy from the sixteenth to the nineteenth centuries, the shift from hand presses to increasingly powerful mechanized printing in the nineteenth century. As a result of these technological and technologized revolutions, the empire of text expanded more rapidly than ever before.

Foucault's attack on repression depends, in part, on a simple statistical error. *Numerically*, Western Europe produced more sexual texts in the eighteenth and nineteenth centuries than ever before; if x is the number of sex texts produced in the sixteenth century, and x + 10 is the number of sex texts produced in the nineteenth century, then obviously x + 10 > x. But this mathematical fact invalidates "the repressive hypothesis" only if the total number of books on all subjects (y) remained constant ([x + 10] ÷ y > x ÷ y). That statistical assumption is demonstrably false. *Proportionally*, sexual representation within the total textual polity almost certainly decreased in the eighteenth and nineteenth centuries: x ÷ y > [x + 10] ÷ [y + 1,000]. And anyone who contrasts the relatively uncensored quarto editions of Shakespeare published in the late sixteenth century with Henrietta Bowdler's expurgated edition of 1807, or contrasts the high visibility of Thomas Middleton and Aphra Behn in the seventeenth century with their almost complete invisibility in the early nineteenth century, or contrasts the obscenely accurate humanist translations of classical authors with their increasingly purged successors, or contrasts the genital frankness of Renaissance art with the "moral improvements" of later owners, should not be quite so quick to dismiss the possibility of "real repression." The rise of the penis, or what Foucault calls "sexuality," overlaps and interacts with the decline of something else.

The Fall of the Scrotum

"Real repression" is what Middleton represents in *A Game at Chess*—in particular, the real repressions, textual and physical, exercised by the Inquisition. Middleton's example provides us, I think, with a way to reconcile the fact that Foucault is right about the rise of a nonreproductive sexual regime, and yet wrong in dismissing individual instances of censorship as merely "local and tactical." The rise of that new sexual regime was not uncontested; it provoked a classic backlash, epitomized by the Counter-Reformation's *Index Librorum Prohibitorum*, first published in 1559, an index that condemned and banned a succession of important books, including not only Luther and Calvin (obviously) but also such things as the 1616 printing of Abelard's works. But that backlash was by no means confined to Catholic countries—because what the Counter-Reformation tried to control was not confined to Catholic countries.

Protestantism was, in a sense, only a "local and tactical" problem. What the Counter-Reformation tried (unsuccessfully) to control was an excess of reproductions, an excess made possible for the first time in human history by the printing press. Foucault pays no attention to the printing press. He is, in some ways, an old-fashioned intellectual historian; he analyzes changes in the thought processes of elites, as though thoughts were wholly unaffected by the merely material world. When he writes of "a completely new technology," for instance, Foucault is not describing a new mechanical device or set of devices, like the printing press; he means by "technology" a set of discursive practices. Foucault's defenders might object that I am indulging here in mere "techno-determinism." And I would agree that technology—including print technology—can never be a simple or sufficient explanation for cultural change. But mechanical technologies cannot be ignored by anyone interested in the powers that change a society, or the changes of power within a society. New technologies do create or magnify differentials of power between persons and between groups, and by doing so they crucially alter the "multiplicity of force relations" and the "interplay of nonegalitarian and mobile relations" of power that Foucault theorizes and analyzes.

A Game at Chess provides an example. The English (Protestant) government could and did shut down the playhouse, penalize the actors, track down and imprison the author; all those operations of repression had been used by regimes for millennia. But the government could not prevent the circulation of printed texts of the play. It had always been possible to identify and punish authors; it proved much more difficult to identify and punish printers. A single setting of type could produce hundreds or even thousands of copies of unidentifiable origin; any one of those copies could, in turn, be used by another printer as the copy-text for yet another edition, of hundreds or thousands of copies. Moreover, theater is an inevitably localized and centralized technology for distributing texts; audiences go to the playhouse, and the censors can go with them. But books are circulated by noncentralized networks of distribution, networks that expanded and ramified as they were fed by a steadily increasing bloodstream of texts pumped out by printing presses. By 1600, the new technology of reproduction and its networks were so well established that successful censorship was almost impossible.

Indeed, the problem that defeated a Protestant regime in London in 1624 had already defeated a Catholic regime in Rome exactly a century before. In 1524 Pope Clement VII ordered the burning of all copies of a printed edition of Marcantonio Raimondi's engravings of Giulio Romano's *I Modi*, sixteen depictions of sexual congress in different positions; the Church also burned a second edition, which had supplemented the images with verse captions by Pietro Aretino—many of them explicitly celebrating nonreproductive sexual acts. But printed editions continued to circulate surreptitiously, so that Middleton could expect his English audience, in 1624, to recognize immediately his allusion to "Aretine's pictures" (2.2.256). Moreover, ironically, those pictures are located, by Middleton, literally *in* "a room" of the Black House. Its opponents equate Catholicism, metonymically, with a sexuality that it had, in fact, tried to suppress.

By the first decades of the sixteenth century, Western European regimes were confronted and defeated by a problem that had never before faced any human society: *too much* (textual) *reproduction*. In the following centuries, the new problem of surplus reproduction surfaced in many spheres: monetary, industrial, mercantile. To understand shifts in attitudes toward human reproduction during that period, we have to understand the historical circumstances that made surplus no longer a simple blessing, but a complicated problem that increasingly exercised the minds of Europeans.

The empire of print dramatically expanded at the end of the seventeenth century, when the Bank of England was given the power to print bills of exchange—thereby introducing paper money. Making money from paper created a temptation to print too much money, flooding the economy with too many (legitimate or counterfeit) reproductions. This macroeconomic problem had been preceded by a proliferation of related microeconomic problems: excess supply of commodities. Again, printing had provided early encounters with this problem. The sudden availability of many more copies of books quickly saturated the market, causing the collapse of most of the printing businesses optimistically established in the first decades after Gutenberg. The trade only stabilized when printers organized into self-regulating guilds—like the Stationers Company of London, loosely formed sometime in the early sixteenth century, and legally chartered in 1557—which controlled prices, partly by placing severe limits on the number of printing presses in operation and the number of copies produced by any single setting of type.

But the problem of excess supply was not limited to the print business; in the early modern period, it spread throughout an expanding European economy, fed by global resources increasingly subjected to Western military power. The English East India Company, for instance, founded in 1600, within only two decades had learned, from bitter experience, that the immediate domestic sale of a newly arrived shipload of commodities from the East Indies disastrously lowered the unit price. More generally, in the words of the economic historian Joyce Oldham

Appleby, by the 1620s the "biblical economy" of scarcity had
begun to seem, to the most sophisticated merchant theorists,
"irrelevant." And Fernand Braudel has characterized the eighteenth century as a demographic turning point that brought to
an end "a long-lasting biological *ancien régime*." By the middle
of the nineteenth century, Karl Marx diagnosed "an epidemic
that would have seemed absurdly paradoxical in all earlier
phases of the world's history—an epidemic of over-production."
Demographically, agriculturally, economically, textually super-
fluity superseded sufficiency.

In all these realms, between the sixteenth and the twentieth
centuries local surpluses became general ones. In Middleton's *A
Chaste Maid in Cheapside* (1613), Touchwood senior laments
his own excessive fertility (2.1.1–63): He has "such a fatal finger in such business" that his marriage produces "every year a
child, and some years two"—not counting escapades abroad.
For his adulteries are fertile too: "I am the most unfortunate in
that game That ever pleased both genders: I ne'er played yet
Under a bastard." Notice that Touchwood senior is complaining, not bragging. The result of this excess fertility is "beggary"
and "barren fortunes." Touchwood here describes a pattern that
has since been documented in many developing societies: As
infant mortality rates decline, more children survive, and the
need to support them impoverishes their parents. Overreproduction undercuts prosperity.

But in *A Chaste Maid in Cheapside* that problem can be
solved because it is only local. Excess reproduction is not evenly
distributed. Touchwood's fertility complements the sterility of
Sir Oliver Kix, and so Touchwood's surplus can supply Kix's
deficiency, leaving everyone happily sufficient at the comedy's
end. But by 1798, such solutions were no longer working,
because the local problem had become a general one. The influential *Essay on the Principle of Population*, by Thomas Malthus,
for the first time theorized the calamitous social consequences of
overreproduction. He did so in a discourse as much economic as
demographic, which conceptualizes the excess reproduction of
human beings in the same terms as the excess reproduction of

printed paper banknotes. "The prejudices on the subject of population," Malthus observed, "bear a very striking resemblance to the old prejudices about" paper money. Malthus gave intellectual and moral authority to new movements publicly advocating birth control. Between 1800 and 1900 the birth rate in America fell by 50 percent; Western Europeans consciously reduced the size of their families until by World War I the average was half what it had been in 1800. These changes preceded, and no doubt in part stimulated, the development of new technologies of contraception.

Foucault had something to say about the rise of the discourses of demographics, "the emergence of population as an economic and political problem" and "the beginning of an era of bio-power" in the eighteenth century. But Foucault was not a statistical thinker. This no doubt explains why literary critics take him more seriously than do economic historians. It also explains why Foucault did not perceive the rise of a new sexual ideology as a problem of *numbers*—in particular, dangerously high numbers of reproductions.

Human regimes have probably always tried to control who reproduces: Witness the eunuch and the elaborate codes that have governed what Foucault calls "deployments of alliance." All such arrangements presumed the essential intrinsic value of reproduction itself. Reproduction was good; like other goods, it was unevenly distributed along lines determined by the fissures of power within a society. But from the sixteenth to the twentieth centuries Western European regimes and dominant ideologies were confronted by a new problem: In certain cases, reproduction itself became bad. Too much reproduction—of texts, of money, of commodities, of people—could be disastrous. And what is the anatomical sign of reproduction in the human male? The scrotum.

"The rise of the penis" was thus complemented, between the sixteenth and the twentieth centuries, by a corresponding "fall of the scrotum." Not only did pleasure, for a variety of reasons, begin to seem more important; reproduction, for a variety of reasons, began to seem less desirable.

A Man's Purse

According to Freud, in the unconscious money equals feces, and so we now describe misers as "anal." But for most of European history money was gendered (as shit is not). The word *male* in the General Prologue to *The Canterbury Tales* means not "man," but "a small bag" (containing valuables). Likewise, the French word *bourse* means both "purse" and "testicles." That seems odd to us, because we associate purses with women. But until recently men controlled the money and carried it in purses (or "moneybags") that resembled the scrotum (and were sometimes attached to their codpieces). Indeed, the Latin *scrotum*, dignified by medicinal antiquity, just means "sack." Hence the epigram published by John Davies in 1617:

Of Phormus his gelded purse

Phormus had in his purse two rubies rich
  When with his Turkesse (damnèd drab) he lay:
  To find which purse and stones, she sought his britch
    While he found sport—for which he dear did pay.
  For when she found his purse, she made no bones
  To geld it, ere he found it, of the stones.

By the usual pun, testicles are (precious) stones, here carried in (another pun) a purse; removing the stones from the purse constitutes gelding. And since eunuchs were, at the time, most strongly associated with the Ottoman empire, the gelding of an Englishman's purse is appropriately performed by a Turkish whore.

Davies did not invent this chain of thought. Shakespeare's Autolycus, in The Winter's Tale, likes "to geld a codpiece of a purse" (4.4.611–612); in Thomas Randolph's comedy *The Jealous Lovers*, an aside promises a rich "Old lecher" that "I will fit you, And geld your bags for this" (3.3)—a threat in context both sexual and financial. A Middleton character explains why con artistry is more profitable than armed robbery on horseback: "We geld fools of more money in one night than your false-tailed gelding will purchase in a twelvemonth's running" (*Puritan* 3.4.56–58).

Freud imagines money as a wad of paper stuffed in a billfold, carried perhaps in a back pocket; when you handle it, the ink on the paper soils your fingers. But until the invention of paper currency, late in the seventeenth century, wealth was measured in precious stones or in precious metals minted into coins: small, round, relatively heavy objects carried inside a leather bag, usually hanging near the waist. Physically, moneybags resembled testicle-bags; symbolically, both stored fecundity. Money breeds. Moreover, financial potency often compensated for physical debility. From Chaucer onward, old men with shriveled testicles but full moneybags acquire beautiful young wives and are duly cuckolded by young men with ripe scrotums and empty purses.

Hence the famous axiom of the entrepreneur in Middleton's *Michaelmas Term*: "They're busy 'bout our wives; we, 'bout their lands" (1.2.112). It is as though the scrotum and the purse were one bag, so that if you filled your sack with one kind of potency, there would be no room left for the other kind. And if men could fill the bag by storing up their money or semen, they could empty it by using either. When Shakespeare the sonneteer agonizes over "the expense of spirit in a waste [waist] of shame," he equates ejaculation with spending. Although we now know that every normal adult male routinely produces enough sperm to impregnate every female on our overpopulated planet, a postcoital male can still be described as "spent." Spending, sexual or monetary, depletes the contents of a man's sack, unfortunately. Most of us have a limited appetite for excrement. But what man ever had too much money? or too much sex?

In the final theatrical image of *A Game at Chess*, "the bag's mouth like hell opens," and the damned characters are piled into it, struggling for standing room and dominance; covetousness and rogue sexuality chaotically jostle one another like coins in a pouch. Instead of the awesome architecture of Dante's *Inferno*, the hell that Middleton imagines is an impatient crowd of selfish semen (*homunculi*, little men) stewing in the cramped hot chaos of the devil's scrotum.

This historical shift from the primacy of the scrotum to the primacy of the penis transformed cultural and psychological life. Foucault was certainly right about one thing: The proliferation of European sexual discourses and typologies in the nineteenth and twentieth centuries (including Freud's) cannot be adequately described by a simple narrative in which an innate human sexual drive gradually overcame the mechanisms of psychological and social repression. But it might be described as a consequence of a gradual and contested shift from an economy of patrilineal reproduction (which repressed everything but marital heterosexual intercourse) to an economy of pleasure (which licensed any enjoyable sex).

I am not claiming that human sexual behaviors generated no pleasure before the nineteenth century or that all regimes organized around patrilineal reproduction are identical or that the now-dominant ideologies of the penis are uncontested. Official Christianity has remained the chief site of resistance to the emergent regime of penises and pleasures; even now, fundamentalist Christians continue to campaign against a proliferation of behaviors that they characterize as "perversions." But what Augustine would have recognized as Christianity has now become a residual and embattled ideology. And that gradual shift from Christian God to secular sex, from reproduction to pleasure, has significantly reorganized attitudes toward the male body.

The scrotum is the locus of male fertility; in a society structured around the sexual economy of the scrotum, orgasms are justified as a means for increasing the fertility of heterosexual intercourse. The penis, by contrast, is the locus of male pleasure. Any hermeneutic for which the penis is standard will emphasize the pleasure principle, selfishness, and sex; it will produce a sexual economy organized toward the efficient production of orgasms, and epitomized by the endlessly repeated "money shot" of postmodern pornography, "the triumph of the dick." As a guide to sexual morality, Saint Thomas Aquinas' *Summa Theologica* yields to Dr. Wilhelm Reich's *The Function of the Orgasm*. As these differences suggest, we cannot use a Freudian or post-Freudian model of castration to interpret sexuality, or maleness, or the gender divide between male and female, in the centuries before Freud. If you shift your attention from the comic baggy balls (of Middleton) to the heroic upright phallus (of Freud), you reconceptualize the male body and its sexual relationships to other bodies, male and female; you forget about reproduction and focus upon masturbation. And you redefine castration.

But you redefine more than castration. Reproduction, unlike pleasure, takes two; it is inescapably social. From the perspective of heterosexual reproduction, the penis is just a delivery system. But from the perspective of male pleasure, the penis *is* everything: the alpha and omega, the beginning and the end.

Where does that leave women?

Contest of Genders
Castrating Women

There is neither male nor female.
—Galatians 3:28

Castration's tentacled centrality to the psychoanalytic model of the human subject was not fully articulated by Freud until "Some Psychical Consequences of the Anatomical Distinction between the Sexes," first published in 1925; but the decisive intellectual turn that culminated in that essay had actually occurred in 1897. By 1895, Freud had an explanation of what nineteenth-century medicine called "hysteria": He diagnosed it as a traumatic reaction to sexual "seduction" in childhood (what we would call sexual abuse, usually of daughters by their fathers). In 1897, Freud abandoned that hypothesis. Although everyone agrees on the importance of this change of direction, scholars are deeply divided over its legitimacy. Freud's critics see his rejection of the "seduction" hypothesis as a moment of denial or of moral cowardice: Freud abandoned his female patients, essentially deciding that they all simply imagined the abuse.

Freud's defenders retort that Freud's critics have no empirical evidence that the alleged sexual abuse ever actually occurred; they simply assume and assert that it did. They also point out that Freud, at various times, did acknowledge that children were sometimes really abused. But by recognizing the importance of sexual fantasy, Freud shifted his theoretical focus "from neurotic abnormality to the general human condition."

Nevertheless, even his defenders have to acknowledge that, after 1897, "Freud had no way to *theorize* the impact of acts of abuse." The sexual abuse of children became, often literally, no more than a footnote; what Freud powerfully conceptualized and represented was not real abuse, but imaginary abuse. But why would anyone imagine such a thing? Because they secretly desired it. And why did so many women imagine the same thing? Because all women secretly desire the same thing. ("What does woman want?"—To be fucked by her father.) Psychoanalysis here reinscribed, with the authority of science, the very ideology of the abuser, forcing women simultaneously to deny what had happened to them and to blame themselves for it. "What is left of reality?" Catherine Clément asks, retracing Freud's history of seduction: "Very little." In the founding phallacy of psychoanalysis, Freud redefined the physical as merely psychical, the historic as merely histrionic.

This is a move Middleton did not make. Witness the difference between Middleton's representation of the White Queen's Pawn (1624) and Freud's theory of female sexuality (1925).

In Middleton as in Freud, sexuality is conceptualized in terms of both castration and incestuous abuse; but Middleton represents both as physical and historical. In Freud's theory, a young female, noticing the difference between herself and a young male, *imagines* that *she* has been castrated. In Middleton's play, by contrast, a young female, noticing the difference between herself and a young male, *observes* that *he* has been castrated. For Middleton, castration is something that happens to men, not women—and, historically, he is right. But the difference between Middleton and Freud here is not only historical; it has profound consequences for what we might call "gender rendering" (that is, the representation of gender as an oppositional binary, a rendering that rends the species in two, a cutting off that separates genders).

In Middleton, "desire is of both genders." In early modern slang, both men and women have a sexual "thing" between their legs. Middleton belongs to a culture that subscribes to what Thomas Laqueur has described as a "one-sex" model of human anatomy, which prevailed from antiquity to the seventeenth century; in that model, there were two genders but only one sex, and the organs we call ovaries were simply an imperfect version of male testicles. Hence, both males and females could be "gelded." But the rise of the penis coincides with the rise of a "two-sex" model (first articulated in 1595), in which male and female anatomy are not variations of one another, but opposites. Hence, by the early twentieth century Freud, structurally and fundamentally opposing male to female, could declare that women anatomically "lack" a biological thing that men have, and therefore foundationally "envy" men. Freud's story of castration defines half the human race as intrinsically defective (as does the "one-sex" model); but where Aristotle and Galen characterized women as immature, Freud characterizes them as intrinsically emotionally malign.

To compensate for this alleged anatomical deficiency, adult women allegedly wish to castrate men. Citing anthropological evidence of widespread taboos associated with virginity, Freud conjectured that the breaking of a woman's hymen forcibly reminds her of her own "castrated" condition, focusing and releasing her pent-up "penis-envy" (*Penisneid*), which culminates in "the wish to castrate the young husband and keep his penis for herself." A particularly "masculine" woman therefore "castrates the man by whom she was deflowered."

Of course, in Middleton's play castration results from a contest between men, not a contest between genders; the literal gelder is male, not female. And Middleton accurately represents the social reality of castration in virtually the whole of human history. Freud himself could not find a single anthropological or mythical text that conformed to his interpretation; he cited as

The Female Eunuch: Aristotle

"All animals when they are castrated," according to Aristotle, "change over to the female state" (*Generation of Animals*, V.vii). In one sense, this statement describes a physiological reality. Normal human bodies produce both male and female hormones, but males produce more male hormones—or rather, more accurately, male hormones produce males. Genetically, the so-called sex chromosome that determines maleness actually only programs development of testes in a fetus; testicular secretions then redirect the embryo's genital development, turning bipotential emergent structures into an unambiguously male penis and prostate gland. Thus, testicles are the biological font of manhood, and the morphology of male sexuality is largely determined by the endocrine system. Since the testicles generate most androgens (particularly testosterone), removing them ensures the dominance of female hormones, produced elsewhere. Femaleness is the default position; without the hormones generated by testicles, a human body reverts, as much as possible, to its naturally female state.

Aristotle was thus, to some extent, right. But his description also had social implications within a society, like ancient Athens, that systematically suppressed women: It justified such exploitation by identifying the natural condition of females with the defective bodies of mutilated slaves. (Aristotle, of course, "scientifically" defended slavery, too.) The Aristotelian equation of women with castrated slaves persisted for centuries. It explains why Chaucer can compare the odious Pardoner to "a gelding or a mare" (as though a castrated male were indistinguishable from a female) and why in early modern English *cut* was slang for "cunt" (as when Shakespeare's Sir Toby Belch declares, "If thou hast her not i' the end, call me cut"). Aristotle's biological theory was trotted out as scientific proof of the

inherent defectiveness of women in every misogynist treatise for more than two millennia. Aristotle was, accordingly,
labeled the "enemy" of women by Lucrezia Marinella, one
of Europe's first feminist writers. In *La Nobiltà et l'eccel-
lenza delle donne, co' difetti et mancamenti de gli uomini*,
published in Venice in 1600, Marinella contended that
"Aristotle goes against all reason . . . when he states that
women are imperfect in comparison to men," and suggested
that "Aristotle was led by scorn, hate, or envy . . . to vitu-
perate and slander the female sex." Marinelli's humanist
feminist treatise was reprinted in 1601 and 1621, but thereafter it disappeared from view; it was not translated into
English until 1999. In the interim, Freud had produced
another "scientific" proof—as misogynist as Aristotle's—
that women are really just "castrated" men.

evidence "a dream" of a twentieth-century female patient and
one nineteenth-century German adaptation of the story of Judith
and Holofernes. He does not provide a text or description of the
dream, which apparently did not include a castration; he admits
that, on the surface, the dream appeared to suggest that the
woman desired not to cut off the penis of her husband, but "pro-
longation and repetition" of his use of it; nevertheless, "some
details of the dream" (which he does not specify) were "evidence
for the graver view" that she *really* wanted to geld him. Thus,
one of the two texts he cites is incomplete, unavailable, and at
the very least ambiguous. His other supporting text is equally
wobbly. In the Book of Judith (c. 135–105 B.C.E.), Holofernes
does not deflower the heroine; in neither the German play nor
the Jewish folktale does she castrate him. But Freud filled this
embarrassing gap by declaring decapitation "a well-known symbolic substitute for castration." Thus, this whole theory depends
upon two modern texts, neither of which explicitly represents a
woman gelding a man, or even explicitly wishing to do so.

The myth of the castrating bitch is no doubt more familiar,
among the general population, than any other aspect of Freud's

Kastrationskomplex. Indeed, even among intellectuals it dominates interpretation. For example, in one of the foundational texts of postmodernist criticism, Roland Barthes analyzed a novella by Balzac, *Sarrasine*. The seed from which that story grows, its center of gravity and mystery, is an operatic castrato; its characters also include the man responsible for gelding him. Nevertheless, when describing the text's structure Barthes rejects the mere "sexual classification" of actual castrator and actual castrated. Instead, it is "the castrating woman" Madame de Lanty who "mutilates men"—because "she is the primal Authority, the Tyrant," endowed with "all the hallucinatory attributes of the Father," including the "power to castrate." Thus, even in a narrative where men literally castrate, Freudianity sees castrating women.

Why? Surely not because Freud's short essay on the subject compels assent by wealth of evidence, force of logic, or brilliance of style. Freud's theory has been so widely embraced because he offers a comforting explanation of "that hostile embitterment displayed by women against men." That bitterness does not spring from any real wrongs suffered by real women at the hands of real men; no, it springs instead, Freud assures his readers, from a pathological female fantasy. Moreover, "the clearest indications" of that pathology—aha!—"are to be found in the writings and ambitions of 'emancipated' women." From the first, the theory targeted women—like Judith—who were seeking to overthrow a male despotism; it expressed, and justified, a conservative backlash against suffragettes. As Virginia Woolf recognized, the campaign for women's suffrage "roused in men an extraordinary desire for self-assertion," so that in the 1920s an observer could hardly avoid noticing the "anger and irritation" in men like "Professor von X." So Woolf's Teutonic misogynist (jabbing "his pen on the paper as if he were killing some noxious insect as he wrote") published texts "protesting against the equality of the other sex by asserting his own superiority."

*Eman*cipating woman means *emas*culating man. So, in the wake of the first political triumph of European feminism, declared Freud. And his theory remains familiar because it continues to serve the same reactionary function. In the autumn of 1999, as the millennium jittered to a close, Dr. Harvey Mansfield, Kenan Professor of Government at Harvard University, fumed that "feminists have mounted an attack on manliness" and announced that "after the feminists get through with [male academics] they are gelded." At the other end of the American social spectrum, black journalist Quinn Eli reports that in his Philadelphia neighborhood "we've got brothers standing on street corners holding their dicks, each one still swearing to anybody who'll listen that . . . it was some woman—usually his mother, but it may be the old lady he's sharing his crib with—who (figuratively) emasculated him and made it impossible for him to function as a man." Neither the Harvard prof nor the brother in West Philly needed to cite (or read) Freud; the psychoanalytic claim had become common knowledge, a shared psychopolitical slogan.

Not surprisingly, objections to Freud's castration theory have primarily come, as he dismissively anticipated, from the adversaries it targets and disarms: "the feminists, who are anxious to force us to regard the two sexes as completely equal in position and worth." Logically, their criticisms should long ago have sunk the entire hypothesis. But every feminist refutation is trapped by the very circularity of Freud's argument. Because he cites feminist resistance to male domination as evidence for his theory, any feminist resistance to the theory itself seems to confirm its premises.

Moreover, the logical attack on Freud's theory has been undermined by social evidence that seemingly supports it. Freud claims that all women everywhere always have wanted to castrate men; that claim is certainly unwarranted. But most people are not historians or psychologists; their ideas about "all women everywhere always" derive from their own local experience. So Freud's theory has been judged on the evidence of twentieth-century female behavior. And more support for this theory has come from that century than from any other. Freud did not accurately describe female attitudes toward castration before his lifetime, but he did predict the new behaviors of at least a few modern women. It's no accident that Freud's "evidence" came from modern texts. Thus, despite its manifest lack of universal validity, Freud's theory might seem to be *locally true*, a compelling description of *contemporary* gender relations.

I am not saying Freud is right; I am saying that his theory *looks plausible* in certain very specific historical and social circumstances. In fact, the apparent congruence between his theory and our experience is illusory. The embittered hostility between the sexes in modern times does not reflect a timeless flaw in the female psyche; it reflects instead the New Woman's resistance to the New Phallocracy (which Freud intellectually legitimated in his transhistorical myth of castration). In the old reproductive regime, one man's scrotum was the enemy of another man's, and amputation of the testicles was a crime men committed against men. But in the new regime of Caesar's (pleasure) Palace, every man's penis becomes, potentially, the enemy of any woman. By 1987, Andrea Dworkin could describe heterosexual intercourse as an act that inevitably violates and degrades women. Increasingly, genital amputation has become an act of rebellion by oppressed women—women like that good Catholic wife Lorena Bobbitt, whose husband's "weapon" was an instrument of sexual tyranny, from which she could only defend herself by amputating it while he slept; women like the hundreds of Thai

---

The Female Eunuch: Germaine Greer

"I am a woman," Germaine Greer insists, "not a castrate." Her feminist classic, *The Female Eunuch* (1970), attacked the physiological definition of females as defective males. Despite what the Western medical tradition from Aristotle to Freud would have her believe, a female is not born broken; instead, she "becomes feminine" by being "castrated" socially. Men insist upon artificially transforming her because "marriage and the family depend on the castration of women."

Yes, yes, I want to say, society warps female development. I cheer from the sidelines as Greer's impassioned wit
demolishes another male target. "Freud is the father of psychoanalysis"—my favorite sentence—"it had no mother."
But it certainly has had daughters (beginning with Anna
Freud, who, when her father was indisposed by illness,
actually attended the 1925 psychoanalytic conference for
him and delivered his famously misogynist paper "Some
Psychical Consequences of the Anatomical Distinction
between the Sexes"). Greer is another of Freud's daughters.
She inherits Freud's assumptions about castration, even as
she rebels against their paternal application to her.

"The characteristics that are praised and rewarded" in
women were, according to Greer, "those of the castrate—
timidity, plumpness, languor, delicacy and preciosity."
General Narses would not recognize himself in that description; neither would Farinelli, the great eighteenth-century
castrato. When Greer complained that the ideal woman of
modern advertising displayed "the lineaments of satisfied
impotence," she described the first seven decades of the
twentieth century allusively and accurately, but she also
echoed Freud's false attribution of powerlessness and com-
placency to castrates. Greer realized that, ironically, the
ideal female of male fantasy "*must not have a sexual
organ*"—but she did not realize that eunuchs *can* have sexual organs. What eunuchs definitionally lack are reproductive organs. And in that respect, of course, they do not at all
resemble patriarchy's ideal woman, whose useful uterus
keeps popping out perfect little progeny.

Females are not eunuchs. Just as important: Eunuchs are
not female. The victims of that particular form of mutilation—as of most other forms of physical violence—have,
historically, been males. Females are not the only humans
whose development is routinely warped by gender expectations.

wives who, in the 1990s, cut off the cocks of their philandering husbands, in some cases attaching the detached member to a balloon, so that it could not be found and surgically restitched. In this sexual new world, the claim that all women secretly want to "castrate" men seems to be confirmed by actual female assaults on penises (not testicles). My own ex-wife used to stand in the kitchen as we made dinner for guests, brandishing a knife and joking about using it in a way that Freud would have found satisfyingly predictable.

Indeed, he had predicted it. Indeed, she might never have acted that way if he had *not* predicted it. Male violence is so routine that it seems natural and therefore largely invisible, a background roar we no longer notice. But Freud's theory gave a new and profound significance to rare acts of female ferocity: Such spikes of rage were not unrelated curiosities or bizarre anomalies, but important confirmation of a universal "scientific" truth. Consequently, any female offensive against the male member is endlessly reproduced, magnified, and analyzed by the printing press and its electronic offspring. A theory about male genitalia, articulated by and for men who felt threatened by uppity women, is thereby "proven" by the riveted male media, telling tall tales of feminist terrorists assaulting some poor defenseless willy. Feminists are handcuffed by the resulting double bind: By ignoring or deploring such incidents, they leave Freud's theory unchallenged, but by contesting the masculinist interpretation of such incidents they increase its discursive mass, its ubiquitous familiarity—and also demonstrate that "one man-hating cock-cutter will defend another man-hating cock-cutter." As theory and practice circulate and intertwine, the endlessly disseminated model of castrating females becomes a pervasively internalized reference point for modern gender relations.

As these examples indicate, women are not the only people affected by Freud's representation of gender. After all, according to Freud, theories of castration govern male sexuality as much as they do female sexuality. One local act of cutting ("castration") metonymically represents, but also enforces, the more general/genderal cutting of the experience of men off from the experience of women.

Like so many other features of the new sexual regime, this postmodernist epidemic of women genitally mutilating men was occasionally anticipated in humanist Europe. In an English play of 1606, a woman, told that her husband is cheating on her, cries, "Bring me my chopping knife, I'll geld the lecherous goat." And such impulses were not always confined to fiction. Robert Burton reports that "a woman in Narbonne . . . cut off her husband's privities in the night, because she thought he played false with her." But before Freud, such moments remained sensational anecdotes, interesting precisely because rare and counterintuitive; they were not theorized or generalized into a paradigm of gender relations. In Middleton's world, women do not cut off men's penises or regard intercourse as invasive or consider men the inevitable enemies of women. We hear the White Queen's Pawn lamenting the castration of the White Bishop's Pawn before we even see him. Because he has lost his testicles, she can no longer marry him. Why not? Not (as we might suppose) because he could no longer satisfy her physically. In fact, the White Bishop's Pawn would certainly have retained his sexual desire and might still have been capable of erections, and thus of intercourse.

Such abilities will seem surprising to any modern reader who has internalized the psychoanalytic equation of "castration" with "sexual impotence." That equation usually applies well enough to males (animal or human) who have been castrated before puberty, and who therefore remain in a permanent prepubescent state. But the White Bishop's Pawn is an adult who has only recently been deprived of his testicles. And castration has very different effects upon male adults than upon male children.

Postpubertal removal of the testicles merely makes a man infertile; it does not inevitably impede penis performance; it does not damp desire; it does not guarantee chastity, physical or psychological. In Shakespeare's *Antony and Cleopatra*, the eunuch Mardian confesses that he still has "fierce affections" and fantasizes about "What Venus did with Mars" (1.5.17–18). If you don't believe Shakespeare, believe the Bible, which tells of "the lust of eunuch to deflower a virgin" and of "the eunuch embrac-

ing a virgin, and groaning" (Ecclesiasticus 20:4, 30:20). The
apparent contradiction was explained by John Chrysostom:
"Many who have been made eunuchs have not been freed from
the flame that burned within them, for the desire resides in other
organs, being seated inwardly in our nature."

What Chrysostom is saying might be paraphrased, less poet-
ically, as the observation that androgenic hormone production is
not confined to the testicles; such hormones, the biochemical
stimulants of sexual desire, are also secreted by the cortex of the
adrenal glands. Eunuchs can lust. And some eunuchs can satisfy
that lust. Although the exact biological mechanisms were not
known until the twentieth century, the physiological difference
between prepubertal and postpubertal castration was recognized
millennia ago. Postpubertal operations were routine in the late
classical world, both in and out of Christianity; their effects were
discussed in medical, theological, and literary texts, texts that
remained available to Middleton and other educated Europeans.
Any reader of Juvenal would have learned that Roman women
sexually preferred young men whose large *testiculos* had been
surgically removed—like the White Bishop's Pawn's—after
puberty. As Dryden energetically translated it,

> when the page, already past a boy,
> Is caponed late, and to the gelder shown
> With his two pounders to perfection grown,

the resulting eunuch is worshiped as a "new Priapus"; "Carved
for his lady's use, with her he lies," giving her "bliss" without
the need for "abortion"—or penis without pregnancy. Where
Juvenal bludgeoned, Martial sliced:

> Why, you ask, is your Celia spending so much time
> With eunuchs? Celia wants to fuck, not mother.

By the same reasoning, Athenaeus and Ammianus (wrongly)
attributed the origin of human castration to the Assyrian queen
Sammuramat (Semiramis), who wanted to satisfy her allegedly

insatiable sexual appetite without the burden of childbearing.
Similar stories were told closer to home. In a notorious poem
written in the 1590s, Thomas Nashe recounted a visit to a prostitute who, frustrated by his premature ejaculation, satisfied herself with a more reliable prosthesis. When Nashe curses
"Eunuch dildo . . . Who (sooth) may fill, but never can beget,"
his equation of dildo and eunuch establishes not only the infertility but also the erectile potential of the eunuch: Both can fill a
woman's vagina, but neither will make her belly swell. For
Juvenal, Martial, Athenaeus, Ammianus, and Nashe, the eunuch
was a human dildo, threatening precisely because he could offer
women just as much sexual pleasure as any uncastrated male.

The White Bishop's Pawn could still give sex, but he could no
longer give "seed." That might be enough, or even especially
attractive, to the whore-with-dildo derided by Nashe, or the
superslut-with-eunuch reviled by Juvenal and company, or the
"wench that will come with a wet finger" described in
Middleton's *The Patient Man and the Honest Whore* (2.5). But
the White Queen's Pawn is not that sort of woman. A male without testicles cannot father children—which means that, within
Christianity, the White Bishop's Pawn could not offer the White
Queen's Pawn any socially legitimated, "virtuous," or "honest"
form of sexual relationship. In 1587, Pope Sixtus V forbade
marriage to any man deprived of both testicles, and retrospectively annulled all such marriages that had already taken place;
he recognized that testicleless men engaged in "fleshly and libidinous acts" with willing wives, but their "filthy lasciviousness"
and "impure embraces" did not constitute true conjugal con-
summation because such men lacked the power to reproduce
(*potentia generandi*). These attitudes were not confined to
Catholics. Calvin—the single most popular author of humanist
England—decreed, "Those who are [eunuchs] by nature, or who
have been castrated by men, are debarred from marriage by this
defect." Likewise, William Perkins, the Elizabethan Protestant
preacher, declared that "deprivation of the parts belonging to
generation" nullifies any engagement or marriage contract. For
orthodox Catholics and orthodox Protestants alike, sexual rela-

tions were justified by reproduction. Hence the continuing Christian hostility to contraception, epitomized by Augustine. He opposed even the rhythm method (once advocated by the heretic Manichaeans); he conceded that intercourse occurred in Eden, but only for reproductive purposes, and without orgasms or lust. Eunuchs can pleasure but not impregnate. That did not disqualify them from contracting legal marriages in ancient Egypt, the Islamic world, or China; but Christianity refused to bless the union of carnality and sterility.

Castration is a social problem, not a sexual or psychological one. The White Queen's Pawn is frustrated not by any female sense of self-lack, but by the combination of male law and male lack. If she envies anyone, it is not men, but other women. Interrogated about "the desire that other women have in ends of marriage," she "must acknowledge" that her marital ambition was primarily motivated by "custom to enjoy What other women challenge and possess" (1.1.166–171). What do women want? What other women have. And what did other women have? Children: "many graceful issues" (3.3.41). The White Queen's Pawn predictably wishes for what the White Queen has: a child. Instead of penis envy, she suffers from pregnancy envy. And even pregnancy envy is not intrinsic, but mimetic—not the inevitable consequence of a natural or biological female desire for motherhood, but a social desire to be what she sees, to acquire what other women already display. (That is still true, of course. Women often decide to get pregnant after they see other women being idolized for their babies.)

Unable to acquire children from the White Bishop's Pawn, the White Queen's Pawn is eventually persuaded to marry the corresponding piece from the opposing side, the Black Bishop's Pawn. Protestant ministers (like the White Bishop's Pawn) could marry; Catholic priests (like the Black Bishop's Pawn) could not. As the Black Bishop's Pawn protests in an aside, "You know I cannot marry, by mine order" (4.1.132). Middleton thus situates the White Queen's Pawn, his Everywoman, between two kinds of eunuch: the White Bishop's Pawn, who has actually been castrated, and the Black Bishop's Pawn, who pretends he has made himself "a eunuch for the kingdom of heaven's sake." As a priest, the Black Bishop's Pawn should be a "spiritual eunuch," the kind of eunuch that Augustine and other orthodox Church Fathers believed that Jesus was describing in Matthew 19:12. *A Game at Chess* juxtaposes this spiritual eunuch with a material eunuch, the allegorical with the literal.

The Reformation attacked clerical celibacy as both a tyranny and a fiction. The Roman demand that priests remain virgins was characterized as a tyrannical act of castration (as we have already seen). But one response to tyranny is evasion. Those who demand the impossible reap the hypocritical. The proposed wedding of the White Queen's Pawn with the Black Bishop's Pawn depends upon two falsehoods: his disguise (which prevents her from recognizing that he is a priest) and his false promise (to marry her, which he does not intend to do, and legally cannot). Rather than sacrificing his genitalia, the priest has simply relieved himself of the obligations of matrimony and monogamy. His sexuality has been not restrained, but released. Hence the comparison between the perpetually randy Black Bishop's Pawn and Priapus (1.1.269–270); hence the Fat Bishop's confession that "there's no eminent trader deals in hole-sale But she and I have clapped a bargain up" (2.2.42–43).

The Catholic House tries to prevent legitimate marriages; it wants the clergy to pretend they are eunuchs. But this policy leads, effectively, to the condoning of extramarital sexual liaisons between priests and women. "Truly, this is the fine fruit which we have reaped from the diabolical system of celibacy," Calvin concluded, "that they who are not permitted to marry a lawful wife can commit fornication without restraint." Unlike ordinary men, priests had regular and unregulated access to unmarried women, giving them unique opportunities to seduce those in their pastoral care. Peter Abelard admitted that, before his castration, he read his young student Heloise "more of love than of any other lecture." In the orientalized Catholicism of Protestant propaganda, the Whore of Babylon actively and structurally and effectively promoted fornication between a clerical "father" and a lay "daughter." *A Game at Chess* thus characterizes the seduction of a woman by her confessor as incest. Like all forms of incest, it breaks down a sacred sexual boundary.

In Middleton as in Freud, a narrative of castration leads to a narrative of incest. But in Middleton's representation the incestuous sexual assault, like the castration, actually happens. The White Queen's Pawn, whom the Black Bishop's Pawn repeatedly calls his "daughter," is told to give herself, sexually, to her spiritual "father." The situation Middleton dramatizes would be familiar to any reader who has studied modern accounts of the sexual abuse of daughters by their fathers. The Black Bishop's Pawn demands sexual satisfaction as proof of "a daughter's duty" (1.1.188, 2.1.1), an obedience owed to him simply as a function of his paternal status; indeed, he characterizes his invitation to intercourse not as an abuse of power, but as a special favor he is showing to her alone: "A favor which the daughters of great potentates Would look of Envy's color but to hear" (2.1.73–74), evidence of his intention "to honor [her] above all daughters" (2.1.70). Again, Middleton characterizes female desire as a function of envy of other women. When the White Queen's Pawn refuses to satisfy his lust voluntarily, he abuses her verbally for her "disobedience" (2.1.54, 83, 99)—a disobedience that must be punished. The punishment of course consists of the forced satisfaction of the very desire she has refused to satisfy voluntarily. The request for sex in the name of obedience, when denied, justifies rape. Continued paternal authority can only be guaranteed if the daughter remains silent about the father's illicit request; her silence can only be guaranteed if she herself is made guilty of fornication, the very crime of which she would accuse the father. After a daughter is raped, she can only accuse the father by admitting that she is no longer a virgin. To accuse him is (in such a culture) to accuse herself.

In *A Game at Chess*, the daughter is fortuitously saved when the father is momentarily distracted by his own fear of discovery. The father's fear of detection on this occasion allows the daughter to escape, and later publicly to accuse the would-be rapist. But, as is also common, the daughter's accusation is not

believed, is redefined as slander of an innocent man with a spot-
less reputation; consequently, the would-be rapist escapes, and
the abused daughter is punished by those to whom she turned
for help. Her judge, the White King, declares—as Freud did,
effectively, to his female patients—"I ever believed rather the
accuser false Than the professor vicious" (2.2.227–228). By the
orders of the ultimate male authority in the White House, the
almost-raped daughter is punished, characteristically, by being
returned to the very house in which she was earlier threatened
with rape, and where she will now be tormented by being
locked, kneeling, in a pornographic prison, "a room filled all
with Aretine's pictures" (2.2.255–260).

Middleton, unlike Freud, represents, emphasizes, and theorizes paternal sexual abuse. He leaves us in no doubt of the
daughter's innocence or the father's guilt. In his configuration,
the Oedipal triangle is not created by the child's (impotent)
desire for the parent, but by the parent's (imperious) desire for
the child. Incest depends upon an inequality of power. And sexual abuse, which takes place in private, thrives upon the maintenance of a rigid distinction between the public and the pubic,
the political and the perverse. Middleton's politico-sexual *Game
at Chess* denies the validity of that distinction; its plots intertwine fingering and kingdoms. The daughter's rejection of incest
is explicitly characterized as a refusal to obey her superiors; that
rejection of the ideology of obedience has immediate and profound political consequences. The White King, who rejects the
daughter's accusation against her father, represents King James
I, who defended monarchic absolutism by analogy with patriarchal absolutism. What for Freud is private is, for Middleton,
intimately political. What for Freud is anecdotal or incidental is,
for Middleton, fundamental.

Moreover, in Middleton the "father" who attempts to rape
his "daughter" is her confessor—who bears an uncanny resemblance to a modern psychoanalyst. In the primal scene of analysis as dramatized by Middleton (1.1), the confessor knows in
advance the answers to the questions he poses—as does, of
course, the psychoanalyst, who is always "supposed to know."

He enters the dialogue armed with the axiom that *every* subject is subject to shameful impulses that can be cured only if confessed. ("Who is so innocent That never stands in need on't, in some kind?") The exchange is thus pre-plotted to expose the vulnerability and desire of a naive female analysand while establishing the authority of an objective and knowing male analyst. ("Daughter, the sooner you disperse your errors, The sooner you make haste to your recovery.")

Of course, Freud would have had an explanation for Middleton's identification of analyst as rapist: He called it "transference." In Freud's consulting room, as in Middleton's play, transference "enters on the scene" when "the work of investigation" encounters "resistance" from the patient. This transference may be negative ("hostile") or positive ("erotic")—indeed, it is usually both. "The hostile feelings make their appearance as a rule later than the affectionate ones"—as happens with the White Queen's Pawn—but the "hostile feelings are as much an indication of an emotional tie as the affectionate ones," and both derive from the same source: the patient's libidinous desire for the analyst. That desire for the analyst is itself a "repetition" of an original "partly unsatisfied" desire for someone else—usually, her father. The doctor dedicates himself to curing the patient (as the Black Bishop's Pawn attempts to do) by "removal of the resistance which maintains the repression."

Some of Freud's analysis fits Middleton's play. The White Queen's Pawn initially transfers onto the Black Bishop's Pawn her unsatisfied desire for the castrated White Bishop's Pawn (or God). But in Middleton, the analyst is as sexually driven as the analysand ("I never was so taken"); there is no point outside sexuality from which sexuality can be objectively understood. Instead, what purports to be objectivity is a technique for subjecting others. ("You will conceive by that my power, your duty.") And this knowledge/power of the analyst is built upon "the current of intelligence," the information acquired by the confessions of numerous analysands and then circulated within the intellectual "Society" of analysts. Each confession contributes to "the great college pot That should be always boiling

with the fuel Of all intelligences possible"; each analysand feeds
the authority of the "Order," which in turn feeds the authority
of the individual analyst. Middleton understands the politics of
analysis, as Freud does not.

Why can Middleton see what Freud cannot?

The seventeenth century can see what the twentieth cannot
because the seventeenth is resisting a powerful but as yet only
emergent ideology. As Foucault recognized, the Counter-
Reformation "continually increased" the scope of the sacrament
of penance, giving more and more importance to "all the insin-
uations of the flesh." As a result, the confessional became, in
fact and in fiction, a sexual site. Of course, sex "must not be
named imprudently," and so the Black Bishop's Pawn is a practiced euphemist who enjoys turning intercourse into discourse:
"A vestal virgin in a slip of prayer Could not deliver man's loss
modestlier" (1.1.153–154). Nevertheless, Foucault is right to
insist that the point at the center of this regime of circumlocu-
tion is sex: "Its aspects, its correlations, and its effects must be
pursued down to their slenderest ramifications." In the early seventeenth century, Catholic instructions to priests about confession include "a shocking catalogue of questions covering every
possible species" of sexual "impurity."

Middleton's representation of this confessional ideology
anticipates Foucault's. But when Foucault claims that the seventeenth century made this transformed sacrament of penance
"into a rule for everyone," Middleton would object. Protestant
England was not Catholic France; it had no Cardinal Richelieu
and would have no Marquis de Sade. Indeed, Middleton's play
seems intent on ensuring that England never become France,
never submit to the power of continental Catholicism.
Middleton sees what Foucault would later see precisely because,
like Foucault (but in space rather than time), Middleton stands
outside the logic of the Counter-Reformation.

And Middleton can see what Freud cannot because the ideology of the penis is only emergent in London in the 1620s; in
Vienna, by the 1890s, it had become hegemonic. Middleton,
accordingly, can project the patriarchally abusive penis onto a

vociferously rejected Other. After all, the old reproductive regime discouraged the sexual abuse of daughters. As anthropologist Margaret Mead observed, human societies regulate sexuality because they need to ensure "reproduction by physically mature" persons. Immature females cannot reproduce; incest with impregnable females tends to produce defective offspring; an immature mother may not be able to tend to her infant properly. In Xenophon's *Memorabilia*, Socrates had explained the reasoning behind the "universal" god-given law that "parents shall not have sexual intercourse with their children nor children with their parents" on the grounds that, by violating the principle of "the right time," such unions "beget badly." This genetic principle was observed very early in human development, in both human and animal populations. Moreover, in addition to this biological consequence, incest had specifically social consequences in patriarchal societies: Pregnancy would shame and thereby reduce the social and financial value of a postpubertal unmarried daughter, perhaps making it impossible for her to marry and reproduce legitimately. If the White Queen's Pawn had been successfully raped, "that contaminating act Would have spoiled all" her fortunes, ruining in particular her projected "marriage" (3.1.317–319).

But the pleasure regime doesn't care about reproduction; a young female may generate male pleasure, long before she is biologically or socially fit to reproduce. The father doesn't need to castrate sexual rivals if he is the only male with access to a particular female—like his own daughter. Daughters, socially subject to absolute paternal power, are transformed from their old status (as the valued products of past reproduction and valued agents of future reproduction) into a new status—as the readiest available mechanism for satisfying the penis in its pursuit of pleasure. I am not claiming that daughters were never sexually abused by their fathers in the old reproductive regime; but I do believe that when the new economy of sexual pleasure overlaps with the old power structures of patriarchy, the paternal sexual abuse of daughters becomes inevitable and, to some degree, legitimated. Hence the demographic shift in the incidence of such relationships, as father-daughter incest, rare in early literary and judicial texts, becomes statistically dominant in postindustrial society. Hence the changing role of incest that Foucault identifies in the eighteenth and nineteenth centuries: No longer "a functionally indispensable" prohibition, incest comes instead to occupy "a central place" in the bourgeois family, "constantly being solicited and refused . . . an object of obsession and attraction, a dreadful secret and an indispensable pivot." Hence the centrality of incest, and the physical abuse of children by their parents, in de Sade.

Hence also the anticipation of de Sade in Middleton's description of the Black House. Consider the intertwining of sanctity, eroticism, and pain in the Black Bishop's Pawn's speech to the White Queen's Pawn:

Upon those lips (the sweet fresh buds of youth)
The holy dew of prayer lies like pearl
Dropped from the opening eyelids of the morn
Upon the bashful rose.

The romantic resonances of Elizabethan love poetry (virgin lips are rosebuds, not yet opened, red because blushing) and classical allusion (the goddess Aurora rising from her lover's bed) are here replayed with an assurance as haunting as ever—but something's wrong: The description, conventional enough in a sonneteer, is here spoken by a priest, and the dew of prayer becomes a precious tear running from the eyes to the lips of a devout young woman observed awakening in bed. The "opening eyelids of the morn" awake to realize what they have done the night before, and that moment of embarrassed awakening is precisely what the observer relishes. Even more blasphemously, the biblical manna (appearing like "holy dew" every morning to feed God's chosen people) pornographically resembles a white beaded fluid dripping onto a woman's lips. He goes on to imagine "How beauteously A gentle fast, not rigorously imposed, Would look upon that cheek," and to recommend ("to beat down frailty") a penance "Whose utmost cruelty should not exceed The first fear of a bride" (1.1.77–85). What excites him, what he turns into exquisite poetry, is a vision of purity shamed and beauty in just a little pain.

Middleton can see all this because the regime of patriarchal pleasure is not his present, but merely a possible future. For Middleton, incest is not, as it would be for Freud, the central shaping fact about human psychological development; for Middleton, incestuous rape is not, as it would become for Andrea Dworkin, "a central paradigm for intercourse." For Middleton, incest is an aberration. It is not fathers in general who so enjoy abusing their daughters; it is certainly not English Protestant fathers. All that sexual abuse is perpetrated by bogus "fathers," oversexed Spanish Jesuits pretending to be fathers, pretending to be eunuchs, pretending to be guardians of the marriage bed.

It is not us; it is them. And what separates "us" from "them"?

The color line.

Castrated White Men

What communion hath light with darkness?

—*2 Corinthians 6:14*

Middleton's play divides the world into blacks and whites. Not an inevitable color-coding of chess. Of course, that binary depends upon (and reinforces) a seemingly self-evident Christian symbolism: white good, black bad. And England has been associated with whiteness since Roman times, at least, because from the Continent it features visibly "white" chalk cliffs. Modern critics have therefore seen no need to interpret the play's color line racially. After all, nobody in the Black House is African.

But this line of reasoning ignores the history of the signifiers *black* and *white* (just as other critics ignore the history of the signifier *castration*). As Kim Hall has demonstrated, even in the love poetry of English humanism *black* and *white*, *dark* and *fair* are seldom used without some awareness of their racial meanings. And Joseph Roach shows that "vortices of behavior" like the early London theaters cannot be disentangled from the complex racial entanglements of the circum-Atlantic "oceanic interculture." In early modern English, "blackness" characterized the complexions not only of Africans, but also of Amerindians, Islamic and Semitic peoples, Gypsies, and inhabitants of the Indian Ocean rim. From the perspective of the late twentieth century, Spaniards may seem unequivocally European, and therefore unequivocally "white." But the skin color of most natives of England differs from the skin color of most natives of Spain; in the United States, racial prejudice stigmatizes not just African Americans, but also dark-skinned "Latinos" (that is, people of Hispanic rather than Anglo-Germanic origin). In what is hard to interpret as anything other than an allusion to skin color, Shakespeare wrote of "tawny Spain"; *tawny* is an adjective he also applied to the child of Aaron the Moor and to Cleopatra—who are both, elsewhere, called "black." Likewise, Edmund Spenser argued that Spain, having been often invaded by "Moors and barbarians breaking over out of Africa," had suffered from intermarital "mixture" with "rude and savage nations"; consequently, the Spanish population, "most mingled," contained "no pure drop left" of European blood. Shakespeare and Spenser here follow the lead of humanist English historians, who routinely racialized Iberian difference, describing Spaniards as "a mixed people descending from the Goths, Saracens and Jews."

A Game at Chess itself leaves little doubt that the darkness of the Black House is not only moral and sartorial, but epidermal. When the White King's Pawn is revealed as a traitor, the (authorial) stage direction reads, "*His upper garment taken off, he appears Black underneath*" (3.1.261.1). Editors apparently or explicitly take this to mean that he is wearing a black undergarment, but the blackness could be skin. Almost immediately, one of the horrified White pieces exclaims, "His truth of their complexion!" (3.1.263). *Their* complexion differs, presumably, from *ours*. The play repeatedly calls White House characters "fair," and in some cases the adjective can only be interpreted as a reference to the lightness of their skin, hair, or eyes. By contrast, men from the Black House are described as blackbirds, monkeys, russet woodcocks, and slaves (3.2.9, 16, 28, 33). And the last Black character thrown in the bag of damnation is the

Black Duke, "a sun-burnt…olive-colored Ganymede" (5.3.211–212). The play's final characterization of the Black House, only seven lines before the collective *Exeunt*, emphasizes dark skin.

So do the title pages of the first editions. These feature an engraving of the Black Knight, which is clearly modeled on a portrait of Count Gondomar. In the original painting, the balding Gondomar, posing before a dark background, is undoubtedly white; in the derivative engraving for *A Game at Chess*, his shiny dome has been covered with a black hat, and his face conspicuously darkened, against a white background. The Black House is not just a theological but a racial category.

The racial binarism of *A Game at Chess* may seem to have little to do with castration, or Freud. But Freud himself was—as he repeatedly insisted—a Jew, and in particular "a godless Jew." For Freud and his contemporaries, Jewishness was not just (or even) a theological category. Jews were sometimes characterized as a separate race in early modern Europe; but that racial typology came to saturate the biological sciences, and the rhetoric of anti-Semitism, in the eighteenth and nineteenth centuries. And "the general consensus in the ethnological literature" from the sixteenth to the nineteenth centuries concluded that Jews were—like Spaniards—"black" or at least "swarthy."

Nevertheless, in the "scientific" discourses of Freud's time, "the most evident sign of the racial difference of the Jew" was circumcision—"a primitive act practiced by culturally inferior peoples such as Jews and African blacks." And for Freud personally, this "primeval custom of circumcision" was a "symbolic substitute for castration." In the pre-history of the primal family, "It was unquestionably the father who practiced castration as a punishment and who later softened it down into circumcision." Consequently—as Freud noticed in 1909 in his case study of "Little Hans," the original basis for his theory—"The castration complex is the deepest root of anti-Semitism; for even in the nursery little boys hear that a Jew has something cut off his penis—a piece of his penis, they think—and this gives them a right to despise Jews."

Obviously, Freud's equation of castration and circumcision

requires and enables his redefinition of castration: Circumcision mutilates the penis, not the testicles. In Western Europe by the late nineteenth century, eunuchs had almost entirely disappeared, but circumcision was routinely practiced in the Jewish community. To that community—and almost all of Freud's early disciples were Jewish men—the shift of attention from testicles to penis would have seemed perfectly "natural."

Race is thus deeply implicated in Freud's thinking about castration. Likewise, race and castration do not simply coexist in *A Game at Chess*; Middleton cannot think one without thinking the other. Indeed, in its combination of racial binarism and castration—as in so many other respects—*A Game at Chess* is eerily proleptic. In the 1890s, while in Vienna Freud was developing a theory of the sexual unconscious, in the United States hundreds of African Americans were being lynched, in the worst decade of extralegal racial violence in the nation's history. Although many white Americans were lynched in the nineteenth century, and although black Americans were lynched for many reasons and in many different ways, the mythical scenario that epitomized and justified southern lynching, in the century after the Civil War, was the rape, or attempted rape, of a white woman by a black man. (Like the attempted rape of the White Queen's Pawn by the Black Bishop's Pawn.) And, as anyone familiar with William Faulkner's *Light in August* cannot forget, the accused black male was typically, and with a ferocious enthusiasm, genitally dismembered. "Now you'll let white women alone, even in hell," Faulkner's castrator triumphantly declares. Faulkner based this incident, in part, on the actual lynching-with-castration of a black man in Oxford, Mississippi, in 1908 (the year Freud formulated the castration complex). Real or imagined, the physical violation of a white woman by a black man produced spikes of communal affect as spectacular as the initial response to *A Game at Chess*.

Of course, in *A Game at Chess* the pawn who has been castrated at the beginning of the play is *white*. But there is a curious error in the only eyewitness account of Middleton's play. Most of the many contemporary responses are secondhand, but John Holles actually witnessed a performance and described it in a letter written the next day. Not surprisingly, he gives an entirely accurate account of the play, except for one detail: Among the black characters put in the bag in the final scene, he writes, is "a Spanish eunuch." Since the play apparently contains no black or Spanish eunuch, scholars have been mystified by this remark.

There are, I think, two possible explanations. First, perhaps it never happened. In that case, Holles' reference to the Spanish eunuch can only be a "Freudian slip"—not an accurate account of what occurred, but a psychologically revealing transposition. The play represents, literally, a castrated white man, but what its audience wants, and imagines, is a castrated black man. The vengeful castration of licentious priests had been celebrated, in the European demotic imagination, at least as early as the medieval fabliaux; the same sadistic glee produced, in the Continental Protestant propaganda campaign of the Thirty Years' War, a 1620 engraving fantasizing a wholesale castration of Jesuits and other Catholic clergy. Closer to home, in a climactic scene of one of the favorite English plays of the seventeenth century, Beaumont and Fletcher's *Philaster* (1609?), a very obviously English crowd captures and threatens to "geld" a lecherous Spaniard who has sought to marry the heir to the throne. Such fantasies were obviously popular, and their circulation may not tell us much about what actually happened on the stage of the Globe in 1624.

Alternatively, Hollis may be telling us something about what audiences saw in the theater. Maybe Hollis took the beardless (Spanish) Black King, the passive sexual partner of the Black Duke, as a eunuch. Or maybe, more dramatically, he saw the White Queen's Pawn geld the Black Knight's Pawn at the end of 5.2. Abelard's castrators were punished by being castrated themselves; he who would rob another man of his manhood loses his own. This would produce an ironic moral economy to be found often elsewhere in Middleton. The biter shall be bitten; yea, and the gelder also, moreover, getteth gelded.

But whether that castration of a "black" male was theatrically imagined by Middleton or was only unconsciously imagined by spectators, *why* was it imagined? Because Middleton, and/or his audience, felt that they could only protect their women by castrating their more powerful male rivals. In 1962, James Baldwin said that the black man is "a walking phallic symbol"; in 1996, Andrew Young attributed white male hostility to the civil rights movement to a "deeply buried but intense sexual fear of black males." That was already true in 1624. The Black males in Middleton's play are, to a man, champions of coitus uninterruptibilitus: a great "codpiece college" (2.1.170) of aggressively horny undergraduates, presided over by Priapus, and routinely more successful sexually than their White nerd counterparts. In Eldridge Cleaver's "Allegory of the Black Eunuchs," the black man has become the Supermasculine Menial, and the white man, the Omnipotent Administrator, has "blundered and clipped himself of his penis." In Middleton's allegory, too, the White House has already suffered castration— just as many southern whites felt humiliated and disempowered by the Civil War and Reconstruction, just as many Englishmen felt humiliated by English impotence in the Thirty Years' War. In 1624, in the play and in the world, Protestant England was the endangered underdog: a militarily, economically, geopolitically, ideologically marginal player. The White House could not help but fear that the Black House might really permanently overpower it—just as, according to Norman Mailer, whites have always feared the "potential superiority of the Negro."

More generally, the entire system of patriarchy is threatened by the emergent ideology of sexual pleasure. As Luce Irigaray argues, "Once the penis itself becomes merely a means to pleasure, pleasure among men, *the phallus loses its power*. Sexual pleasure, we are told, is best left to those creatures who are ill-suited for the seriousness of symbolic rules, namely, women." Moreover, the "rise of the penis" coincides with humanism's rediscovery (in the mid-sixteenth century) of its female-pleasure partner, the clitoris. God, according to Saint Paul, had decreed that a woman who "liveth in pleasure is dead while she liveth" (1 Timothy 5:6). But once pleasure becomes god, why should women limit themselves to one sexual partner? Why not, as de Sade's women propose, "abolish marriages"? Why should a woman "be the captive of a single man" when Nature gave her force enough "to drain the balls of four or five in a row"? Why limit herself to white men when tempted by an irresistibly dark other? Indeed, why limit herself to male partners at all? Why should anyone confine their desires to heterosexual vaginal intercourse? As Augustine recognized, and feared, worshiping the Great Mother leads to a proliferation not only of eunuchs, but of homoerotic "Ganymedes"—like the "olive-colored Ganymede" bagged at the end of Middleton's play.

"A foul injury to Spain," Holles concluded. The Spanish ambassador in London agreed; after describing the play, and the popular enthusiasm for it, he warned his superiors in Madrid that "nothing else but war is to be expected from these people." He was right: England was soon at war with Spain. But he was also right in another sense. The dominant global empire of the eighteenth century would be British, not Spanish, and at the end of the nineteenth century a former British colony would completely humiliate Spain militarily, shattering its status as a world power. By the end of the twentieth century, the White House had become the sign of the planet's only superpower.

Middleton could not know what we cannot ignore. Instead, he and his audience feared that the future might belong to the Black House. But they were fascinated by what they dreaded. Although Middleton may want to insist upon the absolute superiority of whiteness, blackness keeps attracting him. For its first audiences and its most recent readers, the play's most irresistibly interesting character was and is the Black Knight. The White King's Pawn and the Fat Bishop turn out to be, or to become, black; by contrast, none of the black characters turn white. Middleton's protagonist, the White Queen's Pawn, is tempted, from the very beginning of the play until almost its end, to convert. His political heroes, the White Knight and White Duke, travel to the Black House, and until the final moments of the play they appear to teeter on the verge of conversion (just as Prince Charles and the duke of Buckingham had appeared to do when they traveled to Spain in 1623). Middleton couldn't let go of the Black House; revising the play, he brought them all back on for an encore, crammed together in the bag of hell. Something about that rival house, that house of castrators, seems virtually irresistible.

The future of whiteness looks black.

In the representations of Faulkner, Freud, and Middleton, castration intertwines with race. Is that a coincidence? Yeah, right. And it's also just a coincidence that black drivers are more likely than white drivers to be stopped by the police.

In the ancient Mediterranean world eunuchs belonged to the more general category of slaves, and slavery was not systematically racialized. But as Augustine's diatribe demonstrates, eunuchs provoked hatreds as visceral and virulent as anti-Semitism or apartheid: According to an old Roman proverb, "If you have a eunuch, kill him; if you do not have any, buy one and kill him." Moreover, that murderous hostility was partly "color prejudice." In Augustine's description of the castrated *galli*, what is Englished by the Jacobean translation of *The City of God* as "anointed heads and painted faces" was actually, in Latin, "*medidis capillis facie dealbata*"—which would be more accurately translated "oily hair, whitened faces." Augustine here expressed *a prejudice against whiteness*. And the prejudice was not unique to Augustine or to Christian theologians. A similar distaste for the "pallor" of northern European men is expressed by Julius Caesar and by other Romans. Augustine's contemporary, the not-Christian poet Claudian Claudianus, ridiculed the "pale" and "bleached" complexion of a eunuch, so colorless it was "unable to redden" with a blush. Another contemporary, the pagan historian Ammianus Marcellinus, also despised eunuchs and, like Augustine and Claudian, derided their "ghastly" skin color.

Modern clinical studies confirm that castration does produce the epidermal pallor these early texts describe. But the fact of pigment matters less than its effect. Clearly, the color of eunuchs operated, metonymically, as a signifier of separateness; around the paleness of eunuch skin the anti-eunuch prejudice of Augustine, Claudian, or Ammianus erects an entire typology, characterizing the eunuch as radically other, not-us. This is what Freud—victim and analyst of similar prejudices—perceptively labeled "the narcissism of minor differences."

Such visible physical differences, which made it easy to spot eunuchs, also made it easy to discriminate against them. In his satire *Eunouxos* (c. 180), the Greek humorist Lucian has a philosopher argue that eunuchs should be barred from academic appointments, temples, holy water bowls, and all public assemblies; indeed, it was "an ill-omened, ill-met sight if on first leaving home in the morning, one should set eyes on any such person." Earlier in the second century a real eunuch-orator, Favorinus, had been viciously attacked on the grounds that philosophy and rhetoric, the highest achievements of civilized man, "must not be contaminated by practitioners who are imperfect examples of the species." Such prejudices hardened into law. At the end of the first century, the emperor Domitian had decreed that no Roman citizen should be emasculated. He also prohibited the castration of Roman slaves for commercial purposes; in the fourth century under Constantine and again in the fifth under Leo I, this edict was reiterated; in the sixth, Justinian confirmed the prohibition and furthermore mandated freedom for any castrated slave. None of these laws banned or abolished eunuchs, who had become an important part of the social order; but the law insisted that they be imported, not domestically produced. Historians have demonstrated that even these restrictions were ignored, especially in the Eastern empire. But the more important point, surely, is the continuing belief, obsessively enshrined in the legal code, that castration is fundamentally un-Roman.

Also fundamentally un-Christian. In 325, at the Council of Nicaea, self-castration was condemned, and the ordination of such eunuchs forbidden. To reach this decision, the assembled Christians had to reinterpret allegorically—and thereby effectively erase—Christ's apparent praise of those who "made themselves eunuchs for the kingdom of heaven's sake." Their decision belongs to a large and complicated history of Christian beliefs about dismemberment, resurrection, and self-discipline. But it also belongs to the history of prejudice against eunuchs. Consider, for instance, the saintly diatribe of Saint Basil on the "disreputable and utterly accursed race of eunuchs" (εὐνούχων γένος):

> neither feminine nor masculine, woman-mad, envious, of evil wage, quick to anger, effeminate, slaves of the belly, money-mad, coarse, grumbling about their dinner, fickle, stingy, ready to accept anything, disgusting, crazed, jealous—and yet why say more?—at their very birth doomed to the knife! How can their mind be right when their very feet are twisted? They are chaste (thanks to the knife), and it is no credit to them; and they are lecherous without fruition (thanks to their own natural vileness).

Basil—who in the same letter also called eunuchs "lizards and toads"—had plenty of company. For Gregory Nazianzen, "It is all one to call a man a eunuch or a villain," an equation justified by the well-known fact that all eunuchs are "effeminate and unmanly men, of doubtful sex, but of manifest impiety; to whom, I know not how or why, Emperors of the Romans entrusted authority over men, though their proper function was the charge of women." Because some eunuchs became actors, Cyprian could regard them as a symbol of all the "incestuous abominations" of the "degraded" theater: "Men are emasculated, and all the pride and vigor of their sex is effeminated in the disgrace of their enervated body; and he is most pleasing there who has most completely broken down the man into the woman." And Athanasius condemned what he called "the heresy of eunuchs," the Arian heresy, which denied that Jesus was the Son of God; this interpretation of Scripture "receives its support from eunuchs, who, as both their bodies are fruitless, and their souls barren of virtue, cannot bear even to hear the name of son." Given such un-Christian prejudices, how could a man who had voluntarily become a eunuch be considered fit for the priesthood?

In 313, the Edict of Constantine had legalized the practice of Christianity; in 325, Constantine himself called, and presided over, the Council of Nicaea. *Roman* and *Christian* were not antithetical terms anymore. Christian soldiers were no longer supposed to throw away their weapons in pacifist protest. The community of Christ was no longer limited, as its detractors claimed, to "slaves, and women, and nurses, and midwives, and eunuchs," and its doctrines could no longer plausibly be dismissed as "the things a tanner, a purple-seller, a eunuch, slaves, and women believed." Christian apologists were understandably anxious to defuse such bigoted associations. By condemning autocastration and banning self-made half-men from its priesthood, Christianity became more Roman—and at the same time clearly differentiated itself from its rivals, an Oriental cult of emasculated priests worshiping Cybele and Attis. Constantine, taking note of the fact that the Egyptians "were accustomed to offer cult-worship through eunuch priests," issued a decree "that every species of androgyne should be exterminated as a sort of monstrosity." Under the emperor who legitimated Christianity, it was not only illegal to make eunuchs; it was legal—indeed, mandatory—to murder them.

In 325, a Christian council convened by Constantine decreed that eunuchs were not fit to fill certain important offices. At the end of that century, an Egyptian-born Roman poet wrote the most extended, admired, and popular literary description of a eunuch in the ancient Mediterranean world. Claudian's vicious diatribe *In Eutropium* vilifies the eunuch Eutropius, who had been elevated to the rank of consul in the Eastern Roman Empire in 399—the first of his kind to achieve such a rank. Claudian acknowledges that history provides precedents for almost every kind of monstrosity and metamorphosis—except this. Such a prodigy surpasses anything laughable in comedy or lamentable in tragedy: "Never in the world was a spayed thing consul or judge or general!" (*numquam spado consul in orbe / nec iudex ductorve fuit!*). To understand Claudian's apoplexy over "a castrated consul" (*castrati consulis*), you need only imagine the Ku Klux Klan's reaction to "a nigger in the Oval Office." (After his fall, his enemies claimed that portraits of Eutropius might "pollute the sight of those who look at them.")

Of course, not everyone was as vicious as Claudian or the Ku

Klux Klan. Just as America has its racial liberals, so Christianity had men like John Chrysostom, the patriarch of Constantinople in 398–404, a contemporary of Augustine and Claudian, but at the eastern end of Christianity. When Eutropius fell from power, Chrysostom gave the eunuch sanctuary. For Chrysostom, Eutropius illustrated the theme "Vanity of vanities; all is vanity." Eutropius, once powerful, is now powerless; once an enemy of the Church, he is now helplessly dependent on its protection and generosity. Chrysostom acknowledges that "there are many inhuman persons amongst us who are inclined, perhaps, to find fault with me for having admitted him to the sanctuary," but he takes arms against that prejudice: "I parade his sufferings from a desire to soften their hardheartedness." And parade them he does—for Chrysostom makes Eutropius into a human prop, illustrating his sermon. Look there, he tells his Christian audience, and behold "the man who was shaking the whole world, now dragged down from so high a pinnacle of power, cowering with fright, more terrified than a hare or a frog, nailed fast to yonder pillar, without bonds, his fear serving instead of a chain, panic-stricken and trembling." Look, and "ye may see . . . the harlot-face which a few days ago was radiant (such is the prosperity derived from extortion) looking uglier than any wrinkled old woman, this face I say you may see denuded of its enamel and pigments by the action of adversity as by a sponge." A very satisfying sight—so satisfying that any "poor man" who has "gazed at this spectacle does not think meanly of himself, nor bewail himself on account of his poverty, but feels grateful." Better a poor man than a hare, a frog, a wrinkled old woman, a universally despised, trapped, terrified, involuntarily trembling, publicly displayed, pale-faced eunuch.

Of course, even a compassionate liberal cannot guarantee to protect these people forever. Voluntarily or involunarily, Eutropius soon left Chrysostom's sanctuary and, despite assurances of amnesty, was executed.

Contest of Kinds
Confusing Categories

> *Before him shall be gathered all*
> *nations: and he shall separate them*
> *one from another, as a shepherd*
> *divideth his sheep from the goats.*
>
> —Matthew 25:32

Eunuchs were just as much a vilified "race" in the world of Augustine as Jews were in the world of Freud, or Spaniards in the world of Middleton, or African Americans in the world of Faulkner. In all these worlds, the meaning of castration is bound up with the meaning of race.

Freud's apologists might object that I am eliding a crucial difference here: Where these other writers build their representations of the world *upon* a racial prejudice, Freud builds his *against* such a prejudice. And it is true that Freud's theory of castration answers and resists a prevailing theory of race, taking the sign of Jewish racial difference and subverting it, transmuting it instead into a mark of universal identity. But what Freud gains in the discourse of race he pays for in the discourse of gender. His analysis of the relationship between anti-Semitism and circumcision links both to misogyny: "And there is no stronger unconscious root for the same sense of superiority over women. . . . What is common to Jews and women is their relation to the castration complex." This apparent alliance of Jews and women conceals a crucial difference: The "castration" of the circumcised male Jew is in fact superficial, leaving him with an operational penis and testicles, whereas the "castrated" female has neither. As Sander L. Gilman argues, in a persuasive historicization of Freud's logic, "'Normal' Jews, like Little Hans, overcome their anxiety about their own bodies by being made to understand that the real difference is not between their circumcised penises and those of uncircumcised males, but between themselves and castrated females." To Jews as a race had been attributed the weaknesses attributed to women as a gender; Freud divided the category "Jew" from the category "woman," so that "the distinction between male Aryan and male Jew is repressed, to be inscribed on the body of the woman."

One is tempted to say that Freud could only maintain the equality of Jewish men by insisting on the inequality of "castrated" women—to a degree, and with a stubbornness, that clearly embarrasses even his most sympathetic and admiring recent biographers. Women, for Freud, become the racialized other: "The sexual life of adult women is a 'dark continent' for psychology." It isn't Jews who should summon up, for Europeans, the alien incomprehensibility of darkest Africa; it's women.

This peculiarity of Freud's thought may simply illustrate, once again, the principle that every insight depends upon a corresponding blindness. But I think more is involved. After all, the irrational binary is not limited to Freud, or to Jews, or to white men. Castration links—not just here, not just fortuitously or anecdotally, but structurally always—gender and race.

This axiom might be more accurately phrased if in place of "gender and race" I put "gender and *genus*." The word *race* has itself become embarrassing, for certain critics, because by using it we might be thought to confirm the supposed substance of the categorical distinctions it arbitrarily imposes. The Latin word *genus* (Greek γένος) does not carry as much baggage; moreover, it emphasizes that the connection between the two categories (gender and *genus*) is, at one level, etymological. The word *genus*/γένος refers to a family, lineage, breed, gender, class, tribe, people, nation, race, kind, sort, order, species. The simplest and most local of these definitions obviously breeds, temporally and genetically and logically, the most complicated and general senses: The reproduction of an extended family produces a tribe, a people, a race, eventually a species. And those primary biological and linguistic categories in turn become a metaphor for other groupings, other "families" of objects or persons.

The structural relationship of castration to race and gender should by now be apparent. Men need the *genus* "woman" to (re)produce the *genus* "race." And to ensure that the *genus* of their "race" remains unconfused and uncontaminated, men need the *genus* "eunuch" to guard the *genus* "woman." The three categories—"race," "woman," "eunuch"—are structurally intertwined.

But the category "eunuch" turns out to be deeply problematic. Claudian Claudianus describes eunuchs as *"hoc genus"* (1:332, 415). Since eunuchs by definition cannot breed, they cannot produce biological families, which might extend over time into a tribe or people. No, *hoc genus inventum est*: Eunuchs are a "race" or "class" or "kind" not naturally born but instead "artificially invented." And like other inventions, this one has a purpose: *hoc genus inventum est ut serviat*, this race is made for slavery.

Eutropius is a manufactured man. About that much, Augustine and Claudian would agree. Moreover, although for Claudian as for Augustine the female sex may be contemptible in certain respects, at least women are "created by nature," whereas eunuchs are literally "handmade" (*illas praeterea rerum natura creavit, hos fecere manus*, 1:338–339). The eunuch thus blurs the distinction between person and thing: He is "an inert possession" (*inerti mancipio*, 2:55–56). Not surprisingly, therefore, he also blurs the distinction between living being and dead thing, his pale skin suggesting a *"cadaver"* (2:38, 147) or corpse (*funus*, 1:130), stripped to the bone (*nudis ossibus*, 1:121–122), ambiguously alive (*ambiguus vitae*, 1:52). Chrysostom, likewise, compared the eunuch's face to "the countenance of one dead."

Even if we acknowledge that the eunuch is alive, we cannot be sure to which category of the living he belongs, for he blurs the distinction between human and animal. The first word of *In Eutropium* is *semiferos*, "half-beast"; the eunuch represents "the union of human and snail" (*cockleis homines iunctos*, 1:356). Or perhaps he is not human at all, but only a monkey mimicking a man, a "simian simulation of the human" (*humani . . . simulator simius*, 1:303). In either case, the eunuch blurs the distinction between species, like a "swan with black wings or a crow white as privet" (1:348–349). He is, as a result, something prodigious (1:232) and monstrous (2:40), a mix of irreconcilable geographies, a Roman consul who nevertheless resembles "Indian fantasies on Jewish curtains" (1:356–357). Not surprisingly, therefore, even within the category of the human, he blurs the distinction between ages and classes. He is "a mixture of two ages" (*mixta duplex aetas*), combining the attributes of *puer* and *senex*, boy and old man (1:469–470). And this confusion also affects another kind of seniority. Eunuchs create "a novel nobility and sterile senate" (*novi proceres infecundoque senatu*, 1:469), an aristocracy no longer based on long and noble lineages, because it cannot breed at all. Worse than the confusion of patrician and plebeian, the eunuch blurs a distinction even more fundamental for all ancient societies, the division between slave and free; he produces that most outrageous of paradoxes, a "slave king" (*servilibus . . . regnis*, 2:593).

At the same time, the eunuch deconstructs, pervasively and disturbingly, the distinction between male and female. Claudian describes Eutropius as a "woman" once (*muliebris*), as an "old woman" four times (*anus*), as "soft"—which also means "feminine"—nine times (*mollis*). Claudian here speaks for a tradition centuries old: The philosopher Aristotle and the physician Galen had both argued that eunuchs resemble women. But this particular utterly feminized eunuch also, because he is a Roman general and consul, involuntarily reminds Claudian of that ultimate man's man, the founder of Roman manhood, Aeneas: "*arma relinque viris*" (1:281) verbally and rhythmically echoes the famous opening phrase of Virgil's epic, "*arma virumque cano.*"

Eutropius is "male" three times (*mas*); nine times, he is (sarcastically but nonetheless) a "man" or "manly" (*vir, virilis*). This confused gendering is summed up in the twice-repeated word *semivir*, "half-man." Is the eunuch a man or a woman? Both, and neither. He is "neither mother, nor father: one the knife, the other nature, forbids."

Claudian, like Augustine, associates male eunuchs with worship of the female deity Cybele (1:277). Indeed, the language of Claudian is also the language of his contemporary Augustine. Like Claudius (1:280), Augustine calls the castrated male a "remnant" (*reliquus*, 7:25) and "quasi-human" or "half-man" (*quasi hominem*, 7:25). So transformed by subtraction, he no longer belongs to either gender (*nec convertatur in feminam nec vir relinquatur*), but instead "mocks both sexes" (*uterque sexus inluditur*, 7:24). But this excision of sex, this amused androgyny, does not produce the sexual austerity admired by Christians and pagans alike in late antiquity. In the last decade of the fourth century—the decade of Claudian's diatribe against Eutropius—Jerome had insisted that male and female genitalia would be resurrected in heaven, and Augustine concurred, believing even in the resurrection of secondary sex characteristics like beards (which eunuchs do not have). The distinctions of class and gender would be preserved eternally, and the problem of sexual corruption could not be erased simply by removing the genitals, on earth or in heaven.

Hence, according to Augustine the castrating rites of Cybele produce "soft ones" (*mollibus*, 7:26, twice) "in defiance of the modesty of all men and women" (*contra omnem virorum mulierumque verecundiam*). The offense to "modesty" is not just the castration itself, but its consequences; the resulting "soft ones" resemble aristocratic women, whose soft white skin has not been hardened by labor or darkened by exposure to sunlight. Augustine compares this castrated male-who-resembles-a-female to "Ganymede," the beautiful young boy abducted and sodomized by Jove. Augustine here echoes Justin Martyr (d. 165), the first of the Christian apologists, who had accused the eunuch priests of Cybele of being sodomites. For Claudian, too,

Beards

Homo sapiens sapiens is a "weakly dimorphic" species: Although biological males are physically distinguished from females, the distinctions are relatively minor—unlike the northern elephant seal, for instance, where males are typically four or five times the size of females. But the biological distinction is complicated, in humans, by the possibility of cultural interference. One of the few secondary sex characteristics that does differentiate adult males from adult females is facial hair; but, once humans had invented stone cutting tools, such hair could be scraped from a male face, thereby making the species even more weakly dimorphic. Castration before puberty more radically reduces the difference: Eunuchs never grow beards (and never develop male pattern baldness, either). The ancient Akkadian word for eunuch apparently means, literally, "a man without a beard."

For some women, facial hair is an index of masculinity; such women find hirsute men attractive. But there have always been women like "Kate," who, in a song by Thomas Campion, "can fancy only beardless husbands." Indeed, facial hair toughens a man's face, even if he shaves it off. In *The Merchant's Tale*, Chaucer sympathizes with the hapless young bride whose ancient husband "kisseth her full ofte, With thikke bristles on his beard unsofte"—which remained "scharp" even though (or because) he was "schave al newe." Eunuchs not only lacked beards; because they didn't have to shave, they retained the characteristically "soft" skin of children or women. Part of the physical allure of the eunuch, for some women, is precisely that "soft" skin—as Juvenal realized, when he complained about women who "shun the bearded kiss." Beardless men are more like women; that makes them attractive, sexually, to some women.

It also makes them offensive to some men. The Greek philosopher Diogenes, meeting a smooth-shaved man, asked if he shaved because he was upset that nature had made him a man instead of a woman. Church fathers like Clement of Alexandria and Tertullian vilified shaving as a departure from nature and an insult to the Creator, and such criticisms continued into the seventeenth century. John Bulwer, in his *Anthropometamorphosis: Man Transformed* (1650), considered shaving, like castration, "a great indignity and despite to nature" because it removed "the natural ensign of manhood." Indeed, "shaving the chin is justly to be accounted a note of effeminacy . . . as appears by eunuchs, who are not so effeminate in anything than that they are smooth and produce not a beard, the sign of virility." Therefore, men who shave "may be likened" to eunuchs; "not without cause" both can be "called, in reproach, women."

The weak dimorphism of our species permitted a notorious Renaissance theatrical convention: The parts of women were played by boys. Like eunuchs, boys had high-pitched voices and did not have beards; indeed, female parts, played by boys in the Renaissance theater, were played by eunuchs in other theatrical traditions. This interchanging and overlapping of boy/eunuch/woman is most familiar in Shakespeare's *Twelfth Night*, where a boy actor plays a woman who plans to disguise herself "as an eunuch" (1.2.52). In *A Game at Chess*, too, the (small) part of the castrated White Bishop's Pawn might naturally have been played by a (relatively inexperienced) boy actor—thereby emphasizing the eunuch's ambiguous mix of features usually associated with different genders and different stages.

the eunuch is not only *mollissimus* (1:364), but boyish and tender (*tenero*, 1:423), not only soft-skinned but lacking the erectile hardness of an adult male, and thus *ambigui* (1:462). And like Augustine, Claudian associates such eunuchs with sodomy—a practice both writers utterly execrate.

Eunuchs could not procreate. But for orthodox Christians, only reproduction legitimated sexuality; so eunuch sexuality was, by definition, perverse. Not surprisingly, therefore, the official Christian abomination of sodomy—any sexual penetration of a nonreproductive orifice, in either a man or a woman—was often indistinguishable from anti-eunuch polemic. Thus, speaking of sexual relations between men, Chrysostom says that "to continue a man and yet to have become a woman, or rather neither this nor that," is worse than being physically transformed from male to female. Like the eunuch, the sodomite blurred the distinction between sexes, being neither and both. "Thou hast lost thy manhood, and hast neither changed into that [female] nature nor kept that which thou haddest, but thou hast been a traitor to both of them at once, and deserving both of men and women to be driven out and stoned, as having wronged either sex." Better to be transformed into a dog, or a woman, than a sodomite. Indeed, "if you would know the enormity of the evil from other grounds, ask on what account the lawgivers punish them that make men eunuchs, and you will see that it is absolutely for no other reason than because they mutilate nature." So, which is the sodomite, and which the eunuch? Is there any difference?

It is an axiom of contemporary queer theory that "homosexuality" is a modern category. Middleton's Black House—like other xenophobic representations of Catholic Spain and Catholic Italy—recognizes and practices a sin called "Sodomy" and prescribes a sixpenny penance for that sin (4.2.106–107), but the word *sodomite* does not occur in *A Game at Chess* or Middleton's other works. The word *homosexual* was not coined until 1870; although sodomitical practices occurred and were recognized for millennia, such behaviors were not taken to constitute a distinct sexual identity. Until the nineteenth century, "the sodomite had been a temporary aberration," Foucault influentially pronounced; "the homosexual was now a species."

But Claudian had called eunuchs a *"genus"* fifteen hundred years earlier. Their aberrant sexuality was not temporary, but a permanent consequence of a body modification that produced a new, socially recognized, distinctive sexual identity. Eunuchs were men, but they resembled women, partly because of socialized modes of dress, personal adornment, gesture, enunciation, and lifestyle. For sexual relations in the ancient world, as Foucault rightly insists, who penetrated whom was the crucial distinction; the "active" role of penetration was valorized, regardless of whether the person being "passively" penetrated was a woman, boy, or slave. But the penises of males castrated before puberty remain small, immature, and incapable of sexual erections; such males could never adopt the penetrator's dominant role. They were doomed, physically, to the despised category of the *cinaedus*, the catamite, the male who allowed himself to be penetrated. Echoing Foucault's description of the nineteenth-century "homosexual" as "a type of life, a life form," classical scholar Maud W. Gleason concludes that "The *cinaedus* was a 'life-form' all to himself, and his condition was written all over him"; what made him different was "his abandonment of a 'masculine' role for a 'feminine' one."

The identity position of the sodomized male was associated with eunuchs long before Augustine, Claudian, and Chrysostom. An Assyrian law (c. 1300–1100 B.C.E.) decreed, "If a man sodomizes his comrade and they prove the charges against him and find him guilty, they shall sodomize him and they shall turn him into a eunuch." The sodomite's deviant sexuality is made permanent by transforming him into a sodomized eunuch. The *Satyrica* of Petronius (d. 65 C.E.) lyrically summons, "O fairies, O buggers, O eunuchs exotic! . . . With soft little hands, with flexible bums, Come O castrati, unnatural ones!" (Note the emphasis, again, on soft skin.) Petronius, a contemporary of the apostles Peter and Paul, was allegedly master of the revels to the emperor Nero, who fell in love with a young boy named Sporus; the boy's "Genitories he cut out, and assayed thereby to transform him into the nature of a woman"—and then he officially married him, decorating the bride with "the ornaments of the empresses." Eunuchs like Sporus were boys who could never grow up, slaves who could never reproduce, passives who could never be active, males who could never be men but who also could never quite become women, catamites who could never be anything else.

Foucault's two books on sexuality in the ancient world left out an enormous amount of sexual practice and theory, in part because Foucault was not a classicist and was simply ignorant of much of the history and literature of the several related but distinct cultures that developed in the Mediterranean basin over the course of millennia. One of the things left out by Foucault is castration. Foucault barely even acknowledged the existence of eunuchs, as a unique category of male or a unique category of slave, one particularly and systematically stigmatized for "repugnant" sexual relations with other men. But the sodomized eunuch constituted, for thousands of years, what Claudian (and not Claudian alone) called an "other sex" (*alter . . . sexus*, 2:223–224). Produced by sexual transmutation (*sexum mutasse*, 2:552), the eunuch blurs all binary sexual categories. For that reason, Tertullian called eunuchs "a third race," which is "made up . . . of male and female in one," and is therefore "more fitted to men and women (for offices of lust)." An artificial kind, designed for purely perverse purposes.

We might ask of this account of eunuchs what Augustine asks of Varro's account of the rites of Cybele: *Hoc interpretari est an detestari?* (7:24). "Is this an interpretation or an execration?" Both, of course. Augustine and Claudian, Tertullian and Chrysostom, are describing what they detest. And they detest it partly because they find it so difficult to describe. The eunuch stimulates more than distaste for a particular body modification or a particular set of sexual practices. The castrated male, the manufactured man, is the *genus* of *ambigui*, an un-kinned kind, that confuses the very categories upon which all their interpretations of the world depend. The category "castration" not only inevitably infringes upon the categories of "gender" and "race."

It also threatens the very category "category."

Middleton's representation of castration also threatens the category "category." Chess itself is comfortingly categorical; it depends upon absolute distinctions, upon the maintenance of fixed visible sets created by precise rules. But *A Game at Chess* combines this totally ordered universe with the dis-kinded chaos of "a dream" (Ind. 49). Dreams have no rules and no fixed categories. The very clarity and regularity of chess provide a background against which irregularities are conspicuously foregrounded. In chess, for instance, there are two houses, and every player unequivocally belongs to one house or another; *house* can in fact be a translation of the Latin word *genus*, in the sense of "family" or "lineage" (as in "the house of Israel" or "the house of Stuart"). In chess, therefore, the distinction between Black House and White House is always absolutely clear. In Middleton's dream-play, it is not. The White King's Pawn and the Fat Bishop appear to be white, but are in fact black. It is possible, in bed, simply to substitute the Black Queen's Pawn for the White Queen's Pawn; the Black Bishop's Pawn cannot tell the difference.

A Game at Chess depends, like every chess game, upon the play of categories. Categories are constructed by laws, by rules, by what Derrida called "the law of genre." Both castration and the eunuch are—and always have been—legal categories. In the passage from Theophylaktos that I quoted at the beginning of this book, castration is interdicted by "the laws," but "those laws" must be carefully examined because like all other texts they are themselves governed by the "laws" of rhetoric. As this multiplication of plurals suggests, there is always more than one law code, and every law code always contains more than one law, and nothing guarantees that one law will agree with another. Middleton, whose own childhood and adolescence were disrupted by repeated lawsuits over his inheritance, knew this well enough: "Our wills are like a cause that is law-tossed," the White Queen's Pawn punningly realizes; "What one court orders, is by another crossed" (3.3.59–60). Moreover, all laws— and all the categories they define—depend upon meta-laws, on laws that define what "law" is. This doubling, multiplication, and entanglement of enabling legalities produces a disorder in the very attempt to impose order, a chaos of categories, what Middleton calls "the wilderness of law" (2.1.61).

Given such chaos, how can we simply obey the law? In its attack on the Black House, *A Game at Chess*, more than any other play of its time, demystifies and opposes obedience. But this critique of obedience could only be performed through repeated acts of obedience. The White Queen's Pawn is given (by the Black House) a text that instructs her in obedience to her spiritual director; the child actor playing the White Queen's Pawn was given (by the King's Men) a script containing instructions for speech and action. If the actor had not obeyed Middleton's written and spoken directions—if, like the character, he had rejected the book's demands—the play could not have been performed.

Likewise, the play rejects dissemblance, but depends upon it. Actors are, by definition, people who deliberately pretend to belong to categories to which they do not really belong. When the Black Knight says, "What we have done Has been dissemblance ever" (5.3.157–158), his "we" speaks both for the characters of the Black House and for the actors of the King's Men. In this second sense, *all* the actors, on both sides of the chessboard, belong to the Black House. Dissemblance and obedience—the generic marks of the Black House—are also the generic marks of the Play House.

So is the unnatural mixing of sexual categories. A boy actor played the White Queen's Pawn. Boy actors were instructed, by an older male, to dress up in women's clothes and enact scenes of seduction, involving sexual innuendo, touching, fondling, kissing. A male actor playing the White Queen's Pawn pretends to have no penis; a male actor playing the White Bishop's Pawn pretends to have been castrated.

The actor in *A Game at Chess* who pretends to be castrated belonged to a long and influential tradition. The Athenian playwright Menander (c. 324–292 B.C.E.) wrote a comedy called *Eunouchos*; it has not survived, but it formed the basis for a comedy called *Eunuchus*, written by the slave-playwright Terence. The Latin adaptation was first performed in a theater in front of the temple of Cybele, in Rome, in 161 B.C.E., as part of the festival of Megalensia, dedicated to the Great Mother; for a millennium and a half, it was the most popular and influential of Terence's plays. The play's central figure is not a real eunuch, but a lecherous able-bodied young male who disguises himself as a eunuch to gain sexual access to a desired female (whom he then rapes, and at the end of the play marries).

Terence—like Menander before him—wrote for audiences familiar with real eunuchs, but the comic potential of pretended eunuchry was still being exploited in seventeenth-century England. *A Game at Chess* adapts part of its plot from Terence: The Black Bishop's Pawn, by pretending to be celibate, gains intimate access to a desired female (the White Queen's Pawn), whom he then attempts to rape and later proposes to marry. And the plots of several subsequent English comedies—Peter Hausted's *The Rival Friends* (1632), John Ford's *The Fancies, Chaste and Noble* (1638), and William Wycherley's *The Country Wife* (1675)—all depend upon fake eunuchs, even though seventeenth-century England lacked eunuch actors or eunuch slaves. But in all these plays, from Terence to Wycherley, the character pretending to be a eunuch turns out, like the actor, not to be a eunuch after all. There is no real genital disparity between that actor and that role.

The prologue to Terence's comedy asks spectators to pay attention, "so that you may thoroughly know what the eunuch meaneth" (*ut pernoscatis quid sibi Eunuchus velit*). This final line of the prologue is ambiguous: *Eunuchus* may refer to the title of the play itself, or it may refer to the eunuch who is a character in the play, or it may refer to "the eunuch" as a category of person. Centuries before Augustine, Terence is looking for the meaning of the eunuch, and he constructs a play upon the difference between real and pretended castration. Like *A Game at Chess*, Terence's play contains a real eunuch (Dorus, the slave, comparable to the White Bishop's Pawn) and a false one (Chaerea, a young gentleman who disguises himself as a eunuch, comparable to the Black Bishop's Pawn). We derive the "meaning" of "the eunuch" by the juxtaposition of these two signifiers. The "real man" (who is a "fake eunuch") is characterized by three successful actions: deception, rape, and marriage.

But Middleton has transformed the meaning of *The Eunuchus*' plot by transferring it into a different social context. In England in 1624, there is no real eunuch, inside or outside the theater. Therefore, in Middleton's play, an uncastrated actor must represent an actually castrated character, the White Bishop's Pawn. Terence had asked, "What does castration mean?" Middleton also asks, "What does the imitation of castration mean?"

What is the sign for castration? What is castration a sign for? What happens where representation intersects with biology?

Branded and Domesticated
Male Animals

I will write upon him the name of my God.
—*Revelation 3:12*

The human *genus,* at some indeterminable stage of evolution, became grammatological: We learned to make symbolic signs upon surfaces. When Theophylaktos, at the beginning of this book, commanded us to pay attention to "the mind of the inscriptions" (τὸν νοῦν . . . τῶν γεγραμμένων), he used a Greek noun that means "something drawn" and hence "letter" and hence "text"; our words *graph* and *graphic* and *telegram* and *grammar* all derive from that ancient verb and noun. Geometry, mathematics, art, and writing put mind into marks; all kinds of signs branch from this grammatological root, this marking of surfaces.

The epidermal membrane that encloses and contains animal bodies is such a surface, which may easily be marked with signs, deliberate or accidental. The superb writing surface called parchment, for instance, is the skin flayed from a dead sheep or goat. But skins can also be marked with signs while the animals are still alive; domesticated livestock, for instance, are branded to identify their owners. And what humans can do to the skins of animals they can also do to their own skins. Their own skins, after all, were always at hand, many millennia before humans learned to domesticate animals or to cure their hides. Indeed, some humans are born with signs (birthmarks) already marked upon their skins. The relative hairlessness of humans makes it easier to mark their skins and easier to see the marks thus made.

As Michel Thévoz concludes, in our species "there is no body but the painted body." We probably began making deliberate and artificial signs on our own skins—coloring, tattooing, scarring—long before we began signing the walls of caves. Indeed, the silhouette of a human hand that "signs" a cave painting cannot have been made without leaving paint on the hand thereby silhouetted. And since one human hand will produce a different silhouette than another, the sign of a painted hand distinguishes the work of one human from the work of another, just as the birthmark distinguishes the marked child from other children. Moreover, humans, like other animals, from a very early age are particularly sensitive to variations and changes in the physical appearance of other members of their own species. Freud's "narcissism of minor differences" originates in our phylogenetic perceptual apparatus and facilitates "cohesion between members of the community." Signs upon skins, the signs of skins, are thus easily used to distinguish one group of humans from another, one *genus* from another. ("There's no racism," as Derrida insists, without "a system of marks.")

The marks made upon a body need not be beneficent, or reversible, or voluntary, or confined to the epidermal surface. The category "birthmark" overlaps with the category "birth defect." Physical accidents, too, may mark a body irrevocably and involuntarily. And so may deliberate injuries inflicted upon the human body by a human hand. Signs, for instance, are often made by incisions in a surface; tattooing punctures the skin, and what we call writing was often, in earlier periods, literally produced by cutting. Such punctures or incisions, historically acquired during the lifetime of a human organism, may—like genetic defects—affect biological functions. In that case, representation overlaps with biology: The sign both marks and makes a difference.

But there are biological limits to this process of signing the body. You can only mark the available surfaces, and if you want the mark to be read by others, the marked surface must be visible. Moreover, marking the body may alter its ability to perform certain functions—or any functions. Certain markings kill the organism. In "The Penal Colony," Freud's contemporary Austro-Hungarian fellow Jew Franz Kafka imagined a machine that incised the body of a criminal with the sign of his crime, repeating and deepening the mark until it finally killed the victim. Although Kafka's fantasy is bizarrely mechanical and thorough, signs that kill are both ancient and pervasive in human societies. Beheading, for instance, detaches the head from the body, and in doing so identifies an individual as a criminal, someone who has in some way transgressed the code of the community; the head was then, in humanist England as in many other societies, publicly displayed as a sign of the price of deviance. Markings may deliberately be made to transform a living body into a dead one, or markings may be made to signal the distinction between a living human and a dead one—a distinction that matters more than the distinctions of gender, status, age, or race. But in either case representation must attend to biological parameters that preexist the act of marking.

Biologically, humans reproduce through a process that requires the organic interaction of males and females. For the purposes of reproduction, those categories are functionally defined: male = sperm maker, female = egg maker. The categories need have no other meanings socially (though they usually do); "spermite" and "eggite," let us call them, so as to insist upon the biological rather than the social meanings. For reproduction to occur, spermites must find and unite with eggites; therefore, members of one category must be able to recognize members of the other. The two categories are differentiated by certain biological markings (primary and secondary sex characteristics), genetically and hormonally produced. Many insect and animal

species use pheromones for that purpose, but humans are relatively poor at producing or recognizing such chemical stimulants, relying instead on visual signals, on the reading of visual
textual signs. For instance, in humans, as in many other mammals, spermites differ from eggites in the distribution of body
hair. Like all biological differences, these are not essentially but
only statistically distributed; some members functionally belonging to one category may inherit characteristics usually associated
with the other. The correlation is never absolute, and indeed the
mechanisms of evolution depend upon random variation and at
least minimal phylogenetic plasticity. Hermaphrodites of various
kinds are therefore statistically predictable, but also statistically
insignificant.

The biological markings of sex difference, which can be
found in other animal species, are supplemented in humans.
Once humans learned to sign bodies, they could artificially mark
the differences between one set of bodies and another. Those
new signs might either reinforce or change the existing attributes
of the biological grouping; like other signs, they might or might
not affect biological functioning. Given the importance of reproduction to group survival, it is not surprising that humans
began, very early, to signal sexuality in their artificial markings.
The genitals are an obvious, though not the only, site for such
markings. Mutilation of the genitalia of spermite humans—complete or partial amputation of the foreskin, gashing the foreskin
or the entire underside of the penis, removal of a single testicle,
inserting something into holes made in the foreskin—is an
ancient practice, probably dating to the Paleolithic Period, and
widely distributed among human populations from ancient
Egypt to Aboriginal Australia.

By cutting the visible genitalia, all these practices—circumcision, supercision, subincision, and infibulation—clearly distinguish one group of spermites from another. They mark and/or
create a binary opposition. The mutilations often belong to rites
of initiation, which differentiate fertile adults from prepubertal
children and establish stable social identities. But sometimes
mutilation marks another boundary, as the child moves from the

biological world of birth (which belonged to eggites) to the
social world of symbolism (which belonged to spermites). God
said unto Abraham, "Every man child among you shall be circumcised . . . and it shall be a token of the covenant betwixt me
and you . . . and my covenant shall be in your flesh for an everlasting covenant" (Genesis 17:7–13). Circumcision signs the
newborn body, like the signature on a treaty or a business contract, so that every time one of Abraham's descendants looks at
his signed penis he will be reminded of God's covenant with his
people. But God did not tell Abraham to circumcise newborn
girls. The circumcision binary itself depends upon the biological
binary that divides spermites from eggites.

Historically and globally the genital mutilation of eggite
humans seems to be more recent, and less widespread, than
mutilation of the spermite genitalia. As Darwin noticed, in most
animal populations the spermite is more elaborately marked, by
secondary sex characteristics, than the eggite: The marking helps
him to compete with other spermites for the attentions of an
eggite. Human societies may thus have begun with predisposi-
tions, or precedents, for marking spermites rather than eggites.
But in any case, spermite genitals are easier to mark by cultural
means.

Visible genitals are also vulnerable ones. Ancient Egyptians
knew that testicles produce semen, but they did not even have a
word for ovaries or any understanding of their function; neither
did Aristotle. Amputation of the visible external testicles is much
easier to imagine and achieve than surgical removal of the invisible internal ovaries; moreover, because of the differing distribution of blood vessels, orchiectomy produces less bleeding and
fewer fatalities than clitorectomy and other forms of eggite genital mutilation. The results of accidental or deliberate damage to
the exposed vulnerable testicles of animal or human spermites
can be witnessed, and confirmed by repeated observation or
experiment. Such observations will also establish that damage to
the testicles need not be fatal. By contrast, removal of the ovaries
requires surgical invasion of the abdominal cavity—a process
that, before the development of antiseptic and aseptic medical

Circumcision and Anti-Semitism

Christianity did away with ritual circumcision, but the ritual still marked a body's membership in a category. The ritual remained; only the category changed. In the art and thought of medieval Christianity the historical Christ's circumcision (Luke 2:21) signaled his membership in the *genus* "human": The godhead had taken upon itself the vulnerability of all flesh, which can be cut, which bleeds and suffers. By contrast, the continuing circumcision of Jews and Moslems became "a special token or mark of their fond and superstitious sect": Shakespeare can equate "a malignant and a turbaned Turk" with "a circumcisèd dog" (*Othello* 5.2.362–364) and an English humanist traveler pictured himself pursued by a knife-wielding Jew, the rabid rabbi intent on circumcising another Christian victim.

Once the mark of God's chosen people, circumcision became for Christians the mark of a people who rejected God. That redefinition of the sign was crucial to the schism that transformed a Jewish sect into a new religion. By substituting a symbolic "circumcision of the heart" for the Jewish law, Saint Paul made a previously nationalist religion available to the whole world, but this universalism was defined against its originary locale, and Paul's glorification of allegory ("the spirit") would soon lead to condemnation of anyone still committed to literalism ("the flesh"). In his *Tractatus adversus Judaeos*, Saint Augustine condemned what he repeatedly called "carnal Israel" for continuing to live "according to the flesh," insisting upon physical categories rather than spiritual ones. In Antioch in 387 Saint John Chrysostom delivered eight sermons against the "carnal," "lascivious," and "accursed" Jews; the next year, Christians in Kallinikon burned down a synagogue—an action defended by Saint Ambrose. Circumcision is a binary sign dividing the world into two categories (marked/unmarked), and, like all binaries, its polarity can easily be reversed.

technologies in the nineteenth century, almost always killed the victim. In all human cultures, orchiectomy precedes ovariotomy.

But orchiectomy—what a Byzantine physician and a postmodern French psychoanalyst both call "the mark of the cut"—does not just mark the spermite body; it alters it, biologically. Castration permanently prevents spermites from reproducing. It thus not only marks a particular human, or particular group of humans; it disempowers its victims, depriving them of the ability to procreate, and thereby ensuring that the future belongs to someone else. For this reason, castration has often been used as a judicial or extrajudicial punishment, particularly for sexual crimes, from ancient Assyria to medieval Europe to Arkansas in the late twentieth century. For instance, in the Chinese Shang dynasty (1766–1122 B.C.E.), castration was one of several punishments for serious crimes. Like other punishments—beheading; amputation or mutilation of the leg, nose, or ear; piercing of an eye; tattooing or branding of the face—castration both marked and altered the criminal body.

The logic that combines social marking with biological disempowerment is particularly evident in a complex of practices, including castration, among the powerful Carib peoples who gave their name to what is now the Caribbean—and perhaps also gave us the word *cannibal*. They may also explain why *A Game at Chess* associates castration with cannibalism. In a description of an imaginary feast where Spain ambitiously devours the rest of the world, Venice is served "capon-like in white broth" (5.3.88): Venice is first castrated, like a male chicken, and then eaten. Spaniards were the first Europeans to encounter the Caribs, and Middleton (who in this same speech has the Spaniards also feasting upon "Indians") seems to have conflated the discoverers with what they discovered. The Caribs, although cannibals, ate "none but such as they take in the wars" or other strangers; according to European observers, "They eat all the men that they kill and use the women they capture, and the children that they bear—if any Carib should couple with them—are also eaten." By killing the men and eating any children born to captured women, the Caribs not only destroyed their living enemies, but also destroyed their enemies' genetic line (including mixed progeny). "Such children as they take, they geld to make them fat, as we do cock chickens and young hogs, and eat them when they are well fed." Castration here serves a double purpose. First, it ensures that, even if young male prisoners escape, they will not be able to propagate a rival *genus*. Second, it makes human meat more edible—since, as with other domesticated animals, castration alters physiology, producing tenderer and fatter bodies. Rival human spermites are treated as just another domesticated animal: imprisoned, castrated, fattened, and devoured, their blood and flesh nourishing their masters/enemies.

As a routinized social practice, castration—as the Carib example suggests—is intricately bound up with judicial punishment, armies, the domestication and breeding of livestock for slaughter, and slavery or other institutions of extreme domination. Unlike other forms of genital mutilation, it marks and identifies not "us," but "them." Moreover, the anthropological record falsifies Freud's hypothesis that circumcision is a relatively modern "softening" of an originary practice of castration. Castration seems to be the more recent development in human cultures. Medically, castration requires more knowledge of reproductive physiology than genital mutilation. After all, spermites could mark their own penises, for aesthetic or symbolic effect, as soon as they began using tools and making marks of any kind on their bodies. But the more complex castration mark depends upon knowledges and practices that developed very late in the history of the species.

Testicle amputation was almost certainly practiced and perfected upon domesticated animals before humans. Domestication itself proceeded through multiple stages, beginning with certain kinds of mutually beneficial cohabitation between two species of social animals (like humans and canines). The subsequent development of an agricultural and pastoral lifestyle was probably driven by a combination of population pressure and climate change. The earliest zooarchaeological evidence of the controlled breeding of captive populations of herbivores (sheep and goats) locates its origin in mountainous southwest Asia (the area stretching from modern Afghanistan to modern Turkey, between the Caspian Sea and the Persian Gulf) about eight thousand years B.C.E. It "resulted from a rare constellation of environmental, biological and social factors that occurred together only in a very restricted area of the world, namely western southwest Asia, during a short span of time, namely the beginning of the present interglacial period." It then slowly dispersed outward, at the rate of about one mile per year.

Domestication requires sustained breeding of tame populations. But it does not require castration. Domestic animals producing milk are more valuable alive than dead; but pregnant and lactating animals are eggites, and many eggites can be serviced by few spermites. Consequently, all early sites of herbivore domestication give clear evidence of preferential killing of spermites. Most spermites are culled while young, as soon as their growth rate slows down; adult sex ratios are typically in the range of one spermite for ten to thirty eggites. A harem-herd, artificially created and maintained by human intervention.

As long as domesticated herbivores were useful only for their meat or milk, this pattern continued. But the technology that began with sheep, goats, and pigs was eventually applied to cattle (again in southwestern Asia) by 6200 B.C.E. Until about that date the cereal-based sedentary cultures of the Levant (which had already existed for two millennia) show no evidence of the domesticated animals developed farther north and east; there is no necessary relationship between the two technologies (and some conflict). The importation and adoption of animal husbandry explosively altered the existing cerealized societies, creating a newly flexible and sustainable fusion of cultivation and pastoralism. They also created a new opportunity, and a new problem, for animal domestication—what is now called the secondary-products revolution. Unlike rams and billy goats, bulls are big enough to provide significant muscle power for traction (transportation, plowing, and other chores created by increasingly agriculturized and urbanized human communities); they can therefore be used for something besides meat.

But they would only do such work if some way could be found to make them submit to the indignity of becoming "beasts of burden." Large numbers of adult bulls cannot be kept together, or in the company of cows, unless they have been castrated. Thus, by the sixth millennium B.C.E. the farming cultures of southwest Asia had developed, for the first time, a client species that would be made more profitable if many adult spermites could be kept alive without disturbing the herd.

How long did it take to find the anatomical solution to this problem? The evidence is fragile and disputed; it can be difficult to distinguish between the remains of male, female, and castrated cattle. But traction transport and plows, both drawn by bovines, date from the late seventh or early sixth millennium. Some researchers claim that castrated cattle can be identified in eastern Europe circa 4500–4000 B.C.E., and they undoubtedly existed in Babylon by 2300 B.C.E. Anatomically, bovines can be successfully castrated more easily than equines, and cattle almost certainly provided the precedent for horses. (And sheep may have preceded cattle, depending on exactly when they began to be bred for wool as well as meat.)

The civilizations that grew up around these agricultural developments in southwestern Asia were also the earliest known cultures to castrate human spermites. The Greeks located the origins of the practice in southwest Asia. The Hebrew word for eunuch was probably borrowed from Western Akkadian; the Old Testament forbids the gelding even of animals, and associates eunuchs with Assyria, Persia, and Egypt. But eunuchs were never native to, or common in, ancient Egypt (where the domestication of cattle occurred a thousand years later than in the societies around the Persian Gulf). Two texts from the Middle Kingdom (2040–1780 B.C.E.) do refer to human castration: In a battle between the gods Seth and Horus, "the testicles of Seth were cut off," and an execration of the enemies of Egypt includes "all males, all eunuchs, all women." Noticeably, one passage associates the practice with a life-and-death struggle between rival spermites, one associates it with foreign enemies. So castration did not originate in Egypt. The biblical evidence supports the Greek evidence for an origin in what is now Persia, Anatolia, or Mesopotamia.

Within that region, human castration almost certainly originated after the castration of livestock (at some time between 6200 B.C.E. and 4500 B.C.E.) and before the invention of bronze (c. 3500 B.C.E.). All ancient descriptions of the castration of priests of eastern Mediterranean goddesses specify that it was done with a flint knife; that practice must be traditional, and it clearly indicates a Stone Age origin for the ritual.

The geography and chronology of the early distribution of eunuchs overlap, to a remarkable degree, with the pattern of animal domestication and mounted conquest, radiating outward from an area bounded by India to the east, the Mediterranean to the west, and the Persian Gulf to the south. Human eunuchs, probably originating in southwestern Asia by the fourth millennium B.C.E., had appeared in India and China by the second millennium B.C.E. Castration, first of domesticated mammals and then of domesticated humans, is inseparable from the rise of Eurasian urban civilization. Indeed, the Chinese ideogram for castration meant, literally, "palace punishment"; etymologically, the operation was associated with centralized state power. The cult of the goddess first associated with eunuchs, Innin/Inanna/Ishtar, originated in, and always centered upon, Uruk, the largest city in Sumer, the world's first urban society. The early Uruk period (variously dated between 4500 and 3750 B.C.E.) in fact coincides almost exactly with the range of dates for the probable origin of human castration. Writing also apparently originated in Uruk. Symbolic marks were impressed in wet clay by a sharp stylus—just as the symbolic mark of castration could be made in the wet clay of human flesh. Like pottery and cities and writing, castration is a product of progress.

The eunuch was born in the cradle of civilization.

Eunuchs—like wool, plows, yokes, and wheels—are part of the secondary-products revolution. The manufacture of artificially sterile humans can only develop into an institution when there are relatively settled, concentrated, and differentiated human collectivities with a long tradition of animal husbandry. The agricultural revolution that provided the biological knowledge essential to such operations had also transformed social relationships, creating steep hierarchies of wealth between and within peoples. "To be domesticated," as zooarchaeologist Juliet Clutton-Brock observes, "animals have to be incorporated into the social structure of a human community and become objects of ownership, inheritance, purchase, and exchange." Moreover, the transition to a farming culture itself produces demographic change: "Birth rates increase and mortality for the very young and the very old decreases when people cease to be nomadic because greater care can be given to them, family units become larger, and they become owners of houses and property with an established and restricted home range." In the resulting sedentary population boom, the survival of a tribe/*genus* would not be endangered (and might even be enhanced) by doing to humans what was already being done to the animals humans owned: routinely and permanently disabling the reproductive powers of some individuals—without killing them.

Castrating another human being seems, to Augustine and Middleton and us, an act of savagery. But, like slavery, such castrations probably originated as a humane alternative to murder. For most of human history, warriors did not take any prisoners, and certainly not adult male captives; primitive warfare—which is recorded in the earliest cave paintings and continued in some parts of the globe into the twentieth century—resulted in spermite mortality rates that "civilized" states would find completely unacceptable. After all, killing a person (or any other animal) requires less time, energy, and organization than keeping it enslaved. Agriculture led to settlement, which led to walled cities, which led to modern warfare: professional armies, using weapons specially designed to kill humans rather than animals, facing professional armies from rival city-states. These new states and armies were large enough and organized enough to accommodate new conventions of individual and mass surrender. Moreover, because personal relationships in these communities were structured by a hierarchical continuum—virtually everyone was both a "servant" to someone and a "lord" to someone else—human captives could easily be incorporated without disrupting the social system. Indeed, the earliest Sumerian terms for slaves mean, literally, "male from a foreign

country" and "female from a foreign country," and war captives
are represented on a cylinder seal fashioned in Uruk in the second half of the fourth millennium B.C.E.

The eunuch, of course, is a particular kind of slave. But warriors in early cultures (including ancient Egypt) often amputated
the genitals of fallen enemy soldiers to take home as trophies,
and it's a small step from there to the practice recorded in
Herodotus: The victorious Persians entered vanquished settle-
ments and "picked the best-looking boys and castrated them,
cutting off their testicles and turning them into eunuchs."
Moreover, the slave/free distinction has always been inseparable
from issues of reproduction. Linguist Edouard Benveniste
noticed that the Indo-European root word meaning "free" refers
to those "who were born and have developed together"—thus
defining the slave/alien as someone outside that ethnic stock,
without the experience of shared consanguinity and upbringing.
As anthropologist Claude Meillassoux argues, these definitions
reflect the new relationships required by agricultural timetables:
"The labour invested in the land gives rise to delayed production
which compels the members of the community to stick together,
not only during the fallow season but also from one agricultural
cycle to the next." Productive individuals (all adults who can
work) are bound by constantly renewed and lifelong relationships to nonproductive individuals (children, aged parents, dis-
abled adults); they all have been, and may again become,
nonproductive themselves; they are all situated within "the double cycle of material production and human reproduction."

The slave is not. Captured slaves work; they contribute to
production. But they spent their nonproductive childhood years
elsewhere; someone else paid for their upbringing. Slavery thus
reduces the social costs of nurturing a labor force. Those costs
would be further reduced if the slaves did not generate unpro-
ductive children of their own (whose upbringing would have to
be supported before they could work). In general, slaves have
low birth rates, even when they are allowed to marry or breed;
just as many animals do not breed well in zoos, many humans
do not reproduce in captivity. The slave pool must therefore be

renewed by "the constant plunder of human beings from an alien society." Such plunder ensures that the slave class remains permanently alienated: defamilied, depersonalized, desexed, decivilized. In a society bound and made meaningful by kinship relationships, slaves were the "anti-kin."

The eunuch epitomizes the anti-kin. Castration ensures that an alien slave spermite cannot mold a new kinship identity for himself within the society of his masters. He cannot breed with an eggite slave to produce children of his own (thereby creating for himself the status of husband and father). Most important, a castrated slave cannot impregnate a "free" eggite—which would link him and his children to the kinship networks to which she belongs. Castration does not simply deprive spermites of their rights to biological reproduction (as Aristotle recognized); it also deprives them of access to the social rewards of kinship.

Sexual rivalry between one spermite and another is a necessary, but not a sufficient, condition for the evolution of the eunuch. In many early cultures, the desire to steal other men's women motivated war raids (as in the Roman rape of the Sabine women). But such disputes over sexual property can be settled—as other animals settle them—by the death, exile, or cowed submission of one antagonist or the other. Why castrate sexual rivals? Because you want to make use of them, without allowing them to reproduce.

Although performed on an individual, castration is social surgery. That still remains true, even when castration is an anomaly, the illegal expression of one man's hatred for another man's sexuality. In Tennessee Williams' *Sweet Bird of Youth*, a group of white men in a town on the Gulf Coast have "picked out a nigger at random and castrated the bastard to show that they mean business about white women's protection in this state," and at the end of the play Chance Wayne is also "spayed like a dawg"; in both cases castration turns the elected individual into a useful sign, a warning to any other man who might be tempted to ignore the official sexual boundaries.

Maybe the first castrations were acts of revenge or jealousy, like the mutilation of that "nigger" or of Chance Wayne. But they eventually stopped being personal; the act of transformation was itself transformed. When eunuch making is institutionalized, as it was at least four thousand and probably six thousand years ago, its social function becomes primary. Castration self-consciously sets out to improve human society, just as selective breeding had improved livestock. Rather than discarding a surplus or deviant individual, it changes him into something rare and useful. It creates a human equivalent of the drones in social insects, a category of worker that does not breed. Such workers owe no allegiance to their parents and siblings (who sold or abandoned them, or are dead, or far away, and in any case unrecoverable) or their offspring (for they have none); they depend upon, and serve, an assigned master. The allegiances of the anti-kin are arbitrarily social, not biological. Moreover, by facilitating the maintenance of the royal harem, they served a political as well as sexual function: Polygamy made it possible for the monarch to ally himself not with a single important family, but with many families of domestic aristocrats and foreign dynasties. Such lineage clusters consolidated the power of emerging multi-city-states.

Born into one *genus,* the eunuch/slave serves another. Castration can only be institutionalized when one human *genus* regards itself as fundamentally different from another proximate and competing human *genus.* Whether or not such competitors have different skins, they must be sufficiently marked—by physical, linguistic, or ornamental "minor differences"—to constitute a recognizably other "race" or "kind." And if they are not already "naturally" marked in that way, artificial markings, like branding or tattooing, can be supplied.

The Caribs, once again, illustrate the principle. Their castration of boys captured from other islands depends upon a biological fact that also has social consequences in noncannibal and continental cultures. Especially when performed at an early age, castration interrupts production of the hormones that normally trigger development of secondary sex characteristics; it thus short-circuits a process that biologically differentiates prepubertal spermites from adults. These physical side effects, although individually mentioned in passing by many writers, were first systematically catalogued by al-Djāḥiẓ, an Islamic writer living in Baghdad and Basra (c. 776–869). In his seven-volume work on *The Animal Kingdom*, al-Djāḥiẓ notes that human eunuchs never go bald but often suffer urinary incontinence, lack beard and body hair, and have a distinctive vocal register, a strong tendency to obesity, long feet, an ungainly walk, weak musculature, and soft skin that becomes prematurely lined and thin. A cultural marking of the spermite body—castration—thus initiates other changes in the marking of the spermite body, which are not cultural but biological. And that complex bicultural marking of a spermite body produces an organism that is neither spermite nor eggite, neither male nor female, neither child nor adult, but that mixes elements from those otherwise opposed categories. It produces a new *genus*.

The castrated spermite differs from other beings that are sometimes categorized as belonging to a "third sex" or "third gender." For instance, transsexuals—whether the mythological Tiresias or the modern consequence of sex-change surgery—transfer from one existing sex/gender category to another; as such, rather than create a new *genus* they simply contest their membership in the *genus* to which they have been previously assigned. By contrast, the hermaphrodite and the berdache might seem, like the eunuch, to constitute a true third *genus*. The hermaphrodite results from a statistically rare biological condition; the berdache (found in some North American aboriginal cultures) institutionalizes certain social practices like cross-dressing, which enable an organism biologically spermite to sign itself as culturally eggite. Hermaphrodites and eunuchs could both be described, in Latin, as *semivir*, half-men, because they are neither fully spermite nor fully eggite; but unlike hermaphrodites, eunuchs are not produced biologically. Like the berdache, the eunuch is socially produced; but unlike the berdache, the eunuch is not just a collection of reproducible and culturally arbitrary signs, but a biologically altered organism.

The eunuch, the castrated spermite, the male under erasure, results from an inextricable intertwining of biology and culture.

Castration thus calls into question the binary categories of human thought—the binaries of Augustine or Claudian or Freud, obviously, but also our own binaries, the binaries that organize postmodernist academic discourse. The eunuch confuses not only the categories "male" and "female," but the categories "nature" and "accident," "biology" and "culture," "reality" and "representation," "essentialism" and "constructionism."

In two influential studies, the philosopher Judith Butler has claimed that "sex" (she puts the word in quotation marks) is "performative," an enactment of socially constructed and inscribed roles; Butler rejects all "biologically essentialist" readings of the human body. As Butler concedes, "Philosophy is the predominant disciplinary mechanism that currently mobilizes" her writing self; she is, moreover, a particular kind of philosopher, one sublimely indifferent to history and proudly ignorant of biological science. Nevertheless, the historical and biological category of "eunuch" supports certain aspects of her theories. Eunuchs are, in an obvious literal sense, "socially constructed," the corporeal materializing of a dominant discourse that is written onto and in the body. Moreover, castrated spermites may perform a variety of social identities, which do indeed vary from culture to culture: operatic castrati, priests of Cybele, Chinese palace eunuchs, *hijra*s of India, guardians of Islamic harems, Byzantine and Ottoman imperial officers. Indeed, even among other primates "non-hormonal behavioral determinants . . . within the animal's social environment" prove at least as important as biological factors in determining the effects of castration upon individuals living in groups.

On the other hand, despite Butler, the eunuch's performative choices and sexual roles are essentially constrained by biological mechanisms that preexisted the creation of human discourses. Eunuchs cannot procreate. If they have been castrated before puberty, their penis will not expand or stiffen, and their face will not grow a beard; the complexion of their skin, the distribution of their body fat and hair, the pitch of their voice, even the length of their bones, will be biochemically determined. Again, humans in this respect resemble other primates, who experience similar

physiological effects when gonadectomized. By reducing androgenic hormone levels, castration also reduces spermite suscepti-
bility to cardiovascular disease, cancer, and psychosis, and
thereby increases spermite life expectancy, which is otherwise
consistently shorter than the eggite life span. The eunuch combines and overrides the binaries that structure Butler's thought:
both discursive and prediscursive, cultural and biological, arbitrary and inevitable, performative and determined. He is, if you
like, *a determined arbitrariness, a biological construct, naturally
artificial and accidentally essential.*

And he is frightening. In Augustine and Freud, the mere sight
of a castrated spermite, or what is taken to be one, produces
horror. In *A Game at Chess*, castration is the one unforgivable
sin. "I never yet gave absolution to any crime of that unmanning
nature," the Black Bishop's Pawn declares, and promises, "I'll
ne'er absolve" the castrator (1.1.160–163). And as if to insist
that this is not a personal idiosyncracy of the Black Bishop's
Pawn, we are shown in a later scene that castration is not
included in the "*Taxa Poenitentiaria* . . . The book of general
pardons of all prices" (4.2.82–83); "there is no precedent Of any
price or pardon" for such a crime (4.2.122–123). It is not castration itself, of course, that is unprecedented; but even the mer-
cenary Black House can find no precedent for its redemption.
"Wilful murder" is much more readily forgiven (4.2.125–132).

Why should castration produce more outrage than murder?
Because murder simply destroys one specimen of an existing
human *genus*. Gelding, by contrast, creates a new *genus*, something not-human. The play's very first reference to the castration
describes it as "inhuman" (1.1.145), and when "the gelder and
the gelded" first appear onstage, they are introduced as "The
two inhuman enemies" (1.1.205). Both are "inhuman." The castrator by an inhumane action has created a nonhuman being: A
crime "of that unmanning nature" (1.1.163) alters the nature of
both perpetrator and victim, making each an un-man. The castrator perpetrates a violence "That shames creation" (1.1.224),
and as a result the castrated spermite does not "answer his creation" (1.1.151): He can no longer procreate, cannot "answer"

his own creation by responding in kind, cannot father children as his own father fathered him, cannot "answer" to the vocative "man," because he is no longer recognizable as the creature God created, either in Eden or in his own mother's womb. "This 'tis to make an eunuch" (2.1.232).

Mankind was created by God, and only God should be able to create another *genus*. But that of course is precisely what some goddesses did: Cybele and the Dea Syria and Inanna/Ishtar created, and regularly re-created, the sacred *genus* of the castrated spermite. To understand how castration might be celebrated as holy rather than condemned as atrocious, we have to move backward several millennia from an early modern spermite God to an ancient eggite goddess, the *dea meretrix* vilified by Augustine and all of the other early Christian polemicists. By Middleton's time, the real contest of gods fought out in the Mediterranean in the first centuries C.E. was an ancient foregone conclusion; for humanist readers, Mesopotamian antiquity was remembered only as the Babel of Genesis and the Whore of Babylon in the Book of Revelation. Not until the nineteenth century did archaeologists begin recovering evidence of the real ancient civilization demonized in those biblical images. Even now, we can comprehend that civilization only by forcing ourselves to imagine phenomena "characteristic of a certain way of seeing and feeling, which is in no way our own."

Inanna/Ishtar is likely to have inspired the first castration cult. The earliest surviving archive of Sumerian texts comes from her temple complex in Uruk; even in the Protoliterate Period (2900–2750 B.C.E.), numerous captured slaves belonged to her temple household. We do not know if any had been castrated, but she was a war goddess; Sumerians described battle as "the dance of Inanna," so some of the slaves captured in such battles might have been dedicated to her. And Inanna is the only Mesopotamian divinity ever regularly associated with eunuchs. That association begins in myths that all scholars agree are much older than their surviving written forms. In one early myth, "The Descent of Inanna," she is rescued from the Underworld by two specially made sexless beings who are explicitly identified, in

Akkadian texts, as *assinnu* (eunuchs). Although Inanna enjoys
and represents the fruits of urban plenty, she is no goddess of fertility. Instead, Inanna—celebrated in numerous hymns to her
"holy vulva"—incarnates female sexuality without legal or
moral restraint and without pregnancy; endlessly lascivious (and
patron of prostitutes), nevertheless she is somehow never a
mother. Reproduction, after all, belonged to the primitive animal order; for Sumerians prostitution was, like bread and beer,
one of the bounties of a specifically human, specifically urban
civilization.

Sex without reproduction in itself suggests eunuchry, and the
society that worshiped Inanna certainly knew about defective
spermites. A Sumerian creation myth contains a "Man-in-the-
body-of-which-no-male-and-no-female-organ-was-placed," who
is therefore chosen to be a "courtier" who "would stand in
attendance before the king." We may euphemistically call such a
person "genitally challenged"; in prehistoric human groups the
mutant would probably have been treated as a monster and
abandoned at birth. But pastoralists who had learned to breed
domesticated animals would know that a goat or bull born with
defects that would disqualify it for life in the wild might nevertheless serve human purposes well enough, and a prosperous
complex civilization could afford to nourish some deformed
children, especially if their parents were wealthy or powerful;
the "Man-in-the-body-of-which-no-male-and-no-female-organ-
was-placed" appears in a catalogue of handicapped persons—
the blind, crippled, moronic, and congenitally incontinent—for
all of whom a social use is found. But naturally occurring
eunuchs are rare, and once a social use for them—as courtiers,
or guardians of royal harems—had been discovered, the demand
would soon have exceeded the natural supply. At some point
that supply began to be supplemented artificially. Spermites born
normal were transformed into something deliberately abnormal.

The earliest datable text that describes aspects of worship in
Inanna's cult is attributed to the priestess Enheduanna (twenty-
third century B.C.E.), and emphasizes Inanna's powers of sexual
transformation: "She [turns] a man into a woman, She [turns] a

woman into a man." From this text alone we cannot be sure whether her followers were transsexuals or just transvestites. But as they paraded before the goddess the *kurgarru*, to the frenzied beating of drums, mutilated themselves. How? We don't know—but in later cults the mutilations on such occasions were undoubtedly genital. Moreover, these men participated in "abhominations" which included passive homosexual relations, like those which later characterized the Greek and Roman *cinaedus*. Temple singers were also associated with Inanna from the earliest period, and according to one recent authority such singers "probably were always eunuchs." At the very least, the conjunction of gender transformation, ritual self-mutilation, passive homosexuality, and specialist hymn singing anticipates the later profile of castrates. And by circa 1800 B.C.E. a text explicitly declares that the goddess of Uruk "makes eunuchs."

Even this late text anticipates, by more than a millennium, the earliest references to the cults of Cybele and Dea Syria farther west. Besides, the subsequent distribution of eunuch cults and cultures itself suggests an origin in ancient Mesopotamia. The empire of the Persian king Darius, in the sixth century B.C.E., ranged from Libya to India, but of its twenty provinces only Mesopotamia supplemented its annual tribute in gold with an annual tribute in eunuchs. In the third millennium B.C.E. (or earlier), Uruk was linked to both the Elamite civilization in what became Persia and the Harappan civilization of the Indus valley; the self-castrated *galli* of Mediterranean cults resemble in some striking details the *hijra* of India, resemblances which must almost certainly have been meditated through Mesopotamian religious practice.

Why should this particular goddess, Inanna, have originated the connection between religion and castration? She appears to have been first worshiped by shepherds (who culled and castrated animals). She became a dominant figure in the Mesopotamian pantheon, and she is the only Sumerian divinity who was regularly called "holy." But unlike her fellow gods and goddesses, she was never static, never confined to a single human or divine domain. Inanna was, instead, "the goddess of infinite variety"—and, therefore, the goddess of conflict between varieties, of rivalry, jealousy, controversy, war, disorder. As a sexual deity, the icon of mixture (the intersection of bodies); as a war deity, the icon of melee (a different but also intimate intersection of bodies). In a pantheon of stable divine essences, Inanna alone represented instability, mixture without fusion, the intertwining of isolates, the confounding of categories. What better emblem of such divine disorder than the eunuch, the holy slave, the incorporated foreigner, the perfectly mutilated, the neither-spermite-nor-eggite? To some modern minds, it will seem contradictory that the deity of eroticism should be attended by castrates. But contradiction is Inanna's constant. Surely the power that can give sex can also withhold sex—or change it. Castration adds to the variety of human forms and sexualities, and Inanna celebrates variety; indeed, a deity who stands for both cunt and combat herself ambiguously mixes male and female traits. So it makes perfect sense that her priests would "change their masculinity into femininity to make the people of Ishtar revere her." The transformed body was a living sign of the deity's power.

Augustine, of course, denied that the goddesses had any power to transform or create. Augustine instead insisted that the devotee of Cybele was made sterile "by his own hands" (*suis manibus*, 7:24), without any divine intervention. But why should a man voluntarily violate his own body? Why should a free man mark himself with the sign of a slave? Why should a human sign himself nonhuman? For Augustine, self-castration was simply incomprehensible. At least, he refused to acknowledge that he comprehended it. The pagan poet Catullus was perhaps more honest. Five centuries before Augustine, Catullus wrote a poem about the castrated figure of Attis and his castrated worshipers. Catullus attributes the self-mutilation to a moment of "rabid fury" and "wandering wits" (*furenti rabie, uagus animis*, 63:4). Nevertheless, he uses the corybantic measure reserved for hymns to Cybele, and he writes in the voice of the castrated worshiper: "I woman, I young man, I adolescent, I boy" (*ego mulier, ego adolescens, ego ephebus, ego puer*, 63:63). Catullus puts his ego in the position of the eunuch. And at the end of the poem, he reverts abruptly to his own voice, and prays to Cybele (*Dea, magna Dea, Cybebe*) that she stay out of his house: "someone else make elated, someone else make mad" (*alios age incitatos, alios age rabidos*, 63:91–93). Do it to someone else; don't do it to me. Which is to say: Don't make me mad enough to do it to myself.

As Catullus demonstrates, castration does more than transform, physically, the genitals of a few castrated spermites. In any society where spermite genital mutilation has been institutionalized, it transforms the attitudes of all spermites toward their own genitalia. Freud, as a Jew, was circumcised; of course, that fact affected his attitude toward his own penis. But he also recognized that the Jewish practice affected non-Jewish spermites. Sander Gilman argues that, for Freud, the circumcised spermite "is the baseline, the norm. It is the uncircumcised male who looks at the circumcised male and responds. *He does not deny the possibility*; rather he becomes anxious, fearing that he will become a Jew himself" (my italics). But how exactly would this uncircumcised male "become a Jew"? Freud imagines "castration-anxiety" as the young boy's fear that someone else will castrate him. But that is not what Catullus feared. Catullus "does not deny the possibility" that he might, like other men, castrate himself.

Why would anyone be tempted to do that?

Eunuchs were envied. It is impossible, otherwise, to understand the number of stories in which an ordinary human disguises himself or herself as a eunuch. Such stories presume that eunuchs are usually socially identified by signs that can be easily imitated: biological marks like facial pallor or beardlessness, cultural marks like earrings or special uniforms. But the stories also presume that readers or audiences will immediately appreciate why an intact human might want to "pass" as a castrate— just as a homosexual might want to "pass" as straight. In either case, there must be a reward for pretending you is what you ain't.

What does someone gain by "passing"? The ability, the right, to pass through doors that would otherwise be closed. Literally, the eunuch is often the keeper of a door, protector or pimp, the guardian of access to a desired space, sexual or political or religious. A sacred society of eunuchs is still guarding the tomb of the Prophet Muhammad in Madina and has been doing so since the middle of the twelfth century; Inanna's astronomical symbol was Venus, the morning and evening star, appearing at the threshold between night and day, day and night. Symbolically, the eunuch, who straddles categories, is always liminal, always occupying that numinous space "betwixt and between." Sometimes, as in Terence and Wycherley, an imitation eunuch gains intimate access to otherwise inaccessible and desirable females. Sometimes, as in *Twelfth Night*, an imitation eunuch gains intimate access to a powerful and reclusive male ruler. In the fantasies of eunuch imitation, you can gain access to the eunuch's world without making the eunuch's sacrifice, without irreversibly marking your own body. You can put the sign on and take it off. Queen for a day.

But imitation does not always work. A theater audience may let itself be convinced that a boy actor, with no beard and no codpiece, is a eunuch. But a divine audience will not be fooled by signs like face paint or earrings or a high-pitched voice. If you want to gain access to the mysteries of Ishtar or Cybele, you must cut your own skin, you must irrevocably mark your own body. Why? Because deities demand human sacrifices. Sometimes they demand death; the religious immolation of children was still practiced in the Mediterranean world in Roman times. But sometimes the gods will be satisfied with less, with part of a body instead of the whole. The God of Israel told Abraham he would be satisfied by amputation of the foreskin, in place of child sacrifice. European cave paintings demonstrate that the ritual amputation of a finger was practiced at least twenty thousand years B.C.E., and the practice persisted into classical times, as it has persisted in other societies in other parts of the world. Why a finger? Because, like the foreskin, it is dispensable and can be amputated with nothing more sophisticated than a stone knife. But also, perhaps, because hands are quintessentially human: the sign of the sign maker.

Sexual abstinence is often a precondition of proximity to the divine. And if abstinence is good, castration is better, because it makes that temporary condition permanent—but also because it sacrifices to the deity a part of the body, and something much more important than a finger. Such assumptions were by no means limited to the cult of Cybele, practiced in Phrygia and Carthage and Rome and witnessed by Augustine. They justify the cultic castrations of ancient Babylon, Lebanon, Phoenicia, Cyprus, and Syria, the cults of Artemis in Ephesus and of Osiris in Egypt. If you follow these examples, if you transform yourself, you may be raised to "celestial essence, where, they say, there is neither male nor female, but a new creation, a new man, who is androgynous."

And what if you want to gain access to the mysteries of God the Father? What if you want to "pass" through the eye of a needle? To enter the Kingdom of Heaven, must you, as Jesus says, make yourself a eunuch?

What Would Jesus Do?

> *Jesus said,*
> *"He who is near me is near fire,*
> *and he who is far from me is far*
> *from the kingdom."*
>
> —*The Gospel according to*
> *Thomas, 82*

A candidate for president of the United States was recently asked whether, if elected, he would place in the Oval Office the fundamentalist motto "What would Jesus do?" Jesus would, of course, never run for president (and never get elected if he did run), and such questions disturb Americans who think religion should be kept out of politics. But men have been urged, for two thousand years, to model themselves on Jesus.

Men more than women. When Tori Amos sings "I crucify myself," we can believe her, because there has been no shortage of women martyrs; but when she claims to "know it was a girl back in Bethlehem," we all know otherwise. Whether Jesus was the Son of Man, the Son of God, or the son of Joe, he was a *son*. Although politically correct pronouns may neuter the deity, they can't degender Jesus. Early Christianity strongly appealed to women, who might model themselves on Mother Mary or the women at the tomb or—in the apocryphal Gospel according to

Thomas—the "female disciple" Salome; but Jesus himself was
male, and mostly addressed his words to men.

No man can dismiss the question "What would Jesus do?"
without dismissing Christianity. But if we ask the question, how
can we answer it? How can a man determine what Jesus expects
of him? By reading the New Testament, obviously. But reading
alone is not enough. "Whoso readeth," Jesus told those who
would listen, "let him understand" (Matthew 24:15; Mark
13:14). Before we can know what Jesus would do, we first have
to ask "What did Jesus *say?*"—and then "What did Jesus
mean?"—and then, when we have understood what we have
read, "How can I *apply* in my time what Jesus in his time said
and meant?" So a man's search for ethical guidance must begin
with the Greek text of Saint Matthew's account of what Jesus
said to his spermite disciples:

ὁ δὲ εἶπεν αὐτοῖς, Οὐ παντες χωροῦσιν τὸν λόγον τοῦ–
τον, ἀλλ' οἷς δέδοται, εἰσὶν γὰρ εὐνοῦχοι οἵτινες
ἐκ κοιλίας μητρὸς ἐγεννήθησαν οὕτως, καὶ εἰσὶν
εὐνοῦχοι οἵτινες εὐνουχίσθησαν ὑπὸ τῶν ἀνθρώπων,
καὶ εἰσὶν εὐνοῦχοι οἵτινες εὐνούχισαν ἑαυτοὺς διὰ τὴν
βασιλείαν τῶν οὐρανῶν. ὁ δυνάμενος χωρεῖν χωρείτω.

Which could be literally translated into English as:

He said to them, "Not everyone can accept this sentence,
but to whom it is given, for there are eunuchs that are
born so from the mother's belly, and there are eunuchs
that have been eunuchized by men, and there are eunuchs
that have eunuchized themselves for the kingdom of heav-
en. Let who is able to accept, accept." (Matthew
19:11–12)

That Jesus actually spoke those words will not be doubted by
readers who regard the Gospels as a sacred transcript. Of course,
that claim is no longer universally accepted. The current canon
of the New Testament was first fixed by Athanasius in 367 (and
in the West by papal declaration in 405); especially in the first

century and a half after his death, many other texts about Jesus circulated among Christians. I will quote some of those writings, because at the very least they illustrate what some early Christians believed. But their reliability, as testimony of the words and actions of Jesus himself, remains disputed.

However, even secular textual critics must acknowledge the authenticity of Matthew 19:12. The Gospel according to Matthew was given pride of place in the New Testament canon because early Christians (including Augustine) considered it the most ancient of the Gospels, the one closest in time to Jesus himself; certainly, in the first centuries of Christianity it was more widely read and cited than any other New Testament text. Today, most editors believe that Mark antedates Matthew, but a revisionist minority argues stubbornly for Augustine's view. Even those who conjecture that Mark was written first acknowledge that Matthew is the earliest Gospel from the Judeo-Christian communities of Palestine and Antioch, and that it drew upon eastern Mediterranean sources independent of the Roman tradition preserved in Mark. Matthew thus represents, at the very least, the first Gospel to have originated in the area where Jesus lived and where the new religion won its first converts.

Moreover, the general reliability of Matthew is here underpinned by specific evidence of the authenticity of this passage. First, part of it is quoted in the letters of Saint Ignatius of Antioch (written at some time between 105 and 135), and the whole by Justin Martyr in 155. Secondly, the very difficulties of interpretation created by this passage confirm that it is genuine. When preparing the first edition of the Greek Gospels in more than a thousand years, the great humanist Erasmus articulated an editorial principle that has since been substantiated by scholars working in many periods and disciplines: Readings that appear to be "absurd" are unlikely to be interpolations by later copyists, who instead try to smooth away intellectual difficulties. Nuggets of unintelligibility, which the tooth of reason cannot crack, are often discarded by copyists; they are seldom added. For similar reasons, anything "rare" is likely to come from the originality of a great mind, rather than the mediocrity of a mere follower. The content and phrasing of this passage is "unique" and unanticipated in earlier Jewish thought. Moreover, the passive and active Greek verbs ευνουχισθησαν and ευνουχισαν—which I have translated as *eunuchized* and *eunuchize*—are apparently used for the first time in this passage. Jesus himself probably spoke Hebrew or Aramaic, and both those languages have a denominative verb _SRS_ (based on the noun _saris_); that is, they have a verb equivalent to *eunuchize*, based on a noun equivalent to *eunuch*. The Gospel text, in other words, apparently reflects Semitic usage; the Greek language had to be stretched to accommodate an alien linguistic turn. Neither Jewish in its content nor Greek in its phrasing, what Jesus is here said to have said is stamped with a difficult originality unlikely to have come from anyone else.

So Jesus seems to have said it. What does it mean? Our best guides to the sense of Jesus are not polemical theologians living hundreds of miles away and hundreds of years later, speaking a different language; after all, Jesus was as distant a figure to Augustine as Shakespeare is to a twenty-first-century Austrian. Our best guides would be closer to the time and place Jesus himself inhabited. This obvious truth was first fully appreciated by the humanist scholar J. J. Scaliger, who, at the end of the sixteenth century, realized that Jesus was a first-century Jew speaking to other first-century Jews. Scaliger's revolutionary insight informs every modern interpretation of Jesus. Whatever else he was, Jesus was—as Harvard theologian Harvey Cox puts it—"a participant in one of the many Jewish subcultures of first-century Palestine." We know more about those subcultures now than ever before, thanks in large part to the recovery and interpretation, over the last half century, of the Dead Sea Scrolls. "What the scrolls show," according to Hershel Shanks, "is that in almost every respect the message of early Christianity was presaged in its Jewish roots." In particular, the scrolls "tell us a great deal about the language Jesus spoke."

We don't have to decide whether the community at Qumram was the headquarters of the Essene sect, or whether Jesus or John the Baptist ever belonged to that community, to recognize

some striking similarities between the Gospels and the scrolls: a
shared language, ideology, attitude to the Bible, administration,
and eschatology. Both Qumram and the New Testament accept
the canonicity of the Book of Enoch; the most popular books of
the Hebrew Bible at Qumram were also those most frequently
quoted in the New Testament. Most important, the scrolls confirm the testimony of ancient historians that a radical hostility to
human sexuality was one feature of sectarian Judaism in the
Palestine Jesus inhabited. Many scholars believe that the
Qumram community was celibate; certainly, they prohibited
sexual intercourse anywhere in Jerusalem. The first-century
Jewish historian Josephus reported that members of the Essene
sect "disdain marriage," and that in order to maintain their
numbers they were forced to "adopt other men's children." This
claim is confirmed by another contemporary, Philo of
Alexandria ("They eschew marriage. . . . No Essene takes a
wife"), and by Pliny the Elder ("it has no women and has
renounced all sexual desire," creating "a race in which no one is
born"). Like some of their Jewish contemporaries, some early
Christians believed that all "sexual intercourse is polluted." In
the apocalyptic vision of John, "No man could learn that song
but the hundred and forty and four thousand, which were
redeemed from the earth. These are they which were not defiled
with women; for they are virgins" (Revelation 14:3–4); Saint
Paul urged his followers, "Mortify therefore your members
which are upon the earth" (Colossians 3:5). "Woe unto you,"
says the Book of Thomas the Contender, "who love intimacy
with womankind and polluted intercourse with them! Woe unto
you who are gripped by the authorities of your body!"
(144:8–11). "It is fitting to mortify the flesh," says the Gospel
according to Philip (82:28). In the Gospel according to Thomas,
Jesus is said to have said, "If you do not abstain from the world
you will not find the kingdom" (27) and "Woe to the soul that
depends on the flesh" (112).

Some of these Gospels were eventually dismissed as apocryphal, some of these views dismissed as heretical; the Church
did everything it could to reduce the proliferating Christianities

of the first centuries to a single official *genus*. Most believers contracted and consummated marriages, lived in the world, depended on the flesh. Nevertheless, as Peter Brown and Susanna Elm have comprehensively demonstrated, permanent sexual renunciation and lifelong virginity were profoundly important values in the first centuries of Christianity. In the eastern Mediterranean world that Jesus knew and helped to shape, a radical rejection of human genitality was certainly imaginable. Philo of Alexandria, in a lost work, allegedly asserted, "It is better to eunuchize yourself than to rage madly for unlawful sexual intercourse." The works of Philo were widely read by second-century Christians, as were the *Maxims* of Sextus; Sextus urged readers to "cast away every part of the body that misleads you to a lack of self-control, since it is better for you to live without the part in self-control than to live with it to your peril." It's a short step from abstinence to amputation.

Of course, most people would never take that step. What Jesus said about eunuchs is framed, in Matthew's report, by disclaimers ("Not everyone can accept this sentence. . . . Let who is able to accept, accept"). Only a minority would ever take literally the injunction to "eunuchize themselves for the kingdom of heaven." But, after all, only a minority could ever enter that heavenly kingdom: "Strait is the gate, and narrow is the way, which leadeth unto life, and few there be that find it" (Matthew 7:14). How few? In the Gospel according to Thomas, "I shall choose you," Jesus says, "one out of a thousand and two out of ten thousand" (Thomas 23).

However small, that minority did exist. The words of Matthew 19:12 were not always interpreted allegorically. In the apocryphal Acts of John (second–third century), a young man castrates himself with a sickle. In the middle of the second century, Justin Martyr wrote, with apparent approval, of a Christian who wanted to have himself castrated. Montanus (in Phyrgia, c. 156), Origen (in Alexandria, c. 209), and Leontius (in Antioch in the early fourth century) reportedly gelded themselves. These individual acts were systematically encouraged, or enforced, in the Christian sect founded by Valesius (c. 240). Indeed, as I have already observed, by the fourth century, among people considering themselves Christians, self-castration was widespread enough that it had to be attacked by Church councils, Popes, bishops, and preachers.

Obviously, the word *eunuchs* in Matthew 19:12 can be understood literally, and it was often read that way by early Christians. So anyone who wants *eunuchs* here to mean something other than "eunuchs" has to prove that one set of early readers was wrong and that an alternative set of early readers was right. How could that be proven? One strategy, basic to every form of literary criticism, would be to show that the misreading wrenches the sentence from its intended context. "Read in isolation," we might say, "the passage might be interpreted literally; but if we read it properly, in context, we can see that Jesus *meant* the word allegorically." Any nonliteral reading must demonstrate that the literal reading jars with the immediate context of this passage or with the the Gospel according to Matthew or with the four canonical Gospels as a whole.

But *eunuchs*, in its literal sense, does demonstrably fit those larger contexts. Immediately after this λόγον (word, sentence, saying, precept, judgment, formula, rule), Jesus insists that "children" have access to him, "for it is to such as these that the kingdom of heaven belongs" (Matthew 19:13–14; Thomas 46). The child and the eunuch both have special access to God. And what do eunuch and child have in common? By undoing or forestalling puberty, castration artificially prolongs the physical condition of childhood. The eunuch, in eastern Mediterranean mythology, will "always stay a child!" The prototype of Peter Pan.

But Jesus went further than blessing sterility and claiming that the resurrected blessed will be asexual. In the context of a condemnation of adultery, Jesus urged that if a man's [masturbating] hand or [voyeur's] eye offended him, he should cut it off, "for it is better for you to lose one of your members than for the whole of your body to be cast into hell" (Matthew 5:27–30, 18:8–9; Mark 9:43–47). If one body part might be amputated in the pursuit of holiness, why not another? These passages would in fact be cited, in later centuries, as evidence that Jesus recommended castration in the pursuit of chastity; indeed, some recent scholars claim that *hand* was a well-known euphemism for *penis*. In the fourth century B.C.E. Xenophon's Cyrus, taking it for granted that eunuchs were "objects of contempt to the rest of mankind," had concluded that they would serve loyally the "higher power" to whom they owed everything; closer to home, but presumably for similar reasons, eunuchs served in Herod's court. Following the same logic, Jesus of Nazareth endorsed believers who "eunuchize themselves" for a different kind of "kingdom," suffering the contempt of worldly men but being promised a reward for their loyalty to the greatest of all patrons. Jesus was willing to cut the body to save the soul.

How, then, can an allegorical reading of Matthew 19:12 be defended? Champions of the figurative interpretation—who have dominated the Christian establishment since the third century—do not pay much attention to the historical or linguistic context of the passage. Instead, they simply insist that *Jesus could not have meant* his words to be taken literally. Augustine and his fellow allegorists are therefore confident that when Jesus *said* "eunuchize themselves for the kingdom of heaven," he *meant* "make themselves celibate for the kingdom of heaven." Castration, in other words, is a mere metaphor for sexual abstinence. It must be a metaphor because the literal reading is illogical. Of course, this strategy for interpreting Scripture subordinates God to logic; it belongs to a much larger program, epitomized by Augustine, to reconcile a Palestinian religion with Greek philosophy. I don't know that the two are reconcilable; but the more immediately interesting issue here is the logic of castration.

One aspect of the logic of the allegorists can be illustrated by the comments on Matthew 19:12 of Clement of Alexandria, Tertullian, and Ambrose.

The true eunuch is not he who is unable, but he who is unwilling, to gratify his passions.

> What repudiation of ambitious projects does poverty afford? What bridling of lust can the eunuch merit?
> "And there are eunuchs who have made themselves eunuchs," of their own will, that is, not of necessity. . . . And, therefore, great is the grace of continence in them, because it is the will, not incapacity, which makes a man continent.

What Jesus demanded of men, these men contend, is not the mere absence of sexual activity, but the presence of willpower. A man who is physically incapable of sex does not need self-control; therefore, by rendering himself incapable of sex, a man who castrates himself robs himself of any need or opportunity to suppress his immoral physical urges by a moral act of will. By this logic, castration becomes a shortcut to continence, a cheap evasion of temptation, an attempt to cheat God.

Other apologists for allegory take an entirely different tack. They agree that Jesus demands male chastity, but deny that castration guarantees it. According to Basil of Ancyra (medical doctor turned bishop), men who "perversely" castrate themselves "by this very deed make a declaration of their own licentiousness":

> being unable to control themselves, and fearing they might be caught in the act, [they] wholly liberate themselves for sexual intercourse by cutting off the evidence of this activity, that they might act on their desire as they wish.

(The "evidence" they cut off is the pregnancy that would normally result from intercourse.) Cyril of Alexandria and John Chrysostom express the same suspicion: Rather than securing continence, autocastration enables and disguises incontinence.

Obviously, these two arguments contradict one another. Logically, both cannot be right. Nevertheless, they make the same objection to a literal reading of Matthew 19:12. Their reasoning can be expressed by linking two simple syllogisms to each other:

First Syllogism
   1a. Entry into "the kingdom of heaven" depends
        upon sexual asceticism; and
   1b. What Jesus recommends in Matthew 19:12 is
        done "for the kingdom of heaven"; therefore
   1c. What Jesus recommends in Matthew 19:12 is a
        form of sexual asceticism.

Second Syllogism
   2a. What Jesus recommends in Matthew 19:12
        is a form of sexual asceticism; but
   2b. Literal castration does not constitute a form of
        sexual asceticism; therefore
   2c. What Jesus recommends in Matthew 19:12
        is not literal castration.

Castration does not qualify as "a form of sexual asceticism"
(2b) for Clement, Tertullian, or Ambrose because it substitutes
physical incapacity for moral will, and it does not qualify for
Basil, Chrysostom, or Cyril because it does not guarantee chastity; the two sets of theologians disagree about the facts, but they
agree in the logical structure of their repudiation of literal castration. Within its own terms, in either of its forms, this argument is compelling. Castration does not necessarily, logically,
efficiently, or morally control spermite sexuality.
   *But what if Jesus was not talking about sexuality at all? What
if he was talking about reproduction?*

Castration deprives men and other domesticated animals of the
power to breed, and when a man speaks of castration we should
assume he is talking about reproduction—especially if he inhabits a predominantly agricultural society. Jesus calls himself a
good shepherd and a lamb of God; his Gospels teem with sheep,
goats, asses, swine, and oxen (castrated bulls). Although we
anachronistically interpret all three categories of "eunuchs" in
Matthew 19:12 as human, the Greek word εὐνοῦχοι could be
used of animals, too, just as the Greek word μητρὸς could be

used of a man's "mother" or an animal's "dam": Jesus could expect his companions to have seen domesticated animals who were born sterile and livestock who were castrated "by men." The only category of eunuch limited to humans is the third category, those who eunuchize themselves; that is also the only category connected to "the kingdom of heaven." Man differentiates himself from the animals (and from other men), he prepares for heaven, by doing *to* himself what others must have done *for* them.

This passage is immediately preceded by a discussion of divorce (19:3–10; in virtually the same words at Matthew 5:31 and Mark 10:4; paraphrased at 1 Corinthians 7:10). Clearly, Jesus considered "unchastity" the only legitimate grounds for divorce, and also considered remarriage after divorce a form of adultery. Both attitudes emphasize the importance of sexual asceticism. His disciples responded to these injunctions by concluding that it would be better not to marry. He does not disagree (although some translations give the impression of disagreement by interpreting the ambiguous Greek particle δὲ as "but"); instead, he replies with his enigmatic statement about eunuchs. But eunuchs could not contract marriages in first-century Palestine—so his apparent endorsement of voluntary castration also constitutes a rejection of marriage. Certainly, Jesus himself did not marry.

And some early Christians took these verses as a justification for rejecting marriage. According to Clement of Alexandria, "The followers of Basilides" (c. 120–140) claimed that "those who have made themselves eunuchs for the sake of the eternal kingdom are making a choice of reasoned principle in their view because of the incidentals of married life; they are afraid of the amount of time spent on the provision of necessities." And the Gospel according to the Egyptians apparently took the fact that Jesus "praised eunuchs" as evidence that God did not create or approve the division of humanity into male and female.

At the very least, in answering the question about divorce with a statement about eunuchs, Jesus did nothing to encourage his disciples to marry. And his attention to the children who are brought to him, immediately after the statement about eunuchs, follows logically from this indifference or hostility to marriage. A religious movement that forbade divorce, discouraged marriage, and recommended voluntary castration could not count on reproducing itself biologically, and consequently—like the Essenes in first-century Palestine, the Valesians in third-century Arabia, the Shakers in seventeenth-century America, the Skoptsy in nineteenth-century Russia—it would have a strong incentive to adopt other people's children. If interpreted literally, as a statement about voluntary sterilization, the remark about eunuchs follows naturally from the discussion of marriage and leads naturally to the discussion of (other people's) children.

Later in the same chapter, Jesus promises, paradoxically, that in the kingdom of God "the last shall be first," the lowest made highest (Matthew 19:30, 20:16; Luke 13:30; Thomas 4). Who is lower than an enslaved eunuch? Tertullian recognized that Matthew 19:12 constituted a radical elevation of a despised social class: "eunuchs and barren persons used to be regarded as ignominious," but now eunuchs "not only have lost ignominy, but have even deserved grace, being invited into *the kingdom of the heavens*." Jesus, Hippolytus affirmed, "casts away none of His servants as unworthy of the divine mysteries. He does not esteem the rich man more highly than the poor . . . nor does He set the eunuch aside as no man." This was a fundamental difference, Jerome said, between the "the old law" and the new: He contrasted "Blessed is he who hath seed in Zion and a family in Jerusalem" and "Cursed is the barren woman who beareth not children" with the promise, even to eunuchs, that "you have a place forever in heaven."

Jerome was right: In praising eunuchs, Jesus completely reversed the old Mosaic law. According to the Pentateuch, "He that is wounded in the stones, or hath his privy member cut off, shall not enter into the congregation of the Lord" (Deuteronomy 23:1–2; Leviticus 21:20, 22:24). But this ancient law had been challenged by the historical experience of the Babylonian captivity (587–538 B.C.E.), when many Jewish captives were castrated and sold into slavery. The prophets Daniel and Nehemiah were almost certainly "eunuchs in the palace of the king of Babylon" (2 Kings 20:18; Isaiah 39:7; 2 Esdras 11:11). Thereafter "to the eunuchs who keep my Sabbaths, who choose the things that please me and hold fast to my covenant," the Lord promised "in my house and within my walls, a monument and a name better than sons and daughters; I will give them an everlasting name, which shall not be cut off" (Isaiah 56:4–5). Parts of the male genitalia might be "cut off," but what God promised could not be; eunuchs might not be able to father sons and daughters of their own, but God promised them something better than offspring.

Jesus was deeply influenced by Isaiah 40–66, to which he repeatedly alludes. By accepting eunuchs into the community of the chosen people, Isaiah had nullified the Deuteronomic prohibition; but he did not reverse the earlier value system. Eunuchs were once reviled and rejected, and are now accepted, just as foreigners are explicitly accepted in the adjoining verses; a former disqualification is now being disregarded. But physical loss had not itself been reconceptualized as spiritual gain. Nevertheless, that was a logical next step, which close and repeated attention to Isaiah might prompt. The Jewish text that comes closest to doing so is the apocryphal Wisdom of Solomon, apparently written early in the first century; it slipped in and out of the circuit of the emerging Christian canon from the second to the fourth centuries. Its author—probably a Jewish contemporary of Jesus living in Egypt—blessed "the barren woman" and "the eunuch" who have lived without sin, saying, "It is better to be childless, provided one is virtuous" (3:13–4:1).

Jesus is also said to have said, "Blessed are the barren" (Luke 23:29) and that "in the resurrection they neither marry, nor are given in marriage, but are as the angels of God in heaven" (Matthew 22:30; Mark 12:25; Luke 20:35–36). This radical hostility to heterosexual marriage and reproduction can also be found in some of the apocryphal Gospels. Consider, for instance, some surviving fragments from the Gospel according to the Egyptians:

When Salome asked, "How long will death maintain its power?" the Lord said, "As long as women bear children."

The Savior said, "I am come to destroy the works of the female."

When Salome asked when she would know the answer to her question the Lord replied, "When you trample underfoot the integument of shame, and when the two become one and the male is one with the female, and there is no more male and female."

The human "body is a domestic animal," according to the Book of Thomas the Contender, and it will perish, "just as the bodies of domestic animals perish."

Does it not derive from sexual intercourse like that of the domestic animals? If it too derives from intercourse, how can it beget anything different than they do?

This desire to transcend the biological binary of spermite and eggite also shows up in the Gospel according to Thomas, the most important of the apocrypha. Composed circa 50–125 and attributed to the brother of Jesus, the Gospel according to Thomas was written in the same language, the same area, and about the same time as the Gospel according to Matthew, with which it often overlaps; indeed, most scholars now agree that in the many places where it contains material that also appears in the canonical Gospels, the Gospel according to Thomas "almost always appears to have preserved a more original form of the traditional saying."

Yet I have said, whichever one of you becomes a child will be acquainted with the kingdom and will become superior to John [the Baptist]. (46)

> Jesus said, "Blessed are the solitary and elect, for you will
> find the kingdom." (49)

An adult spermite can only "become a child" again by undoing
puberty; a man who is "solitary" has neither wife nor children.

> Jesus said, "I myself shall lead her [Mary] to make her
> male, so that she too may become a living spirit resem-
> bling you males. For every woman who makes herself
> male will enter the kingdom of heaven." (114)

Just as a man by self-castration makes himself a (feminized)
eunuch to enter the kingdom of heaven, so the woman who
makes herself male will enter the kingdom. "When you make the
two one and . . . when you make the male and the female one
and the same, so that the male not be male nor the female female
. . . then will you enter [the kingdom]" (22). And if you abolish
the distinction between spermite and eggite, you abolish reproduction.

Even if these apocryphra do not record anything that Jesus
himself said, they do demonstrate that the ministry of Jesus was
understood, by many early Christians, as a campaign against
reproduction. The eunuchs of Matthew 19:12 are, at the very
least, compatible with that message. They are also compatible
with a hostility to family life articulated in this same chapter:

> And every one that hath forsaken houses, or brothers, or
> sisters, or father, or mother, or wife, or children, or lands,
> for my name's sake, shall receive an hundredfold, and
> shall inherit everlasting life. (Matthew 19:29; Mark
> 10:29–30)

Thanks to the political rhetoric of American fundamentalists
and papal encyclicals against birth control, Christianity is now
associated, by most people, with the defense of "family values."
But Jesus hated families:

He that loveth father or mother more than me is not worthy of me: and he that loveth son or daughter more than
me is not worthy of me. (Matthew 10:37)

The disciple said to him, "Your brothers and your mother
are standing outside." He said to them, "Those here who
do the will of my father are my brothers and my mother.
It is they who will enter the kingdom of my father."
(Thomas 99; Matthew 12:46–50; Luke 8:19–21)

And call no man your father upon the earth: for one is
your Father, which is in heaven. (Matthew 23:9)

Jesus said, "Whoever does not hate his father and mother
cannot be my disciple. And whoever does not hate his
brothers and sisters and take up his cross in my way will
not be worthy of me." (Thomas 55; Luke 14:25–27)

Families are necessarily biologically hierarchical; they contain
large powerful adults who must impose decisions on small helpless children. Families also contain socially ranked siblings: some
older, some younger, some male, some female. By "family values" conservative politicians mean "hierarchical values,"
imposed not only on children but on lots of adults, often puni-
tively. "Family values" forcibly infantilize most of the population. Jesus rejects families in part because he insists upon a different hierarchy: God is the father, which means that all humans
are children, which means that humans are equal in relation to
one another. Hence the impulse among some early Christians to
free their slaves, give away or share their property, dismantle the
ladders of gender and class; hence the historic appeal of
Christianity to disempowered peoples.

That slaves were attracted to Christianity is not surprising.
Beginning with Paul, Christians described themselves as "slaves
of God" or "slaves of Christ." In doing so, they followed a tradition of "sacred slavery" also found in Mesopotamian, Persian,
Egyptian, and Greek cults. So did Jesus: "Whoever would be
first among you must be your slave: even as the son of man came

not to be served but to serve" (Matthew 20:27–28, 23:11). More generally, of course, his parables often figure humans as bondservants of God. By enslaving oneself to a deity, in Christianity or other religions, one denied the authority of any human master. And just as, in the ancient world, slaves were almost always branded (like livestock) or tattooed as a sign of their servile status, so too the slaves of a god were often marked with tattoos (literally, τὰ στίγματα, "stigmata"). Paul claims, "I bear the marks [τὰ στίγματα] of Jesus branded to my body" (Galatians 6:17). In Revelation, the name of the living God is written on the forehead of his slaves (7:3), so that at the end of days God's slaves can be distinguished from the slaves of the Beast (who bear his mark). A good many Christians in the first centuries apparently endured the pain of marking their bodies with tattoos to show that they belonged to God—as did the devotees of Cybele. By the same logic, some Christians (again, like the devotees of Cybele) endured the pain of castration to mark themselves as a particular kind of slave.

Against the biological family, with its inevitable inequalities, Jesus sets the slave, the eunuch, the anti-kin. Historically, the institution of the slave-eunuch has repeatedly been used to protect a monarch from rivals in his own family and to break the political power of aristocratic families. Within human structures of governance, the eunuch (who stands outside heredity) begins the attack on hereditary privilege. The eunuch breaks the chain of generation that links generations; the eunuch walks outside the hierarchical walls of biology and family. Against the inherited body the eunuch sets stigmata, the artificially produced sign: against the birthmark, the tattoo mark. The eunuch substitutes chosen affiliations—to a God or a kingdom or an elected community—for that unchosen spiderweb of kinship into which we are thrust at birth and into which in turn we thrust our own helpless squalling offspring.

In doing so, the eunuch rejects a culturally inherited and enforced understanding of time. That ancient concept of cyclical temporality is embodied in the rite of circumcision (not only in Judaism but in many other traditional societies). As anthropologists since E. R. Leach and Claude Lévi-Strauss have argued, all rituals reduce the unique to the representative; this individual moment, this momentary individual, becomes one of the innumerable interchangeable parts in a fixed and unchanging order; time does not pass, its evanescence is irrelevant. But circumcision in particular—which marks without disabling the male organ of generation—"makes the living identical to the previous and succeeding generation" of a particular *genus* (family, tribe, nation). As anthropologist Maurice Bloch argues, familial descent thereby becomes "denial of time through denial of the relevance of death and, by implication, birth. This is because descent is an image of the true social unit, which endures for ever. The living are mere representatives of a force that they have received from the dead and that only truly belongs to the dead."

By contrast, the moment of castration deliberately differentiates and alienates a eunuch from his progenitors; if they had been like him, he would never have been born. At the same moment, by the same act, the self-made eunuch also ensures that he will father no descendants. By refusing to link a past generation to a future one, by insisting on the sovereign agency of his own present instant, the autocastrate breaks the circle of generations and the circle of time. He ends a world.

And Jesus, of course, promised to do just that. He did not bring peace, but a sword; and with its sharp edge he set "a man at variance with his father," daughter against mother, the present generation against their forebears; he defined "a man's enemies" as "they of his own house" (Matthew 10:33–36). the Gospel according to Matthew, like the War Scroll of the Qumram community and the Book of Revelation, is structured by an apocalyptic eschatology; it anticipates the imminent end of the world. "Verily I say unto you, This generation shall not pass, till all these things be fulfilled" (24:34). In the coming final contest between good and evil, the enemies of God will be cast into fire (Matthew 3:10–12, 7:19, 13:40–50, 25:41–46). To avoid that "everlasting bonfire," it would be better to "cut off" your hand or your foot (18:8–9). The end of days will not be kind to those who continue breeding: "Woe unto them that are with child, and to them that give suck in those days" (24:19). This ambiguous curse might seem to apply only to those actually pregnant or micturating when the end comes. But the Gospel according to Luke (and the Gospel according to Thomas) undo the ambiguity: "For behold, the days are coming, in the which they shall say, 'Blessed are the barren, and the wombs which never conceived, and the breasts which never gave milk'" (Luke 23:29; Thomas 79).

Jesus blesses barren women, just as he blesses men who eunuchize themselves. In both cases, he condemns reproduction. What's implicit in the man's case is explicit in the woman's. Reproduction belongs to the mundane order of circular agricultural time, which is about to perish. Therefore, do not stop to plant or reap; break the cycle; stop the wheel. Jesus is said to have said, "I have cast fire upon the world, and see, I am watching over it until it blazes" (Thomas 10). A time is coming when time will end. The Son of Man is coming.

The Gospel according to Matthew—and the New Testament as a whole—begins with "The book of the generation of Jesus Christ," a long genealogy, a numbing repetition of begettings that begins with Abraham and finally produces "Joseph the husband of Mary." Begat begat begat. But there the genealogy ends. Unlike Abraham, unlike Mohammad, the Son of Man had no children.

What would Jesus have you do?

Die childless.

Castrate yourself.

That is not a message Christianity as a world religion—or a political agenda—wants to hear. "Seek," the Gospels promise, "and ye shall find" (Matthew 7:7; Luke 11:9). But not necessarily what you expected. In the Gospel according to Thomas, Jesus elaborates on the canonical formula: "Let him who seeks continue seeking until he finds. When he finds, he will become troubled" (2). Certainly, "there are eunuchs who have eunuchized themselves for the kingdom of heaven" is a finding that has troubled the official guardians of Christianity since the fourth century. Dostoevsky's Grand Inquisitor would indeed have to sentence Jesus to death as a heretic whose words threaten the survival of the Holy Church.

The rise of Christianity from a Jewish separatist sect to an imperial religious monopoly in part depended, as sociologist Rodney Stark has demonstrated, upon the fact that Christians outbred polytheists. Ignoring the pronouncements of Jesus, official Christianity encouraged reproduction. It adopted the Jewish hostility to contraception and infanticide—in contrast to pagans, who had low birth rates and were especially prone to discard female infants. The surplus of marriageable Christian females helped fill the pagan gender gap because—unlike Judaism—Christianity was not confined by ethnicity; as redefined by Saint Paul, it stressed the voluntary association of religious "brethren" rather than the biological lineage of a circumcised "chosen people." Well-trained Christian girls could thus furnish exogamous brides for pagan husbands—who were then often converted, or at least allowed their children to be raised Christian. In this way Christians systematically infiltrated pagan kinship networks—and religious conversion almost always travels along the roads of preexisting social networks (particularly kinship). This demographic logic explains how, beginning with perhaps only a thousand adherents in the decade after the crucifixion, the Christian population managed to keep expanding until, by the middle of the fourth century, it probably constituted half the total within the borders of the Roman Empire.

In *Cultural Selection*, I argue that culture consists not of what happened, but of what gets remembered; not of the achievements of heroes, but of the memorials created by survivors after those heroes die, to transmit their achievement out of one time into another. The Gospel according to Matthew was such a memorial, and it became, for early Christians, the most venerable of venerated texts, lovingly preserved, faithfully copied. But new memories compete with old memories, and rival contemporary memories, for mental and social space, and some memories are likelier to survive than others. In culture as in biology, the difference between survival and extinction is numerical. Jesus himself might have been satisfied with "one out of a thousand, two out of ten thousand"—but Saint Paul was not. In the transmission of cultural memory, the first generation of survivors is the most important, and Paul's aggressively expansionist proselytizing among the gentiles ensured that the story of Jesus was reproduced and dispersed in hundreds and then thousands of new memories, biological and artificial; Paul guaranteed that a single local disaster, like the Roman destruction of Jerusalem in 70 C.E., could not wipe out the vulnerable new *genus*.

Sociobiologists like Richard Dawkins and E. O. Wilson have spoken about human memory as the cultural equivalent of DNA; on the analogy of genes, they have been christened "memes." Whatever the limitations of this analogy, it is certainly true that in the competition between memes (or between genes), those that create built-in incentives for their own reproduction have an advantage over those that do not. Matthew may have accurately remembered what Jesus said about eunuchs, and Jesus might have been right about castration—but those who remembered and acted upon that advice would not reproduce. By contrast, those who forgot or ignored that advice would keep reproducing. As a result, those who wanted to allegorize Matthew 19:12 would rapidly outnumber those who insisted on what Jesus actually said and what Jesus actually meant. In this competition, demographics was destined to triumph over truth: It was mathematically inevitable that the allegorical misreading would become orthodox.

Mainstream Christian commentators, preachers, and theologians have therefore always insisted—and they are still insisting—that the word *eunuch* in Matthew 19:12 is simply an "image" used in "a figurative sense," a metaphor for "voluntary celibacy." The English Protestant Bibles of the sixteenth century, which formed the foundation of Christianity in the English-speaking world, routinely translated the Greek words εὐνοῦχοι (eunuchs) and ευνουχισαν (eunuchize), used five times in this single verse of Matthew, as "chaste." Such allegorizing translations and commentaries effectively cut out of the New Testament the objectionable word *eunuchs*. They castrate the text, in order to prevent that literal word *eunuchs* from impregnating the minds of impressionable, potentially fertile, meme carriers. At the same time, by excluding authentic alternative traditions—and particularly the early Gospel according to Thomas—the guardians of orthodoxy castrated the New Testament canon.

The triumph of Christianity has depended upon the castration of Jesus.

But if memories, "memes," are like genes in their vulnerability to the reproductive imperative, then like genes also they can lie dormant for long periods. In *Cultural Selection*, I point out that the invention of writing radically altered the dynamic of cultural memory. When an oral tradition is repressed, or dies out, it cannot be reconstituted. By contrast, because writing is an artificial memory system, it can preserve a memory even after all its living carriers have died (or been murdered). Writing permits original meanings to resurface at any time—as the Gospel according to Thomas resurfaced at Nag Hammadi, as the Dead Sea Scrolls resurfaced at Qumram. Writing creates the possibility of "recessive memes"—suppressed memories, which in the right circumstances may be recovered again. The apocalyptic eschatology of Jesus and his first disciples, for instance, has remained dormant for most Christians in most periods, but because it survives in all texts of the New Testament it remains available in times of crisis, or anticipated crisis. Humanist Europe was full of apocalyptic sects and impulses. Middleton's first play, *The Phoenix*, imagines the exposure and punishment of wrongdoers by a king's only son, returning in glory; the pattern reappears at the end of his last play, *A Game at Chess*. Middleton here exemplifies an eschatology that can also be found in the literary works of Spenser, Shakespeare, Dekker, Milton, and Marvell, in the explosive prophetic enthusiasms of the English Civil War and Interregnum—and in the mission of the Puritans who helped found America.

The literal meaning of Matthew 19:12 is another recessive meme, which despite its official suppression has stayed available to any Christian with access to a text of the New Testament. The Byzantine Christian Church included many castrated monks and bishops and was sometimes led by castrated patriarchs. The brother of Theophylaktos, the twelfth-century archbishop of Ochrida whom I quoted at the beginning of this book, was a eunuch, and it was for his brother's sake that Theophylaktos wrote his *Defense of Eunuchs*; he compared eunuchs to holy ascetics living "a life beyond nature." In 1772 authorities discovered a religious sect of self-castrators, the Skoptsy, which flourished for a century and a half in Russia and Romania, allegedly surviving until 1970. In Pennsylvania in the nineteenth century, George Rapp castrated himself and founded the Harmony Society of utopian Christians. In Mississippi in 1932, Faulkner told the story of a castrated man named Christmas, a man clearly modeled in many ways upon Christ, a man who calls sex "a sewer," a man who, once mutilated, "looked up at them with peaceful and unfathomable and unbearable eyes" and then "rises soaring into their memories forever and ever."

What do all these men have in common? The desire to transcend an abject corporeality. By castration they achieve a non-human state by which they gain privileged access to the divine. Such access can only be gained by sacrificing some part of yourself to something you value more than yourself. That is how the White Bishop's Pawn in *A Game at Chess* understands his own castration: "My suff'rings for her . . . Are sacrifices to her worth and virtue." And what has he gained by such sacrifice? "Though confined, in my religious joys I marry her and possess her" (1.1.199–204). Physical "suff'rings" earn "religious joys."

The castrate in *A Game at Chess* belongs to the City of God, not the city of man; he is the *White* Bishop's Pawn, an exemplary English Protestant in a play performed by and for English Protestants. Unlike Augustine's eunuchs, Middleton's is saved, not damned. Indeed, given the biological pallor universally associated with eunuchs, whiteface and body paint would have been an obvious theatrical expedient for identifying the White Bishop's Pawn as a eunuch. The gelded character in Middleton's play is not simply white; he is, quite possibly, the whitest of the white. And when the White Queen's Pawn finally "takes" the Black Knight's Pawn, she rejects the Black House by embracing celibacy: "For thy sake . . . I'll never know man further than by name" (5.2.116–118). Symbolically, she castrates herself, thereby sealing her "spiritual marriage" with her original betrothed, the castrated White Bishop's Pawn. Unlike the promiscuous breeders of the Black House, neither will have any children. Like Heloise and Abelard, they might as well be buried together.

But this collocation of eunuch and childless woman, at the end of Middleton's last play, had already been anticipated at the beginning of his career. When Middleton was only seventeen, he published his longest work, a poem twice as long as any of his plays, *The Wisdom of Solomon Paraphrased.*

> The soul of virtue is eternity,
>   All-filling essence of divinest rage;
> And virtue's true eternal memory
>   Is barrenness, her soul's eternal gage:
> O happy soul, that is engagèd there,
> And pawns his life that barren badge to wear!
>   (4.13–18)

What others despise, barrenness, is "virtue-worthy" and "founded on a rock" (4.29–36), more reliable than the fertility that others praise: "Bareness and barrenness is virtue's grace" (4.8). The original Wisdom of Solomon came closer than any other book of the Old Testament to a position on procreation comparable to the literal words of Jesus in the Gospel according to Matthew; but Middleton's very expansive paraphrase goes further. The Jewish original praises a barren woman in one verse and a eunuch in the next, but Middleton intertwines them in a single stanza.

> The eunuch never lay in vice's bed,
>   The barren woman never brought forth sin;
> These two in heaven's happiness are led,
>   She fruit in soul, he fruit in faith doth win:
> O rare and happy man, for ever blest!
> O rare and happy woman, heaven's guest!
>   (3.139–144)

The barren woman and the eunuch have become a couple, like the White Queen's Pawn and the White Bishop's Pawn. Middleton's admiration for a barren woman and her eunuch consort stretches from the beginning of his career to its end; so does his admiration for an engaged soul willing to pawn his life to the signifier of sterility.

Like Catullus, like the actor who plays the part of the White Bishop's Pawn, Middleton puts himself in the place of the eunuch; uncastrated, he imagines himself uttering a castrated male's high-pitched "I." He tries on the sign of the cut. His masculinity is shaped, not only by the fear, but also by the temptation, of castration; not only by his physical vulnerability, but also by the possibility of a transformation that would render him invulnerable. The eunuch is not-human; but so is God. What if the castrated male is not less but more than human?

What if the manufactured man is an improvement?

THE FUTURE OF MAN

Therefore if any man be in Christ,
he is a new creature. Old things are
passed away; behold, all things are
become new.

—*2 Corinthians 5:17*

"It's a boy!"

The first words that greeted my first child as he emerged from the warm womb were also the first that had once greeted me. But that standard identification of an infant by its genitals presupposes that other unspoken questions have already been answered. After all, most humans are born headfirst—"coming out of my mother upside down," as Tori Amos sings—so the genitalia arrive late. One of our best friends had given birth to a dead baby; without breath, sex is irrelevant. So my own first thought was "It's alive!" And that is what I remembered most vividly when, later, I tried to describe for Isaac the night of his birth.

> The midwife handed you to me,
> as though I had a clue
> what fatherhood should do.
> What wisdom could I claim to give

your oh so helpless oh so free
your oh so alien serenity?
I just said "Live!"

Oh so imperially unafraid
then for the first (and last) time, you obeyed.

I wrote that to celebrate Isaac's twenty-first birthday, a moment
conventionally described as his official entry into "manhood."
Given the occasion, it seems surprising to me now that the poem
itself gives no indication of the gender of the child. But gender
was, at the time, the last thing on my mind. It was a British hospital, so Isaac was not subjected to that pointless painful amputation of the foreskin that had welcomed me (and most
American spermites of my generation) into this world. No knife
and blood and screaming forced his genitals on my attention;
indeed, because he was immediately wrapped in a blanket, the
little things weren't even visible while I held him. In contrast, his
head was huge, by proportion to his body—as, indeed, is the
head of every newborn baby. I looked at his face, amazed. His
face was neither male nor female. It was human.

Freud's mythical story of castration begins when a boy dis-
covers that a girl's genitals differ from his own. That is, it begins
after the child has already learned the social and linguistic categories "boy" and "girl"; only then does he discover that those
categories have a genital corollary. Boys know they are "boys"
before they learn they are spermites. Freud thought this discovery typically takes place between the ages of two and five; I was
four when I made it, playing doctor with a neighbor girl in South
Carolina. Long before then, of course, I had learned to speak.
Parents almost always remember, and cherish, the moment when
a child crosses that threshold into language, the moment when it
demonstrates the talent peculiar to our semiotic species, the
moment it becomes human. Not just a demanding animal crawl-
ing around the floor, putting things in its mouth, but a true
member of the *genus*. The categories of gender always presuppose—usually unconsciously—the categories of the *genus*. We

want to know that the newborn is alive and that it has the right number of appendages and organs in the right shapes and places. We want to be assured that our child is not a monster.

For spermites, the categories "human" and "male" often get confused, because in our language (as in many others) one word stands for both. The ambiguity of "man" presumes that what is not properly male is not properly human. By this line of reasoning, eggites are monstrous—and so are eunuchs. But eggites are born; eunuchs are made. Eunuchs are a human invention, using human raw materials. Eunuchs, in other words, are not human, but the capacity to make eunuchs is uniquely human.

What are eunuchs? Nonhuman monsters.

And what are humans? Monster makers.

Or, if you prefer a more neutral terminology: manufacturers of altered species.

As a Stone Age technology for transforming humans into cyborgs, castration was crude; you could castrate a human spermite with a sharp object or a piece of cord. We now have more sophisticated tools, and we know that the infertility produced by castration can be guaranteed by much simpler means: Rather than removing the source of semen, one need only interrupt the flow of semen from the testicles to the penis. This interruption can be achieved by cutting or closing the vas deferens. This procedure, like castration, was performed upon domesticated animals before being tried on humans. In 1823, the London surgeon Sir Astley Cooper gave his pet dog the first recorded "vasectomy." Similar operations were subsequently performed, in 1847 and 1884, by other European physicians on other animals. In 1894, the procedure was performed on human males, in both England and Sweden. In subsequent decades, various bizarre (and often racist) claims were made about the advantages of this innovation, and the operation became increasingly popular; Freud was interested in the procedure and considered getting a vasectomy himself. By the middle of the twentieth century, vasectomies had become a medically routine form of birth control. Between 1965 and 1971 seven million voluntary vasec-

The End of Castration?

"Act so that you treat humanity, whether in your own person or in that of another, always as an end and never as a means only." Immanuel Kant's categorical imperative, articulated in *Foundations of the Metaphysics of Morals* (1785), is perhaps the summit and epitome of Enlightenment philosophy. Certainly, it delegitimates any institution that castrates children. It articulates the principle behind Jean-Jacques Rousseau's condemnation, in his *Dictionary of Music* (1768), of "barbaric parents" who have their children "mutilated" in order to fit them for careers as musical castrati: "the voice of modesty and humanity . . . vociferates loudly against this horrid custom," which should be abandoned for the sake of "the preservation of the human species."

Organized castration originates alongside monarchies, capital punishment, and slavery. All four decline in tandem. Judicial torture, long enshrined in European law codes, was effectively abolished in the eighteenth century. In England in the seventeenth century, in America and France in the eighteenth, monarchies were overturned by republics; by the end of the twentieth, only symbolic remnants of hereditary absolutism remained. In 1857, slavery and the slave trade were prohibited in the Ottoman Empire; slavery and castration were simultaneously outlawed in Egypt in 1877; by 1887, there were only thirty-eight eunuchs left in the Persian royal harem; the Vatican, which had for centuries provided a market for musical castrati, banned their use in church music in 1902; the palace eunuch system in China was ended in 1924; harems and their attendant eunuchs were outlawed in India in 1955.

Before we congratulate ourselves on our moral superiority, we should recognize that our high-minded resolve no longer to treat humans as though they were mere tools was made possible only by the mass production of new and improved tools. Machines make better slaves than people do, and they are even more obviously outside the kinship system. I do not have to dictate this book to an indentured scribe because I can write it on a personal computer, which I treat "always as a means only, and never as an end." This machine is, quite deliberately, infertile; it reproduces the texts I want copied, but it has no parents and cannot reproduce itself. Indeed, in the founding nightmare of our global technostate—Mary Shelley's *Frankenstein*, written in the very middle of that parade of enlightenment I have just rehearsed—the artificially constructed new species rebels against his human creator precisely because he is not allowed to breed. If the new species began to breed, *Homo sapiens sapiens* would soon go the way of the Neanderthal. Frankenstein's monster is a eunuch, and we want him—and all our other inventions—to stay that way.

tomies were performed in India alone; in the "emergency" of 1975–1977, India sterilized 7.6 million men, not so voluntarily. In North America, it has been estimated that a third of males eventually get a vasectomy. The operation efficiently controls reproduction, without the hormonal side effects produced by earlier methods of disabling the testicles; it might be described as an artificial male menopause (without hot flashes). It has—believe me—absolutely no effect upon a man's sexual appetites or abilities.

But vasectomies were only the beginning. The early twentieth century also witnessed the rise of eugenics. Positive eugenics provided incentives to encourage those with desirable traits to reproduce; negative eugenics discouraged or forbade reproduction by those with undesirable traits. In 1888 the phrase "sterilization of the unfit" entered the medical vocabulary; within another decade it had also entered the legislative vocabulary. A sterilization law was proposed in Michigan in 1897 and adopted in Indiana in 1907; by the late 1920s, twenty-four states had involuntary sterilization laws; under them, perhaps 70,000 Americans were legally deprived of their ability to reproduce between 1907 and 1945. Many of them were black; eugenics, in America, has always been closely allied to racism. Similar laws were passed in Switzerland in 1928 and Denmark in 1929; over 8,500 "unfit" Danes were eventually sterilized. In July 1932 the Mexican state of Veracruz legalized eugenic sterilization of idiotic, insane, incurably ill, and delinquent persons; in April 1933 the Canadian province of British Columbia authorized "a surgical operation . . . for sexual sterilization" of certain institutionalized persons—not necessarily voluntarily.

All this legislation predated the Law for the Prevention of Genetically Diseased Offspring passed by the German government in July 1933. That notorious statute (which inspired a German Jesuit, Peter Browe, to write a history of castration) mandated a compulsory "surgical operation" to sterilize persons with certain physical and mental illnesses, including chronic alcoholism; but it was often applied to persons who were neither physically nor mentally diseased, but simply, from the point of view of the regime, "asocial" or "alien." Criminals could also be sentenced to "removal of the gonads"; castration was mandatory for sex offenders. The Nazis turned eugenics into a program for permanently improving the human gene pool—restoring the purity of Christian Europe by eliminating any undesirable *genus*, including Gypsies, Jews, and homosexuals. Within only a dozen years, 1 percent of the German population was involuntarily sterilized.

Hitler's Brownshirts are the Black House of twentieth-century nightmare. But our nightmares, like Middleton's, are in part simply projections of what we see ourselves becoming. The topic of involuntary sterilization was being debated in scientific, political, and popular discourse in the Weimar Republic and in many other countries for decades before the National Socialist coup d'état violently usurped and redirected an agenda that had, until then, cut across the divide between conservatives and progressives. The postwar communist regime in Romania controlled

reproduction as systematically and brutally as its fascist prede-
cessors had elsewhere in Europe. The anti-Semitism of Nazi
Germany is not an aberration, but only the most notorious
exemplar of a twentieth-century pattern of "ethnic cleansing"
that has repeatedly sought to produce enclaves of (racial, religious, ethnic, ideological) purity. In Turkey, Yugoslavia,
Rwanda, and Cambodia, social planners self-consciously and
programmatically sought to create a superior monoculture by
"weeding out" disdained subvarieties.

Nor should that surprise us. We are already living in a
"eugenic" ecosystem, surrounded and supported by enslaved
animals and plants bred for certain preferred features.
Increasingly, the foods we eat and medicines we take are "biological constructs." And as with castration and vasectomy and
artificial insemination, what we have first tested agriculturally,
in our domesticated monocultural ecologies, we will sooner or
later apply to ourselves. The eugenics movement in the United
States actually began as a natural extension of an agricultural
organization; to the American Breeders Association, genetic
improvements of livestock demonstrated what could be done to
improve the human race.

If you don't trust ranchers, ask an anthropologist. Plant and
animal husbandry is double-edged: It domesticates the domesti-
cators. Humans are compelled to co-adapt to the needs of the
species we adopt and exploit, and at the same time we become
increasingly dependent on all our biological prostheses. The
paradoxes of the master-slave relationship, described by Hegel,
apply as well to the farmer-livestock symbiosis. The perfectly
domesticated little woman requires, for her support and maintenance, a perfectly domesticated little man. Precisely the breed of
spermite that, Nietzsche warned, our civilization has "willed,
bred, *achieved*: the domestic animal, the herd animal, the sick
animal man—the Christian." Because of that progressive degeneration, "the European of today is of far less value than the
European of the Renaissance." To a continent of castrated
sheep, Nietzsche offered his vision of the Superman, the Anti-
Christ, the High Priest of Power. And what is the first thing any

Superman worth his cape will do? Castrate as many of his contemporaries as possible. Witness Hitler. Witness Heaven's Gate.

The twentieth century tried to apply the new eugenic para-
digms in a crude way; the twentieth-first century will, no doubt,
develop more sophisticated methods. It was a scientific team in
Germany in 1935 that first synthesized testosterone. Many
Germans deeply involved in Nazi eugenics quietly moved into
respectable positions in the postwar scientific establishment.
Moreover, American democracy's insistence upon personal freedom lends itself to eugenic reasoning as easily as the National
Socialist slave state's cult of the fatherland. To the extent that
you separate sexual pleasure from reproduction, reproduction
becomes a choice: not an uncontrollable biological corollary of
sexual instincts, but a lifestyle option. The women of
Middleton's Black House have already liberated themselves of
the burden of reproduction. In the first scene of *A Game at
Chess* the Black Knight's Pawn, having castrated his sexual rival,
expects "To gather fruit" (both sensual reward and the offspring
of legitimate marriage) but he instead finds

> nothing but the savin tree
> Too frequent in nuns' orchards, and there planted
> By all conjecture to destroy fruit rather.
>   (1.1.216–218)

According to a tradition that dates back to first-century Rome,
the juniper (savin) tree induces artificial miscarriages. The nuns
of the Black House, allegedly dedicated to celibacy, are instead
devoted only to infertility; they have accordingly planted a tree
that (like an early modern "abortion pill") rids them of
unwanted fetuses. In the final scene of the play, the Black Knight
brags that "venery" is "the only fruit we have here" in the Black
House; as confirmation, he notes "at the ruins of a nunnery once
Six thousand infants' heads found in a fishpond," and proceeds
to cite historical documents to substantiate the genocidal statis-
tic (5.3.127–137). Whether these skulls testify to abortions
deliberately induced, or postpartum infanticide, hardly matters

to him. The women of the Black House want sexual congress without sexual consequence: penises without testicles. The White Bishop's Pawn would be welcome.

Middleton's Black House has again anticipated us. In a regime legitimated by individual pleasure, the hegemony of the penis is virtually uncontested; every man has a right to erections, as the instant cult of Viagra has demonstrated. But the residual claims of the scrotum oppose those of the emergent clitoris. On the side of the clitoris, some Americans vehemently insist that women have as much right as men to pleasure without reproduction ("the right to choice"); they are appalled by the prospect, imagined in Margaret Atwood's *The Handmaid's Tale* (1986), of a future of compulsory breeding. But on the side of the scrotum, other Americans passionately defend the imperatives of reproduction ("the right to life"). Ironically, most of these people defending the fetus call themselves Christians.

The noisy and violent disputes about abortion, which have torqued American domestic politics for a quarter of a century, are not simply arguments about sexual morality; they are also the most conspicuous precursor of a looming struggle over the micromanagement of our collective biological destiny. In another part of the same cultural forest, the rights of adoptive parents challenge those of biological parents, while surrogate mothers create a new legal category; both developments separate "the right to parent" from the biological capacity to reproduce. They also separate one kind of *genus* (family) from another kind of *genus* (race). My own adopted children, a brother and sister born to a Hispanic mother, lived for three years in an African American foster home before joining our Caucasian family— thereby transforming us into a hybrid household, an "unnatural" mixed *genus*. The adoption of dark-skinned children by pale-skinned families is itself controversial; advocates and opponents rage against each other, each accusing the other of bigotry. But what is really being contested is the prerogative of biological reproduction over artificial forms of *genus* making.

The successful experimental cloning of mammals—first accomplished as I was writing this book—brings us only a step away from a world in which testicles are completely irrelevant, even to reproduction. Again, people calling themselves Christians have most vehemently opposed these "unnatural" reproductive technologies. But the conception of Jesus was hardly natural. (Twentieth-century humanist joke: What did the midwife say when Mary gave birth to Jesus?—"It's a god!") Certainly, Jesus himself had little enthusiasm for the age-old "natural" method for producing babies. "I and my Father are one," Jesus said, in the Gospel according to John (10:30), imagining a form of sonship impossible in two-parent reproduction. And the Gospel according to Thomas, genuine or not, eerily anticipates the possibility that a spermite might be born without any eggite participation:

> Jesus said, "When you see one who was not born of woman, prostrate yourself on your faces and worship him: it is that one who is your father." (15)

> Jesus said, "Blessed is he who came into being before he came into being." (19)

A clone, of course, existed in another body before he existed in his new one.

Whether celebrated or deplored, Christian or demonic, all these recent developments in the technology and law of birthing presuppose a prosthetic sexual freedom liberated from the obligations of biological reproduction. But the same logic also makes it possible to separate sexual rights from reproductive rights. You can offer one while taking away the other. China and India, in their different ways, have already tried to restrict, programmatically, the freedom to breed. As I write this chapter, the human population is topping the six billion mark, and we are rapidly approaching ecological catastrophe. Even the ever-equable Arthur C. Clarke imagines a future of "Breeder Lynching" and the Vatican burning; the rock group Harvey Danger complains, "I've been around the world and found That only stupid people are breeding, The cretins groaning and feeding." I find myself wincing at the sight of yet another Christian couple towing its large litter of uniformed Aryan children. They remind me of E. O. Wilson's observation that a biologically wired "hard-core" attachment to our own kin and tribe "is the enemy of civilization." As the planet becomes increasingly over-crowded, as the perils of excess reproduction become increasingly evident, more and more people will sacrifice their right to reproduce, voluntarily or involuntarily. In the name of Gaia, the great mother, we will cut ourselves (or cut others).

Or we will slice and splice genes. The just-completed mapping of the human genome will make it possible to mark our bodies by interventions less crude and macroscopic than castration or vasectomy—but no less socially and ethically problematic. In 1933, one of the hereditary ailments that the Nazis specified as grounds for compulsory sterilization was Huntington's chorea; by 1987, the single gene responsible for that condition had been isolated. Genetic screening would now make it possible to abort any fetus containing that gene. Indeed, it will not only be possible, in the next few decades, to alter the human genome; it will be impossible *not* to alter it. What society will be able to resist, permanently, interventions to eradicate genetic disabilities? How long will any court be able to deny a woman's "right to choose" a healthier genome for her offspring? If individuals have a "right to reproduce," how long can we insist on one form of reproduction rather than another? How long before the "right to life" includes the right of every fetus to the best genetic opportunities money can buy? Indeed, what right has a parent to "neglect" a child by failing to provide for it the synthetic genetic foundation that will eventually seem just as normal and necessary as a modern education or modern medical care? In the 1998 film *Gattaca*, a well-groomed future discriminates against the children of fundamentalist couples who insist on the old-fashioned chromosome lottery; they are freaks, doomed to the menial jobs of a genetic undercaste.

We have already irrevocably entered the world of what E. O. Wilson calls "volitional evolution," the era of Homo proteus, "shapechanger man." Actually, we began deliberately changing our biological shapes with the invention of the eunuch, perhaps six millennia ago, but in the last century the pace and nature of such change has suddenly accelerated. Soon, literally amputating the testicles will be a superfluous gesture. Involuntary surgical castration is already almost universally condemned as brutal and ineffectual; voluntary testicle amputation may eventually be condoned as a personal freedom, just another example of kinky body sculpting, like tattoos or nipple rings or penis studs. You can already find on the Internet autobiographical narratives of autocastration and an introduction to a subculture of "cutters," epitomized by a gay man living in south Florida who calls himself "Gelding." Dr. Felix Spector of Philadelphia, America's leading castrator, charges $1,600 for such surgery, which is perfectly legal. Autocastration remains rare, of course; the corporeal sign still marks a minority. But it literalizes a larger transformation which one cutter calls "the emasculation of our society." The separation of scrotum from penis, of reproduction from pleasure, of manhood from biology, is already normal and may eventually become universal.

The mixed nature of the eunuch (human and not human, male and not male) will also be universalized by the future production of hybrid humans. At MIT, Steve Mann has already developed a form of portable computer that works in "extremely close synergy with the human user," so that "the user becomes one with the machine over a long period of time." We are entering what Arthur Kroker and Michael Weinstein call "the beginning of recombinant history." In the future of flesh, where "the organic body has been fitted with a customized nervous system," a new "third sex" will be made possible by "the archiving of the human function in the form of monstrous hybrids" and "new body constructs."

The manufactured man is, for us as for Middleton, a specific incarnation of the not-me, not-present: the Other as future. The Black Queen's Pawn claims that she possesses a "magical" looking glass, which through the "mystery" of ancient (orientalized) Egypt enables her to foresee the future (3.1.316–332). The White Queen's Pawn should know, as a good Protestant, that such miraculous claims are always false—but she finds it impossible to resist the temptation to look in that mirror. Middleton's play, like that "speculative" mirror, like any encounter with the future/other/me-to-be, "does require A meeting 'twixt my fear and my desire" (3.3.70).

Science fiction writers have been mesmerized by that mirror for almost a century. (Science fiction is to us what commercial theater was to the Renaissance: our most inventive, and least legitimate, literary genre.) In the socialist dystopia of Evgeny Zamyatin's 1920s *We* only women who fit the required maternal norm were eligible for impregnation; in 1932, Aldous Huxley dreaded the future *Brave New World* where humans would be hatched from incubators; in 1964, Robert Heinlein contrasted the individualist white American *Farnham's Freehold* with a post-nuclear-holocaust global racial state, where an entirely black governing class maintains its power by systematic castration, particularly of whites; in 1976, Kingsley Amis worried about *The Alteration*, a small but decisive change in history (Martin Luther, co-opted by the Vatican, is made Pope, thereby castrating the Reformation) that results in a small but decisive change in his protagonist's body (at the end of the twentieth century, boys are still being castrated for papal choirs).

But after all these male nightmares, fear began turning into something like desire, at least among women. By 1975, the prospect of *The Female Man* clearly delighted Joanna Russ, describing with unembarrassed glee the male-free mode of reproduction prevailing in the feminist future of "While-away." In 1977, a female CIA analyst followed Heinlein in sending white American men into a post-apocalypse future; but for her the old testosterone boys were not heroic, as they had been for Heinlein. Their semen might be a useful diversification of the genetic stock available to a "humanity, mankind" entirely composed of female clones, but socially the men were at worst brutal, at best superfluous, and the solar system a happier habitat without them. In 1978, Suzy McKee Charnas envisioned a mother teaching her daughter "to bite out a colt's balls with my good front teeth" in a post-apocalyptic world divided between the hetero horrors of the Holdfast (male masters, female slaves) and the utopian lesbian liberties of nomadic female clones, clearly no longer the same species. And species metamorphosis is the central experience of *Xenogenesis* (1987–1999), a trilogy by the African-American novelist Octavia E. Butler. The human race, for Butler, is epitomized by a black woman abducted by a race of aliens; the racial encounter begins with slavery ("She did not own herself any longer. Even her flesh could be cut and stitched without her consent or knowledge"), abjection (their alien "captors" treat people the way people "used to treat animals"), and castration ("His manhood was taken away"; "the ooloi acted like men and women while the males and females acted like eunuchs"). But by the third novel the meeting of fear and desire has created a burgeoning third race; not a replacement for the first two, but an addition, a supplementary synthesis, an expansion of biological and social possibilities.

By now, even Anglo male novelists can relish a future in which their familiar biological machinery has been transformed. Iain M. Banks has offered his readers, in a series of novels published since 1987, a "Culture" where the species has been genetically engineered to improve and prolong orgasms, and where harems are stocked with women "genofixed before conception . . . to be stunningly attractive to a wide variety of humanoid males," producing "highly accentuated aphrodisiac pheromones." In 1995, Charles Pellegrino and George Zebrowski anticipated a twenty-first-century cult of Resurrectionists, using fragments of preserved DNA to produce clones of Jesus and Buddha (who soon say things their modern followers can't stomach). And in *The Golden Globe* of 1998, John Varley jauntily trots Shakespeare around the solar system, beginning with a performance of *Romeo and Juliet* out near the orbit of Pluto, featuring "the fastest sex-change since Roy Rogers gelded Trigger." Our bard's most famous femme is played by a male actor—who fortunately, by the grace of biotech, has a retractable penis. As for "the family jewels," they are

> in a safe-deposit tube in a Lunar hospital, near absolute zero. My father taught me that testicles were God's joke

on the male species, good only for procreation and the delivery of agony. Testosterone comes in pills.

Thus happily castrated, with his penis turned inside out to form a serviceable vagina, our hero is ready to play an anatomically convincing Juliet in the mandatory onstage live-sex scene. "Yes, I hear you, all you purists out there . . . but the public demands realism." Which purists? the textual ones? or the sexual ones? (And why are such creatures performing *Romeo and Juliet*, when *A Game at Chess* would obviously be more appropriate?)

These futures may be less fictional than you think. "The end of the world as we know it" was announced, by R.E.M., way back in 1987, in a tongue-twisting rush of random unintelligible now-outdated data. (Do they still "feel fine"?) The data tide keeps pouring in. Today, as I am finishing this book, I hear about a new soft-porn website where you can look at the "Helen of Troy Collection" of miracle models willing to sell their eggs to any spermite interested in siring gorgeous test-tube offspring. Frozen ovaries have been successfully reimplanted. It is relatively easy, we have discovered, to make men lactate; fathers may soon be nursing their children in public (as Jesus, in medieval art, suckled the faithful at his breast). Already, vending machines in some London nightclubs dispense napkins saturated with sex pheromones. A New England biotech company claims to have grown human embryonic stem cells (taken from the tongue) in cow cytoplasm; bioethicists debate the resulting "human-animal hybrid" and the legal status of embryonic material; the company promises a technology that "could eventually be used to grow replacement body tissues of any kind from a patient's cells, side-stepping the increasing scarcity of organs available for transplant and the problems of immune rejection."

The amputated penis of John Wayne Bobbitt was found and reattached, using new microsurgical techniques; curiosity about America's most famous lost-and-found organ launched his career as a porn star; the movie career then financed another medical miracle, whereby the Bobbitt whatsit was transformed from short feature to Hollywood epic. But what if the amputated penis had not been found? What if Lorena, like Sudjai Panitphan, had drugged her husband's food, cut off his penis while he was unconscious, thrown it down the drain, and then refused to tell police where to look? Don't worry. The new tissue-culture technology, if successfully developed, would enable any mutilated spermite—whether the victim of an angry eggite, or a racist mob, or a dictatorial regime, or a sexual rival—to regrow and reattach amputated genitals. But once we can do that, it will not be long before consumers can order new body parts, replacing original organs with customized replacements. Indeed, there is already a thriving global market in body parts appropriate for transplantation.

This humane service is provided by an international crime syndicate, which acquires its commodity-organs by stealing them from living bodies. As a species, we are still willing to murder and mutilate others for our own convenience, still driven to genocide by that "narcissism of minor differences." We may have an inherited predisposition to such xenophobias. After all, within the evolution factory, the person most likely to replace you is sitting right next to you: a species well adapted to the same niche, with an ability profile remarkably like your own, but differing in one or two little respects. Too little to do any harm, surely? No? If the difference gives your odd neighbor an advantage, it could kill you, or kill your children. Hence the trail of extinct progenitors *Homo sapiens sapiens* has left behind it: Deliberately or inadvertently, each new model has clobbered its progenitor. In ancient Greek and Hittite myths, the child-god castrated the father-god. So every little variant from us might be a threat to our genetic future. Which is why we are frightened by "monsters."

Monsters like eunuchs, the un-kinned kind, confusing categories. The emperor Constantine and the poet Claudian Claudianus called eunuchs monstrous; even the exemplary Enlightenment philosopher Diderot included eunuchs in his long discussion of "monsters" in *The Dream of d'Alembert*. But in his *Elements of Physiology* Diderot concluded his survey of the human body by asking, "What is a monster?" and answered, "A being whose time is incompatible with the existing order." A being living in an inhospitable moment. "But," Diderot continues, "the general order changes ceaselessly . . . without one's being able to say that everything improves or degenerates. Improvement and degeneration are terms relative to the individuals of a species," and can't be applied to the differences between species, between orders.

A monster embodies a conflict between one time and another; consequently, what is monstrous in one age, or one place, will not be monstrous in another. For many "Christians" in our time, nonreproductive sex remains monstrous; they are grossed out and outraged by even the thought of oral or anal intercourse, one spermite kissing another spermite, lesbian lovemaking. But Freud was surely right—and courageous—to acknowledge "the inate *variety of sexual constitutions*" among humans. Many of those varieties (which Middleton so perceptively dramatized) are obviously recessive survivals of our own phylogenetic heritage. For instance, other primate spermites mount from the rear and openly copulate in front of others; in some species, eggites mate not with one but with every spermite in the group. To the extent that humans insist on differentiating themselves from other species, they will sanctify privatized missionary monogamy and pathologize "doing it doggy-style," exhibitionism and group sex. But most humans are probably born with propensities to such alternatives, although the strength of the impulse will vary from one individual to another and will be encouraged or repressed from one society to another.

All of us are more like other primates than some of us can admit. It is now forbidden to teach evolution in the Kansas high school from which I graduated, perhaps because in Kansas there are few nonhuman primates around to shatter the fundamentalists' illusion of God-given uniqueness. The illusion is harder to maintain in Africa. In the sixteenth century, for the first time, Europeans began encountering chimpanzees in their natural habitats. In Middleton's lifetime a Portuguese Jesuit in what is now Sierra Leone reported that some of the indigenous people "claim to be descendents of this animal, and when they see it they have great compassion; they never harm it or strike it, because they consider it the soul of their forefathers, and they think themselves of high parentage. They say they are of the animal's family." Even the Jesuit had to admit, "This creature is almost human," and he imagined it "appearing in a theater in Europe!" A pet monkey of some sort did appear on the English stage in 1605. One by-product of the increasing European trade with Africa was a fashion, in some aristocratic households, for exotic pets. In *A Game at Chess*, a white pawn, having captured a black pawn, assures him that he knows how to feed a pet "monkey" (3.2.27). Twenty years before, another Middleton character had said that "an old Lady delights in a young page or monkey"—equating the two sorts of accessory, and suggesting that the delight was not entirely innocent. Monkeys, after all, lacked some of the sexual inhibitions so carefully instilled in humans, and therefore they quickly developed a reputation for lechery. But lechery did not necessarily distinguish them from humans. In Philip Massinger's play *The Bondman*, a character, regretting his past lust, reflects, "Had I been gelded then . . . I had not been transformed, and forced To play an o'ergrown ape." As he says this, he is standing on stage "in an ape's habit" (presumably, an early version of the modern ape suit); we have just seen him led in "with a chain about his neck" and ordered to perform tricks and take the woman's part in a dance. But if gelding saves a man from becoming a monkey, doesn't that suggest that monkeydom is his natural, ungelded condition? Middleton—whose family coat of arms featured an ape with a chain around its neck—summed up the Renaissance as "a monkey-tailed age." In a more charitable (or cynical?) mood, he confessed that "love makes us all monkeys."

Why should we be bothered if other consenting adults are monkeying around? After all, I am in no way affected by the sodomy that might, for all I know, be happily happening next door. On the other hand, as traditional African wisdom and Hillary Clinton insist, "it takes a village to raise a child." When other people engage in *reproductive* sex, it *does* affect me; it affects everyone in the global village, because we all have to deal with the human consequences of *their* fucking fertility. The Monty Python film *The Meaning of Life* contains an unforgettable scene, culminating in the song "Every Sperm Is Sacred," which features a grotesque drag "mother" so ever-pregnant that she hardly notices when one more soiled baby drops out between her legs. Four centuries earlier, Edmund Spenser had imagined "Error" as a disgusting breeding machine: An "ugly monster" with a "beastly body," her "fertile slime" is surrounded by her greedy multiplying brats, "ten thousand kinds" of monstrous spawn, "sucking upon her poisonous dugs." Her own brood eventually kills her—sucking her blood, "making her death their life." Do we want the future of the human race, of life on this rare and precious planet, to be determined not by who thinks most wisely but by who breeds fastest? I am viscerally revolted by the thought. To me, in our time, eunuchs are natural; binge breeding nauseates.

It probably seems perverse to label something as "natural" as reproductive sex perverse. But as long ago as 1974, in his prize-winning novel *The Forever War*, J. R. Haldeman imagined an overpopulated future in which heterosexuality was stigmatized as a disgusting animalistic fetish. If, as a species, we wish to distinguish ourselves from animals, why should we keep propagating ourselves like so much meat on the hoof? The erotic allure of heterosexuality—as in the rock refrain "I want to fuck you like an animal"—surely in part depends upon our sense of its necessary bestiality. Perhaps actual bestiality only literalizes what is always latent. *Hetero-*, after all, means "other." Heterosexuality, by definition, involves "fucking the alien." That is, in fact, the "pretty crazy thought" that comes to one of the speakers in Diderot's *Dream*. "Maybe man," she ventures, "is just the monster to woman, and woman the monster to man." Diderot then provides a precise technical description of the genitals, showing that those of one sex are just malformed versions of the other's. Thus, the "other sex" can never be the "opposite sex," precisely because they are not clearly different but also clearly not the same, simultaneously alike but alien, *heterohomo.*

Freud believed that the discovery of that vertiginous ambiguity initiated the castration complex. But our sharp, thick, and twisted feelings about the difference between eggite and spermite cannot spring from ideas about castration. Castration is a very late, artificial, specifically human development; primate hetero-sexuality, by contrast, precedes and informs our species. *Homo sapiens sapiens* could only have evolved, in fact, because one ancestor who was genetically normal and traditional mated with another ancestor who was genetically odd, thus perpetuating that new oddness, the monstrous novelty that became us. The moral of this story is not just that our normality was once abnormal, but that the originary monstrousness *attracted* some-one not-monstrous. The biological imperative that enables both the reproduction of existing species and the evolution of new ones encourages an erotic attraction to otherness—which finds expression not only in practices as widely accepted as hetero-sexuality (the union of the *genus* spermite with the *genus* eggite) and exogamy (marriage outside the familial or tribal *genus*), but also in practices as widely condemned as gold digging (sex between classes or castes), adultery (sex with "the other woman" or "the other man"), miscegenation (sex across races), and bestiality (sex across species). It also explains why eigh-teenth-century Englishwomen were sexually attracted to Italian castratos: They were not only sterile, but strange, tinglingly exotic. More like a woman than other men, but also somehow less like a human being. Deliciously un-.

Why do so many of us have this furtive impulse to mate with the un-us? The biological payoff for cross breeding is genetic diversity. That is a lesson humans learned, and systematized as a practice, from our experience with breeding domesticated live-stock. From our cattle breeding we learned about genetic drift. (Darwin is the author not only of *The Origin of Species*, but of *The Variation of Plants and Animals under Domestication*—a work less frequently contested by fundamentalists.) From our cattle breeding we learned about castration, too; from our cattle breeding we have now learned that cloning can be successfully performed on higher mammals. These technologies, by contrast to cross breeding, restrict genetic drift: They attempt to stabilize an existing *genus* by reducing alien interference. Those who want to preserve the pristine integrity of *Homo sapiens sapiens* should, logically, advocate cloning. Those who are horrified by miscegenation should also, logically, advocate isosexuality. After all, mating with members of your own sex is the ultimate form of endogamy.

Most humans seem to prefer sex with aliens. But, whatever its biological motives, that impulse and its satisfaction do not constitute an inbuilt breeding instinct. Animals, after all, have sexual drives, without connecting their mating pleasures to later reproductive consequences. Insofar as our sexual impulses are phylogenetically inherited, they cannot be centered around reproduction. Of course, humans are intellectually capable of making the connection between pleasure and pregnancy, and we may have developed such impulses during the last few hundred thousand years. I can remember, as a teenager, being sexually excited, once or twice, by the idea of "impregnating" a particular female. The fantasies of that time seem alien and bizarre to me now, in this time. And such fantasies are, not only personally but socially, relatively rare—much less common, for instance, than threesome or group-sex fantasies, which according to surveys are very widespread, especially among men. As Celia R. Daileader has pointed out, pornography ignores pregnancy, and the ubiquitous "money shot" is sterile. In my own sexually inexperienced 1960s Catholic teenage fantasy, "impregnating" a high school girl had little to do with childbirth or child rearing; the thought was exciting precisely because not using birth control made transgressive unmarried intercourse even more transgressive, and because impregnation would mark her, socially, as a not-virgin, someone who had "gone all the way." Not, I must confess, a very nice fantasy. It pretty much conformed to the pornographic impregnation scenaries I have occasionally encountered since, in print or conversation, in men and women. In them, impregnation—unlike lovemaking—is something a man does to a woman, and that he can do to her without her consent. And its excitement derives not from biology, not from any sense that impregnation is "natural" (after all, the thrill of unprotected sex presupposes the ready availability of reliable contraceptive technologies), but from a sharp appreciation of social deviance and transgressive sign making. Human hetero-sexual intercourse with an intent to impregnate can be nastier, and less natural, than anything that animals do.

Of course, the fact that birds do *not* do it, bees do *not* do it, the flowers and the trees do *not* do it the way *we* do it might be taken as a proof that impregnation fantasies are good because they are specifically and only human. Likewise, the suggestion that impulses like exhibitionism may derive from our primate heritage will not recommend them to people who still deny the evidence of evolution, or people who accept it but nevertheless insist that we should strive to rise above our animal inheritance. But why should we always insist on differentiating ourselves from other species? The word *humanism* resembles words like *racism* and *sexism*; all three attitudes presume the entitled supe-riority of our own *genus* over all others. When a bioethicist like Peter Singer argues for animal rights or redefines "person" to include some animals (chimpanzees, dolphins) and exclude some humans (fetuses, newborn babies, brain-dead patients artificially maintained in a vegetative state), he is labeled a fascist. But who is the fascist? The philosopher who challenges our complacent self-definitions, or the self-righteous people in Germany and Austria who harass and threaten anyone who wants to teach, or even discuss, Singer's arguments? Singer dares to ask, "What are we?"—and many people do not want that question asked. But we will not much longer be able to avoid asking it. Or answer-ing it.

Do we have a moral and genetic obligation to insist on pre-serving the boundaries of our kind? To impose a single definition of humanness, or maleness, on our six billion neighbors? Maybe some "real men" and "feminine women" think they can. But to do so, they will have to turn themselves into monsters. The mon-sters, for Middleton, are those who want to impose a "universal monarchy." *A Game at Chess* champions localism against the assaults of a global unifying imperialism, dressed up in the vest-ments of "monster holiness." (That's one of the many reasons I prefer Middleton to Augustine.)

The universe, Diderot concluded, is just "an assemblage of monstrous beings," and men—spermites, humans, *hommes*—are "imperfectible animals." The worst monsters are the animals who imagine they are perfect, who refuse to acknowledge their own monstrousness, and want to put their own noses on everyone else's faces, their own penises in everyone else's pants.

What does manhood mean in the twenty-first century?

Well, son, that depends on who wins the battles you will be forced to fight.

Once upon a time, the signs of manhood, like the signs of race, derived the authority of their allegories from Nature. But it is now our Nature to choose which Nature we prefer, and if we don't like any of the available Natures, we can design a new one. Biology itself is becoming a cultural choice, an elected arbitrary sign. Anatomy may still be destiny, but we are increasingly able to alter our anatomies and shop for our destinies. The human race is about to transform itself into a radical biological construct, a bioengineered new *genus*. On the stage we are about to enter, at that unavoidable meeting 'twixt our fear and our desire, we will all, like Middleton's Black Knight's Pawn, discover what it means "to make an eunuch" (2.1.230)—because Everyman will be hand-made.

Jesus was the first clone.

The eunuch was the first post-human.

Thomas Middleton and
A Game at Chess

The importance of *A Game at Chess* to theories of castration has not until now been recognized, largely because Freud himself never read it (or anything else by Middleton). Of course, Freud was not alone; except for specialists in English Renaissance drama, few people today even recognize the title. But the play was once as well known as anything by Middleton's contemporary and sometime collaborator, William Shakespeare. Middleton's last play had the longest consecutive run, the largest initial attendance, and the greatest ticket revenue of any play of the English Renaissance. In nine days in August 1624, *A Game at Chess* was seen by perhaps one-seventh of the total population of London, and many more who did not see it heard about it, or heard the "extraordinary applause" and "extraordinary concourse" of its audiences. It stimulated more immediate commentary than any play, masque, or pageant of its age. Accounts of it were dispatched to Brussels, Florence, Madrid, Paris, and Venice. In England, it was rumored to have received a secret performance at court; certainly, it provoked legal action by the king, the lord chamberlain, and the Privy Council. It survives in more manuscript texts and appeared in more editions in one year (and in more surreptitious editions) than any other early modern play. And it was the first individual English play published with an (expensive) engraved title page—in fact, it was published with both the first and the second such engraved title page (because the third printing supplied a new engraving).

In other words, the play generated in its first spectators and readers an unparalleled excess of affect. Such an uncanny mismatch between stimulus and emotional response would suggest, to any psychoanalyst, that something about this text provoked an eruption of the unconscious into consciousness. Even more suspiciously, after this initial (excessive) response, the play was almost immediately repressed: The theaters were closed, the play banned, the actors interrogated, the author imprisoned. With unparalleled intensity, *A Game at Chess* both excited and discomfited the humanist mind—more than *King Lear*, *Macbeth*, or *The Merchant of Venice*, texts that Freud found suitable for psychoanalytic interpretation. It clearly belonged, in its time, to the class of works Teresa de Lauretis characterizes as "public fantasies."

A Game at Chess could so uncannily embody the private fantasies of its public because, although in some respects unique, it was in other respects profoundly representative of its time. That period dazzled its contemporaries and still dazzles us. Harold Bloom has hyperbolically, unhistorically, and hysterically claimed that we owe to the plays of those years "the invention of the human"; it would be more accurate to say that those years laid the foundation of the canon. No one can deny that the decades on either side of 1600 produced an outpouring of literary achievement unparalleled in English, an achievement that has since risen to global preeminence. The England of Middleton's lifetime punctured the equilibrium of Western cultural evolution; *A Game at Chess* flourished within an extraordinarily rich, competitive, and powerful literary niche.

Within that niche, Middleton's work occupies a position comparable in importance to Shakespeare's. That comparison

seems strange to modern readers, because in the intervening centuries Shakespeare has been canonized and Middleton largely
ignored. But that difference in their reputations reflects not a
fundamental difference in artistic achievement, but the accidents
of history that affect all cultural memory. For instance, the inhibitions and prohibitions affecting public discussion or representation of sexuality, which increasingly dominated English culture
from the late seventeenth to the early twentieth century, affected
Shakespeare much less seriously than they did Middleton, precisely because sexuality saturates Middleton's work in a way it
does not saturate Shakespeare's. Moreover, Shakespeare worked
for a single theater company for virtually his entire professional
life; after his death, the leaders of that company (his lifelong
friends) could collect and publish all his plays in one volume.
Middleton, by contrast, wrote for many companies, in many
venues, for many kinds of audience; that variety contributes to
the range of his work, but it also meant that, after his death, no
one person or company owned all his plays, and as a result his
work remained uncollected for more than two centuries.

The new *Collected Works of Thomas Middleton*, published
by Oxford University Press, will for the first time assemble all of
Middleton's plays in a single volume; readers can then assess
Middleton in the same way they have been able to assess
Shakespeare since 1623. In some sense, the Oxford edition can
be read as a massive appendix to this book—not simply because
it collects all his texts, but also because it surrounds those texts
with a body of scholarship and criticism produced by more than
sixty scholars in a dozen countries. In that context, claims about
the cultural importance of Middleton's achievement do not seem
so eccentric as they otherwise might.

Within the Middleton canon, *A Game at Chess* occupies the
same position that *The Tempest* occupies in the Shakespeare
canon: a final full-length work that sums up and epitomizes
many of the themes of a lifetime of writing. But even that comparison is inadequate, because *The Tempest* was not especially
popular or controversial in its own time. And so, from another
perspective, *A Game at Chess* is to the Middleton canon what
Henry the Fourth, Part One is to Shakespeare: its author's most

popular work in his own time—and also the work that got its author in the most trouble politically. When Middleton's plays were rediscovered in the mid-nineteenth century, *A Game at Chess* was immediately recognized as "the solitary work with which the Elizabethan drama fairly attempted to match the political comedies of Aristophanes." In 1927, T. S. Eliot singled it out—in an influential essay on Middleton that actually mentioned only seven of his more than fifty works—as "that perfect piece of literary political art."

The word *political* has dominated, indeed virtually monopolized, previous scholarship on *A Game at Chess*. I have myself elsewhere written at length on the play's micro-politics. But many of the play's most obviously political elements are later additions to the text; Middleton began with a dream about a castrated pawn. Moreover, even in the expanded final text, the pawn plot dominates. More of the text is entirely devoted to the pawns than is entirely devoted to the politicos. The first chess piece to speak, and the last to speak, is a female pawn. The chess allegory begins with a scene between pawns; one or more of the four key pawns appear in all but two of the play's thirteen scenes—and one of those two exceptions, 3.2, is entirely populated by other pawns. Although critics have obsessed about the "real" political identity of the characters, only seven of the play's twenty-one speaking chess pieces can be confidently linked to historical persons.

The kings, dukes, knights, and bishops of the subplot do demonstrate that the play has a political meaning. But "politics" is a larger category than satiric impersonations of local politicians. After all, the lynching and castration of a black man accused of raping a white woman is a political act as well as a sexual one. Moreover, humanist culture allegorized chess not only as the game of politics, but also as the game of mating—as can be seen easily enough in the onstage eroticized chess matches of Middleton's own *Women Beware Women* (1621?) and of John Fletcher and Philip Massinger's *The Spanish Curate* (1622). Traditional readings of the "politics" of *A Game at Chess* anachronistically isolate the category "politics" from the category "sex." After Monicagate, it should be obvious to everyone that the two often cannot be separated.

Plot Summary

Readers unfamiliar with the play may find it helpful to know how its scenes, discussed separately in various chapters, fit together as a narrative. [Material in brackets is absent from one or another version of the play.] For convenience of reference, after each scene I indicate the pages of this book in which that scene is separately analyzed.

Induction The ghost of Ignatius Loyola (Spanish founder of the Society of Jesus) wakens the allegorical figure of Error, who tells of his dream "vision" of *A Game at Chess*. Loyola asks to be shown the game. All the chess pieces appear; Loyola recognizes the Jesuit Black Bishop's Pawn and Black Queen's Pawn. Pp. 26, 29, 45, 64, 155.

1.1 The chess game begins with an exchange between women; White Queen's Pawn desires the confident faith apparently possessed by Black Queen's Pawn. (The relationship of imitation and rivalry between these two women initiates and sustains the entire pawn plot.) Black Queen's Pawn introduces her White friend to Black Bishop's Pawn. Under his questioning, she confesses her frustrated love for White Bishop's Pawn, who has been castrated. His castrator, Black Knight's Pawn, enters, and is rejected by her and Black Bishop's Pawn; the castrator seeks reconciliation with his victim, and they exit together. Black Knight enters; Black Bishop's Pawn gives White Queen's Pawn a book to read, and she leaves. Black Bishop's Pawn and Black Knight discuss the larger struggle between Black and White Houses; White King's Pawn (who is secretly working for Black House) plots with Black Knight. Pp. 3, 25, 27, 41, 62, 70, 80–81, 83, 86–87, 89, 121, 124–29, 131–32, 156, 176–77, 207, 218, 242, 255, 286.

2.1 Black Bishop's Pawn attempts to seduce White Queen's

Pawn; when rejected, he threatens to rape her. She escapes when he is distracted by sounds of someone's approach (faked by Black Queen's Pawn). Afraid that public exposure of his crime will politically discredit the Black cause, Black Knight and Black Bishop organize a cover-up. After they leave, Black Knight's Pawn enters, looking for them; he and Black Queen's Pawn briefly discuss his gelding of the White Bishop's Pawn. Pp. 43, 60, 70, 80, 81, 83, 87–88, 126, 128, 136, 138, 156, 157, 177, 233.

2.2 [Fat Bishop presents to White King his new book attacking the Black House.] In front of both houses, White Queen's Pawn publicly accuses Black Bishop's Pawn of attempted rape. Black Knight produces (forged) evidence that the accused man was miles away at the time of the alleged crime; White King's Pawn seconds Black Knight; White King condemns her and hands her over to the Black House for punishment. White Knight plots with (castrated) White Bishop's Pawn to prove her innocence. Pp. 28, 80–81, 102, 125, 127, 266.

3.1 [Black Knight convinces Fat Bishop to change sides.] Black Knight's Pawn forewarns Black Knight that the cover-up has been discovered. Both sides enter, and White Knight presents evidence proving White Queen's Pawn's innocence; after she is released, Black Queen's Pawn confirms her story, thereby increasing embarrassment of Black House. In retaliation, Black Knight takes White King's Pawn [and Fat Bishop switches to Black side]. After others leave, Black Queen's Pawn tells White Queen's Pawn why she prevented the attempted rape: She wanted to save White Queen's Pawn for a marriage that had been magically prophesied. White Queen's Pawn is surprised but curious. Pp. 43–45, 81, 83, 91, 130, 134, 137, 222, 242, 257.

3.2 [An anonymous White Pawn takes from behind a Black Jesting Pawn; White Pawn is then taken from behind by an anonymous Black Pawn.] Pp. 80, 134, 228, 238, 276.

3.3 Black Queen's Pawn shows White Queen's Pawn a magic mirror in which she sees her supposedly destined future husband (Black Bishop's Pawn in disguise). Pp. 124, 155, 223, 275.

4.1 Black Knight's Pawn seeks absolution from his confessor, Black Bishop's Pawn, who tells the castrator that he must seek absolution from higher ecclesiastical authorities. Black Queen's Pawn introduces White Queen's Pawn to (disguised) Black Bishop's Pawn; they plan an immediate engagement. Pp. 81, 124–25, 157, 242, 255, 275.

4.2 Black Knight and Black Knight's Pawn discuss their respective past crimes. Pawn learns from Black [or Fat] Bishop that castration cannot be forgiven, but murder could be. Pp. 80–81, 152, 176, 242, 273, 287.

4.3 Mime of Black Queen's Pawn conducting White Queen's Pawn to a bedroom, then conducting Black Bishop's Pawn to a different bedroom, then (after putting out the light) entering his bedroom. Pg. 155.

4.4 Black Knight leads White Knight and White Duke toward the Black House. White Queen fears the white pieces have been lost, and is attacked by Black [or Fat] Bishop, then rescued by White Bishop. Pp. 89, 266.

5.1 Black House ceremonially welcomes arrival of White Knight and White Duke. Pg. 275.

5.2 White Queen's Pawn, awaiting the arrival of her bride-groom and a priest, meets undisguised Black Bishop's Pawn, who reveals that he was the man who had sex with her the night before and sneers at her for not even being a virgin. Black Queen's Pawn reveals that he had not had sex with White Queen's Pawn but with her, his old discarded lover, who had substituted herself in the dark. White Bishop's Pawn enters and takes Black Bishop's Pawn; White Queen enters and takes Black Queen's Pawn. Black Knight's Pawn (the castrator) enters to kill White Bishop's Pawn (the castrated); White Queen's Pawn inter-cepts him and takes him. [See note below.] She vows lifelong chastity. Pp. 43, 47, 70, 89, 137, 207, 242–43, 256.

5.3 White Knight and White Duke discover, and then publicly expose, the hypocrisy of Black House, and thereby checkmate Black King. Other White pieces enter triumphantly. [Black pieces are thrown in the bag.] Pp. 81, 108, 135, 137, 139, 156, 165, 206, 218, 232, 243, 276.

[**Epilogue** Spoken by White Queen's Pawn.]

Note on Action in 5.2

In the final scene of the play's pawn plot, the Black Knight's Pawn is defeated by a woman, the White Queen's Pawn, his alter ego. The Black Knight's Pawn is more like the White Queen's Pawn than any other character; a frustrated encounter with her begins and ends his part. His castration of the White Bishop's Pawn initiates, for both of them, a search for some new form of self-validation. She seeks it first in obedience to a religious superior, then in marriage; he seeks it first in absolution from that same religious superior, then in murder; neither alternative works for either.

These two characters meet, for only the second time, at the end of 5.2. In the terminology of chess (and sex), she "takes" him (5.2.116); onstage, she might take away the weapon with which he intends to commit murder (just as he had taken away the "weapon" of the White Bishop's Pawn). Given the phallic symbolism elsewhere attached to weapons, her disarming of him might well be interpreted as a symbolic amputation. Indeed, her action might be said simply to complete the play's ongoing transformation of the Black Knight's Pawn from a man into a woman. Middleton's language has already repeatedly effeminated the Black Knight's Pawn. In his very first speech, he declares, "I'll give my part now for a parrot's feather" (1.1.210)—"part" being a typically Middletonian genital pun. Having gelded another man, he develops a "tender" conscience (3.1.116), a sense of compunction that is easily "pricked" (3.1.123), so that "a soft, rare, poor-poached iniquity" can "ride" upon him (4.2.21–22); he is followed by a "worm" and lacks the "courage" to any longer "ply [his] game" (4.1.19–24). Linguistically, the Black Knight's Pawn is no longer a real man. And maybe such effeminacy is intrinsic to his crime. Any castrator must take hold of the victim's genitalia, and when one man handles another man's genitals the suspicion of homoerotic desire inevitably rears its head. By taking the sexual place of a woman, such a man loses his virility.

But maybe this verbal unmanning of the Black Knight's Pawn

was also physically enacted. This literalistic interpretation might be supported by a prefatory poem printed in the first edition of the play and probably written by Middleton himself:

> . . . and so at last,
> The game thus won, the Black House (cast
> Into the bag, and therein shut)
> Find all their plumes and cocks-combs cut.

Cock already meant "penis" in early modern slang; the castration of male chickens prevents the development of the rooster's distinctive coxcomb. What exactly were the black "cockscombs" that were, at the end of the play, cut?

Acknowledgments

Biologically, evolution proceeds by interaction, and that has also been true of this book. Conversations with others have taken me in directions I would never otherwise have imagined. Many of those conversations have been with Isaac, Joshua, and Michael Taylor; I had never really thought much about manhood until I had three sons. Isaac has also been, over the last year, an invaluable research assistant. The project was transformed by the intellectual fertility of students (male and female) in two graduate seminars, one on literary theory at Brandeis University, the other on male sexuality at the University of Alabama. I also learned a lot from audiences at Brown University, the Center for Literary and Cultural Studies at Harvard University, and the Group for Early Modern Cultural Studies conference in Coral Gables. Over the years I have been blessed by energetic research assistants—James Casey, Leah Guenther, Abigail Scherer, Raphael Seligmann, Ron Tumelson—who will notice pieces of this puzzle they put in place. Every exchange with William Germano at Routledge has inspired and energized me.

At the University of Alabama, I have profited from the intellectual generosity of many colleagues. Richard Rand read the entire manuscript; Elizabeth Meese, an early draft. Particular questions have been helpfully answered by: Philip Beidler, Peter Logan, Don Noble, and Diane Roberts (English); Michael Murphy (anthropology); Vernon James Knight (archaeology); Nicklas Sven Vollmer (film); the especially helpful Maarteen Ultee (history); Beverly Thorn (psychology); Barbara Galli (religious studies); and Carol Pierman (women's studies). Fabulist Andy Duncan recommended science fiction novels I hadn't read and reminded me of others I had read long ago. My work on Middleton over the last decade would have been unthinkable without the close collaboration of John Lavagnino (King's College, London). Claudia Daileader passed on tidbits from the *Bangkok Post*. For long-distance alleviation of particular ignorances I am indebted to: Dennis Allen, Bruce Boehrer, Marjorie Garber, John Jowett, Paul Morrison, Stephen Orgel, Debora Shuger, Brandie Siegfried, and Daniel J. Vitkus. Among the many pleasures of writing this book has been the unfamiliar terrain into which it has taken me: This is the first time I have had the need or opportunity to acknowledge assistance from two Assyriologists (Jerrold Cooper, Gonzalo Rubio), a biblicist (Gary A. Rendsburg), an Egyptologist (M. A. Leahy), a historian of Christian antiquity (Susanna Elm), a veterinary surgeon (Karl W. Kersting), or a zooarchaeologist (Brian Hesse).

None of these people (some of whom know me only over e-mail) is responsible for what I have done with the information they gave me. I hope none of them is too horrified by the results.

And then there is Celia R. Daileader, my co-conspirator and co-explorer in the gender jungle, whose mind has so often impregnated my own that I have lost count of the names and numbers of her progeny. In the entangled lineages of intellect, there is neither male nor female, just this delicious play of difference, this rocking recognition.

To the reader: These notes are extensive, because no previous history or theory of castration has been adequately documented, and because analysis of the subject must draw upon many scholarly disciplines. The notes are keyed to page numbers and names or topic phrases in the text; when the note identifies a quoted passage, I generally give the final words followed by closing quotation marks (as in **raspberry swirl**"). This system enables you to track my sources; but it also allows you to browse the notes without having to flip back and forth constantly between different parts of the book. Full references are given only on the first occurrence of a title; but if you are intrigued by an abbreviated reference and don't want to trawl backward through all the notes to find the full details, you can find that first occurrence in the Index.

Four texts are central to this book. Throughout these notes, references to Freud cite volume and page numbers of *The Standard Edition of the Complete Psychological Works of Sigmund Freud*, tr. James Strachey et al., 24 vols. (1955–1974). I use the Latin text of Augustine's *De Civitate Dei* in William M. Green's edition of *The City of God against the Pagans*, 7 vols. (1963); I do not generally follow his translation, however, preferring either my own or John Healey's translation, *Of the City of God*, rev. W. Crashawe (1620). References to *A Game at Chess*, unless otherwise noted, correspond to the text of "A Later Form" in *The Collected Works of Thomas Middleton*, gen. ed. Gary Taylor (Oxford University Press, 2001); citations of other works by Middleton adopt the text, titles, line numbering, chronology, and canon of that edition. The Bible is cited (unless otherwise noted) from the so-called "King James" or "Authorized" translation, first published in 1611. Throughout the book, I have modernized the spelling and punctuation of quotations.

What Does Manhood Mean?

1   Charles Ancillon, *Traité des Eunuques* (1707), tr. Robert Samber and published anonymously as *Eunuchism Display'd* (1718), x.

1   **1999 hit single** Christina Aguilera, "Genie in a Bottle," on *Christina Aguilera* (1999).

2   **Pointer Sisters**, "Slow Hand," on *Black and White* (1981).

2   **Snap**, "Believe in It," on *The Madman's Return* (1992).

2   **raspberry swirl"** Tori Amos, "Raspberry Swirl," on *From the Choirgirl Hotel* (1998).

3   **"star-fuckers"** Tori Amos, "Professional Widow," on *Boys for Pele* (1996).

3   **Germaine Greer**, *The Female Eunuch* (1970), 307.

3   **challenge and possess"** Middleton, *A Game at Chess*, 1.1.171.

4   **birth control** On the central role of women in braking birth rates, see Angus McLaren, *A History of Contraception: From Antiquity to the Present Day* (1990), 193–251.

4   **fifty percent** Leslie Lafayette, *Why Don't You Have Kids? Living a Full Life without Parenthood* (1995), 18. She has an excellent chapter on men's resistances to fatherhood (132–154).

5   **on my back"** Alanis Morissette, "Right Through You," on *Jagged Little Pill* (1996).

5   **restaurant** Alanis Morissette, "I was hoping," on *Supposed Former Infatuation Junkie* (1998).

5   **playing God** Morissette appeared as God in the film *Dogma* (1999), directed by Kevin Smith.

6   **office as a fashion runway** Nancy Friday, *The Power of Beauty* (1996), 377–449.

6   **cosmetic surgery** Edisol Wayne Dotson, *Behold the Man: The Hype and Selling of Male Beauty in Media and Culture* (1999), 103–111.

6   **Hollywood films** Celia R. Daileader, "Nude Shakespeare," in *Shakespeare and Sexuality*, ed. Stanley Wells (forthcoming).

6   **gay subculture** Naomi Wolf, *The Beauty Myth: How Images of Beauty Are Used against Women* (1991), 288–289; Susan Faludi, *Stiffed: The Betrayal of the American Man* (1999), 505–529.

7   **chastity movements** Eric Werner, "The Cult of Virginity," *Ms.* (March/April 1997), 40–44; Adam Davidson, "The Joy of No Sex," *Rolling Stone* (October 15, 1998), 81–82.

8   **Michel Foucault**, *The History of Sexuality*, volume I: *An Introduction*, tr. Robert Hurley (1978), 43.

8   **modes of affectation"** John Cleland, *Memoirs of a Woman of Pleasure* (1749), ed. Peter Sabor (1985): There is "a plague-spot visibly imprinted on all" men "of that stamp," who are "stript of all the manly virtues of their own sex, and fill'd up with only the very worst vices and follies of ours," producing thereby a "monstrous inconsistency" (159–160).

8   **Eve Sedgwick**, *Between Men* (1985).

8   **Marjorie Garber**, *Vice Versa: Bisexuality and the Eroticism of Everyday Life*

(1995), 167–206. The particular quotation comes from Freud's last case study, "The Psychogenesis of a Case of Homosexuality in a Woman" (1920), 18:157; but in fact Freud suffuses Garber's book, and is its central figure.

8   Lee Edelman, *Homographesis: Essays in Gay Literary and Cultural Theory* (1994), 173–191.

9   Susan Faludi, *Stiffed*, 9. This (unanalyzed) image of "emasculation" is often reiterated: 144, 507, 524, 529, 532, etc.

9   **"Me and a Gun"** Tori Amos, on *Little Earthquakes* (1991).

10   **more than a dildo"** Greer, *Female Eunuch*, 307.

11   **Mesopotamian myth** "The Descent of Ishtar," in *Ancient Near Eastern Texts Relating to the Old Testament*, ed. James B. Pritchard, 2nd ed. (1955), 109; also in *Myths from Mesopotamia*, ed. Stephanie Dalley (1989), 159. This Akkadian version is first attested to in Late Bronze Age texts (c. 1650–1150 B.C.E.), but most scholars believe that the cuneiform tablets redact much earlier oral traditions. "The shadow of a wall" was a stereotypical locale for prostitutes; taverns were also brothels; so the eunuch is being cursed to the life of a homosexual male whore, whose drunken customers beat him ("smite your cheek").

12   **Albert Camus**, *The Stranger*, tr. Matthew Ward (1988), 92.

13   **Plato**, *Euthyphro*, tr. Benjamin Jowett, in *The Trial and Death of Socrates: Four Dialogues* (1992), 12; for the Greek text (and commentary), see *Plato's Euthyphro*, ed. Ian Walker (1984), 12a7.

14   **Augustine**, *Of the City of God*, tr. John Healey, rev. W. Crashawe (1620), 271, 285. This "corrected" second edition differs from the first (1610) edition, which does not contain the phrase "what does that mean now" (188).

14   **enigmatic passage twice** Augustine, *Confessions*, tr. F. J. Sheed, intro. Peter Brown (1993), II.2 (p. 24), VIII.1 (p. 130).

15   **emasculate the world"** Tertullian, *De cultu feminarum*, II.9.7; *On the Apparel of Women*, tr. Edwin A. Quain, in *Disciplinary, Moral and Ascetical Works* (1959), 142.

15   **hostile to life"** Friedrich Nietzsche, "Morality as Anti-Nature," 1–3, in *The Twilight of the Idols* (1889), tr. R. J. Hollingdale, in *A Nietzsche Reader* (1977), 163.

16   **federal intellectual space** Gary Taylor, "Farrago," *Textual Practice* 8 (1994), 33–42.

16   **Edward O. Wilson**, *Consilience: The Unity of Knowledge* (1998).

17   *Entmannung* Freud rarely used the German word equivalent to the English "unmanning." See *Konkordanz zu den Gesammelten Werke von Sigmund Freud*, ed. Samuel A. Guttman et al., 6 vols. (1995), and *Gesammelten Werke*, ed. Marie Bonaparte, Anna Freud, et al., 18 vols. (1968–1978): *Interpretation of Dreams*, 4:256 (*entmannt*) and 4:256, note 1 (*Entmannung*). More often, he used the word *Kastration* even when his sources more precisely use *Entmannung*: See Jay Geller, "Freud v. Freud: Freud's Readings of Daniel Paul Schreber's *Denkwürdigkeiten eines Nervenkranken*," in *Reading Freud's Reading*, ed. Sander L. Gilman et al. (1994), 180–210.

17   **history of the eunuch** Twentieth-century histories of the eunuch include: Peter Browe, *Zur Geschichte der Entmannung: eine religions- und rechtsgeschichtliche Studie* (1936); Peter Tompkins, *The Eunuch and the Virgin*

(1962); Charles Humana (pseudonym of Joseph Jacobs), *The Keeper of the Bed: The Story of the Eunuch* (1973); Victor T. Cheney, *A Brief History of Castration* (1995). The three most recent "histories" were all written by amateur scholars with sometimes peculiar agendas. Tompkins, for instance, systematically championed the eccentric sexual theories of Wilhelm Reich (including the "orgone"); Jacobs included sixteen (mostly soft-porn) illustrations, uncritically accepted the universal validity of Freud's castration theories, and began and ended his book deploring "the certainty" of vasectomy becoming "compulsory in a future era" (8), thereby producing "dull generations of future sterile males" and "submissively sterile" husbands (198). There is, of course, no evidence that vasectomies produce dullness or submissiveness. Cheney is a retired Air Force officer who advocates judicial castration "as a remedy for serious sex offenders" (viii); his own sexual politics can be inferred from statements like "homosexuals . . . and other sexual deviates" (8), or "polygamy evolved with the laudable objective of safeguarding the continuation of the family and the racial strain" (25–26). Typically, these books collect references to castration in many cultures (often cited at second hand, and usually without documentation of any kind), but they do little to analyze the textual sources or the historical phenomena, and they pay little attention to current scholarship on the texts they cite or the cultures they describe; they are essentially sensational and anecdotal.

17   **treatise on eunuchs** Theophylacti Achridensis, *Orationes, Tractatus, Carmina*, Corpus Fontium Historiae Byzantinae, vol. XVI/1, ed. Paul Gautier (1980), 289 (*Eun*. Pro. 20–25); Gautier provides a parallel French translation, but I have translated directly from the Greek. The only English translation of the whole treatise ("The Justification of Eunuchism") is by Cheney, in his *Brief History of Castration*, 101–120; but Cheney translates from Gautier's French text.

18   **always contested** Gary Taylor, *Cultural Selection* (1996), 14, 260.

Contest of Texts

22   **result of castration"** Freud, "The Infantile Genital Organization" (1923), 19:144.

22   *quasi hominem"* "*Defecit interpretatio, erubuit ratio, conticuit oratio*": *De Civitate Dei*, 7:24.

22   **horror instead of pleasure"** Freud, "On the Sexual Theories of Children" (1908), 9:217. This draws upon Freud's treatment of "Little Hans," chronologically anterior but not published until the following year: "Analysis of a Phobia in a Five-Year-Old Boy," 10:1–147. Early articulations of the theory are also found in *The Freud/Jung Letters*, tr. R. Manheim and R. F. C. Hull (1988), 159 (21 June 1908) and 265–266 (21 November 1909), and in Freud, *Leonardo da Vinci and a Memory of His Childhood* (1910), 11:95–96.

22   **infantile civilization** Freud, "The Dissolution of the Oedipus Complex" (1924), 19:173–179; "Some Psychical Consequences of the Anatomical Distinction between the Sexes" (1925), 19:248–258; "Fetishism" (1927), 21:152–157; *Moses and Monotheism* (1939), 23:79–84, 91, 99, 122. Freud retrospectively interpolated these theories into later editions of *The Interpretation of Dreams* (1900) and *Three Essays* (1905).

22   **primary and universal** For a critique of this psychoanalytic assumption, and

a counterargument that "medieval secular eroticism (courtly love) is itself modelled on the analysis of spiritual longing," see Debora Shuger, *The Renaissance Bible: Scholarship, Sacrifice, and Subjectivity* (1994), 167–196.

23 **sustain themselves**" *Of the City of God,* tr. Healey, 286.

23 **Afghanistan** Jacobs, *Keeper of the Bed,* 192 (citing a 1971 report from the Anti-Slavery Society).

23 **Istanbul in 1931** I owe this anecdote to scholar Cyrus Gordon (private communication, 10 December 1999); he promises to elaborate in his forthcoming autobiography, *A Scholar's Odyssey.*

23 **Russian religious cult** See Laura Engelstein, *Castration and the Heavenly Kingdom: A Russian Folktale* (1999).

23 **Richard Millant,** *Les Eunuques à Travers les Âges* (1908), a "histoire générale de l'eunuchisme et des eunuques" (4). Though never translated into English, Millant's book is a major source of the historical material on castration in Tompkins, Jacobs, and Cheney.

24 **other people's texts** For Freud as literary critic, see Taylor, *Cultural Selection,* 199–201.

24 ***Oedipus the Tyrant*** In his first formulations of the Oedipus complex, in letters of 15 October 1897, 5 November 1897, and 15 March 1898, Freud explicitly referred, each time, to "*Oedipus Rex*," the play rather than the legend; in fact, on the third occasion, he resolved to "read up on the Oedipus legend," making it clear that until that time he knew the play but not the larger mythological context. See *The Complete Letters of Sigmund Freud to Wilhelm Fleiss,* tr. and ed. Jeffrey Moussaieff Masson (1985), 272, 277, 304. His first public exposition of the theory, in *The Interpretation of Dreams* (1900), also explicitly and repeatedly refers to "Sophocles," "*Oedipus Rex*," and the "play" or the "tragedy" (4:261–264). And Freud persisted in emphasizing that his theory was a critical "reading" of the play-text, specifically: See *The Psychopathology of Everyday Life* (1901), 6:178, *Totem and Taboo* (1913), 13:80, *Introductory Lectures on Psycho-Analysis* (1917), 16:330–331, "Some Additional Notes on Dream-Interpretation as a Whole" (1925), 19:132, and "Dostoyevsky and Parricide" (1927), 21:188.

24 **Uranos by Kronos** Freud, *Interpretation of Dreams,* 4:256 ("Zeus emasculated his father"). Freud recognized his error, and its relevance to its own filial attitudes, in *The Psychopathology of Everyday Life* (1901), 6:218–220.

24 **succession myth** Hesiod, *Theogeny,* ed. M. L. West (1966), lines 175–176, pp. 18–31. Hesiod discusses gelding of livestock in *Works and Days,* ed. West (1978), lines 790–792.

24 **metaphors for castration** Freud, "Notes on Medusa's Head" (1922), 18:273; *An Outline of Psycho-Analysis* (1938), 23:190.

24 **Freud never read** *A Game at Chess* has never been translated into German; Freud never mentions the play or its author. See *The Concordance to the Standard Edition of the Complete Psychological Works of Sigmund Freud,* ed. Samuel A. Guttman, Randall L. Jones, and Stephen M. Parrish, 6 vols. (1980). I have also checked the individual indexes to available editions of his published correspondence, and accounts of his personal library: See Nolan D. C. Lewis and Carney Landis, "Freud's Library," *Psychoanalytic Review* 44 (1957), 327–328 (and facsimile of bookseller's catalogue, 28 pp.) and Harry Trosman and Roger Dennis Simmons, "The Freud Library," *Journal of the*

American Psychoanalytic Association 21 (1973), 646–687, esp. pp. 674–675 (English literature, in original and in translation).

25 **evading censorship** "A writer must beware of the censorship, and on its account he must soften and distort the expression of his opinion": Freud, *Interpretation of Dreams*, 4:142. For this strategy in relation to literature particularly, see Annabel Patterson, *Censorship and Interpretation: The Conditions of Writing and Reading in Early Modern England* (1984).

26 **First Folio"** Kenneth Tynan, *The Observer*, 8 July 1963.

26 **depth-psychology** John Stachniewski, "Calvinist Psychology in Middleton's Tragedies," in *Three Jacobean Revenge Tragedies: A Casebook*, ed. R. V. Holdsworth (1990), 228.

27 **heterosexual sodomy** See Celia R. Daileader, "Backdoor Sex: Renaissance Gynosodomy, Aretino, and the Exotic," forthcoming in *English Literary History*.

29 **Cathar heresy** Malcolm Lambert, *The Cathars* (1998); Carol Lansing, *Power and Purity: Cathar Heresy in Medieval Italy* (1998).

30 **Leo Steinberg,** *The Sexuality of Christ in Renaissance Art and in Modern Oblivion* (1983). As critics have pointed out, the "sexuality" of Steinberg's title should be "genitality," since Jesus is not represented acting sexually.

30 **Montaigne,** *Essays* (1588), III, 5, in *Oeuvres Complètes*, ed. Robert Barral and Pierre Michel (1967), 348 ("châtra tant de belles et antiques statues . . . châtrer et chevaux et ânes, et nature enfin").

30 **plays of those decades** Statistics compiled from the Chadwyck-Healey database of Literature Online for the words *eunuch(s), geld, gelded, gelder, gelt* in plays first performed within the period 1580–1642.

30 **1600 and 1640** I have checked all the plays listed under castrato, eunuch, and gelder in Thomas L. Berger's *An Index of Characters in English Printed Drama to the Restoration* (1975). To Berger's list I have added Edward Sharpham's *Cupid's Whirligig,* Matthew Gwinne's *Nero* (Sporus), and the anonymous tragedies *The Eunuch* and *Claudius Tiberius Nero* (Spado); but I have subtracted *Twelfth Night*, where it is clear that, whatever she says in 1.2, Viola is not disguised as a eunuch at Orsino's court.

30 **African and Asian** Leo Africanus, *Descrizione dell' Affrica* (1550), tr. John Pory (1600), ed. Robert Brown, 3 vols. (1895), III, 724, 828; Manuel Álvares, *Ethiopia Minor and a Geographical Account of the Province of Sierra Leone* (c. 1615), tr. P. E. H. Hair (Liverpool: privately published, 1990), chap. 7 (folios 69[v]–70). Marco Polo was first translated into English in 1579; after the founding of the East India Company, the English had increasingly frequent contact with Asia. See, for instance, the incident in Bantam reported in *The East India Company Journals of Captain William Keeling and Master Thomas Bonner, 1615–1617*, ed. Michael Strachan and Boies Penrose (1971): "As I went to court I met two of the nobility, led by the King's command to be deprived of their testicles for not being ready with fire before the King's elephants at the appointed hour" (23 May, p. 138).

30 **Ottoman harems** Ottaviano Bon, *The Sultan's Seraglio: An Intimate Portrait of Life at the Ottoman Court,* tr. Robert Withers (1625), ed. Godfrey Goodwin (1996); Jean Baptiste Tavernier, *Nouvelle Relation de l'interieur du serrail du grand seigneur,* tr. J. P. (1677).

30 **histories of castration** Joannes Heribertus (or Teofilo Raynaud), *Eunuchi*

nati, facti, mystici ex sacra et humana litterature illustrati (1655); Hieronymus Delphinus, *Eunuchi conjugam; hoc est, scripta varia de conjugio inter eunuchum et virginem juvenculam anno 1660 contracto* (1908). On the bibliographical history of eunuchs, see N. M. Penzer, *The Harem* (1936), 150–151.

31 *History of Sexuality* For a critique of Foucault's published statements about medieval sexuality, see Karma Lochrie, "Desiring Foucault," *Journal of Medieval and Early Modern Studies* 27 (1997), 3–16.

31 **Shakespeare** See Gary Taylor, *Reinventing Shakespeare: A Cultural History from the Restoration to the Present* (1989), 410–411: Shakespeare "has become a black hole" who "no longer transmits visible light. . . . We find in Shakespeare only what we bring to him or what others have left behind; he gives us back our own values."

Contest of Males

33 **marriage bed** *A Greek-English Lexicon*, ed. Henry George Liddell, Robert Scott, and Henry Stuart Jones (1968), 724.

33 **power to breed"** Aristotle, *Generation of Animals*, ed. A. L. Peck (1953), 717b2. The translation is my own (οὐ δύνανται γεννᾶν τὰ ἐκτεμνόμενα). The Assyrian word for eunuch, *šūt rēši*, refers to one "who does not breed": see J. E. Reade, "The Neo-Assyrian Court and Army: Evidence from the Sculptures," *Iraq* 34 (1972), 92.

34 **sexual rivalry** Charles Darwin, *The Descent of Man, and Selection in Relation to Sex* (1871), ed. Paul H. Barrett and R. B. Freeman, 2 vols. (1989), 215–68, 579–630; David C. Geary, *Male, Female: The Evolution of Human Sex Differences* (1998), 38–45, 59–71, 88–90, 139–44. Standard evolutionary theory here can be summarized in the formula "male competition and female choice"; the harem reduces both. Some rival males are castrated, and used to guard against intrusion by other rival males; female choice is, as far as possible, eliminated.

34 **cheating on you** The joke appears in Poggio Bracciolini's *Facetiae* LXXXVIII (1470), in Lodovico Guiccardini's *L'Hore di Recreatione* (1568; English translation, 1573), and in Edward Sharpham's play *Cupid's Whirligig* (1607; reprinted 1611, 1616, 1630). See *A Critical Old Spelling Edition of the Works of Edward Sharpham*, ed. Christopher Gordon Petter (1986), 349. Mark Breitenberg analyzes another example, reported by Robert Burton, but he discusses it in terms of a putatively transhistorical Freudian "fear of castration" without recognizing this historically specific context: See his *Anxious Masculinity in Early Modern England* (1996), 15–17.

34 **Birgitta Sillén-Tullberg and Anders Møller**, "The Relationship Between Concealed Ovulation and Mating Systems in Anthropoid Primates: A Phylogenetic Analysis," *American Naturalist* 141 (1993), 1–25.

35 **shared child rearing** Jared Diamond, *Why Is Sex Fun: The Evolution of Human Sexuality* (1997), 63–88.

35 **Emperor Mawlay Ismāïl** Wilfrid Blunt, *Black Sunrise: The Life and Times of Mulai Ismail, Emperor of Morocco (1646–1727)* (1951), 94.

35 **eastern and western Eurasia** For eunuchs in China, see Taisuke Mitamura, *Chinese Eunuchs: The Structure of Intimate Politics*, tr. Charles A. Pomeroy (1970), and Mary M. Anderson, *Hidden Power: The Palace Eunuchs of Imperial China* (1990).

35   1305 B.C.E. Martha T. Roth, *Law Collections from Mesopotamia and Asia Minor* (1995), 198. I emphasize that this is the earliest *unequivocal* evidence; it is very likely that eunuchs were used much earlier to guard Mesopotamian harems, but the key lexical terms remains contested among specialists.

36   **Herodotus,** *Historiae,* ed. Charles Hude, 3rd ed. (1927), 8.105–106. Herodotus also refers to eunuchs at 1.117 ("most trusted"), 3.4 ("most trustworthy"), 3.77 (eunuchs who die defending their king), 3.92, 3.130, 4.43, 6.32, 7.187 (eunuchs listed between women and draft-animals).

37   **Inanna** "The Descent of Inanna," in *Ancient Near Eastern Texts,* 109, and Dian Wolkstein and Samual N. Kramer, *Inanna, Queen of Heaven and Earth: Her Stories and Hymns from Sumer* (1983), 64.

37   **Assyrian empire** Simo Parpola, "The Assyrian Cabinet," in *Vom Alten Orient Zum Alten Testament,* ed. Manfried Dietrich and Oswald Loretz (1995), 379–401.

37   **Byzantine generals** On eunuchs in Byzantine history, see John Julius Norwich, *Byzantium: The Apogee* (1991), 129–130, and Lawrence H. Fauber, *Narses, Hammer of the Goths: The Life and Times of Narses the Eunuch* (1990).

37   **Cheng-ho** Cheney, *History of Castration,* 20.

37   **Keith Hopkins,** *Conquerors and Slaves: Sociological Studies in Roman History* (1978), 172, 181.

37   **African state of Oyo** Claude Meillassoux, *The Anthropology of Slavery: The Womb of Iron and Gold,* tr. Alide Dasnois (1991), 196–198.

37   **sultan's seraglio** Bon, *Sultan's Seraglio,* 80–81, 92.

38   **castration joke** See *Three Turk Plays from Early Modern England,* ed. Daniel J. Vitkus (1999), 5, 46.

38   **Xenophon,** *Cyropaideia,* ed. Walter Miller (1914), VII.v.59–65. Since *Cyropaideia* was revered by sixteenth–century humanists, I quote from the first English translation: *The School of Cyrus,* tr. William Barker (1567), ed. James Tatum (1987), 179.

38   **Persians valued castrates** Herodotus, *Historiae,* 8.105. The men here contrasted with eunuchs are usually translated as "perfect" or "complete," but the Greek word is ενορχεων, literally "entesticled" (also used of uncastrated rams). For eunuch trustworthiness see also Bon, *The Sultan's Seraglio:* "Eunuchs generally prove . . . of the greatest judgment and fidelity; their minds being set on business, rather than on pleasure" (85).

39   **unique vocal register** Patrick Barbier, *The World of the Castrati: The History of an Extraordinary Operatic Phenomenon,* tr. Margaret Crosland (1996), 15–17; F. D'Amico, "Evirato," in *Enciclopedia dello Spettàcolo* (1954–1965), IV, cols. 1719–1723. The term *evirati* (an alternative to "castrato") might be translated as "the unmanned."

39   **al-Djāḥiz,** *K. al-Hayawān,* I, 113. This work has never been translated into English; the section on eunuchs was translated into Spanish by Miguel Asín Palacios in "El 'Libros de los animales' de Jahiz," *Isis* 14 (1930), 42–54, and there are summaries of the relevant material in the article on khāsî ("castrated man, eunuch") by Ch. Pellat in *The Encyclopedia of Islam: New Edition,* vol. IV (1978), 1087–1093.

39   **Christian choir** Socrates, *Ecclesiastical History,* VI:8, tr. A. C. Zenos, *A Select Library of Nicene and Post-Nicene Fathers of the Christian Church* [second series], ed. Philip Schaff and Henry Ware, vol. 2 (1890), 144; Sozomene,

Ecclesiastical History, tr. Edward Walford (1855), VIII:8.

39   **Roman Catholic choirs** E. Celani, *I cantori della Cappella Pontificia nei secoli XVI–XVIII* (1909); Angus Heriot, *The Castrati in Opera* (1956); John Rosselli, "The Castrati as a Professional Group and a Social Phenomenon, 1550–1850," *Acta Musicologica* 60 (1988), 143–179.

39   **Stephen Greenblatt,** "Mutilation and Meaning," in *The Body in Parts: Fantasies of Corporeality in Early Modern Europe*, ed. David Hillman and Carla Mazzio (1997), 221–241. Greenblatt is not talking about castration. The Skoptsy equated the crucifixion with castration (Engelstein, *Russian Folktale*, 18).

39   **early Christian martyrs** Eusebius, *The Martyrs of Palestine*, 8, tr. H. J. Lawlor and J. E. L. Oulton (1927), on castration as torture. Martyred eunuchs included Eugene, Hyacinthes, Protas, Indes, and Theodore the Stratelate: See Theophylactus, tr. Cheney, 118.

40   **Origen** Eusebius, *The History of the Church*, tr. G. A. Williamson (1965), VI, 8. Although for most of Christian history Origen's castration has been taken as fact, some scholars now dispute the reliability of the story: See Jon F. Dechow, *Dogma and Mysticism in Early Christianity: Epiphanius of Cyprus and the Legacy of Origen* (1988), 128–135.

40   **Chrysostom and Theodoret** John Chrysostom, "Homilies on the Acts of the Apostles," Homily XIX, in *A Select Library of Nicene and Post-Nicene Fathers of the Christian Church* [first series], ed. Philip Schaff, 14 vols. (1886–1890), 11, 122; Theodoret of Cyrrhus, *Dialogues*, III ("The Impassible"), in *Nicene and Post-Nicene*, II, 3 (1892), 230.

40   **Athanasius,** *Festal Epistles*, XIX, 5–6, tr. W. H. Burgess, in *Saint Athanasius: Historical Tracts* (1873).

40   **Jerome,** *Against Jovinianus*, I:12, in *Nicene and Post-Nicene*, II, 6, 356.

40   **Richard of Bury,** *Philobiblon*, tr. E. C. Thomas, ed. M. Maclagan (1960), 145. Bury also praised Origen, "who chose rather to be unsexed by the mutilation of himself, than to be made effeminate by the omnipotence of woman," but Bury objected to Origen's "hasty remedy, repugnant alike to nature and to virtue, whose place it is not to make men insensible to passion, but to slay with the dagger of reason the passions that spring from instinct" (139). Bury's praise of Origen and the eunuch is cited by Carolyn Dymshaw in her analysis of what she calls "Eunuch Hermeneutics"—in *Chaucer's Sexual Poetics* (1989)—but she does not examine the historical specificity of castration. Moreover, her claim that Bury "commends Origen as an exemplary reader" (160) is misleading, because Bury does not mention Origen's reading at all (simply citing him in a paragraph with Plato, Jerome, and Xenophon), and singles him out only for condemnation of his self–mutilation.

40–42   **Peter Abelard** "*Historia calamitatum*," in *The Letters of Abelard and Heloise*, tr. Betty Radice (1974), 77. Abelard here echoes Jerome, who had called Origen "the greatest teacher of the early church after the Apostles."

41   **act of "revenge"** The Black Knight's Pawn's action is described as "revenge" at 1.1.159 and 4.1.26, but the play never explains what it revenged; Abelard's castration was "cruel vengeance" for his seduction of Fulbert's niece (*Abelard and Heloise*, 75).

41   **they both love** Abelard repeatedly emphasizes Fulbert's "boundless love" for Heloise (*Abelard and Heloise*, 66, 67, 68); he also speaks repeatedly of the

"jealousy" of his enemies (60, 61, 63, 64, 83, 85, 94).

41   **sexual rivalry** Middleton's use of the story of Abelard and Heloise would also explain one detail of the text which is otherwise inexplicable and confusing: In the climactic final moments of the pawn plot, the Black Queen's Pawn asks, "Whose niece was she you poisoned with child . . . When 'twas indeed your bastard" (5.2.105–107). She means herself, but none of the known sources explains this description of her as an unidentified someone's "niece"; in my experience in ten years of teaching and performing the play, this detail confuses readers and audiences. But Heloise, who did give birth to Abelard's "bastard," was Fulbert's "niece." This question is immediately followed by the entrance of the (castrated) White Bishop's Pawn.

41   **two different editions** *Petri Abaelardi, . . . et Heloissae conjugis ejus, . . . Opera, nunc primum edita ex mss.*, ed. François d'Amboise (1616). See also Charlotte Charrier, *Héloïse dans l'histoire et dans la légende* (1933); Wanda Cizewski, "The Legend of Abelard and Heloise in Seventeenth-century France," *Studies in Medievalism* 3 (1987), 71–76. Middleton read Latin and French and wrote other plays based on texts published in France but not England.

41   **Take Shakespeare** *A Midsummer Night's Dream* 5.1.44–45; *Twelfth Night* 1.2.52–54; *Two Noble Kinsmen* 4.1.130–131 (a passage by Fletcher); *Coriolanus* 3.2.112–15 ("My throat of war be turned, Which choired with my drum, into a pipe Small as an eunuch or the virgin voice that babies lull asleep"); *Cymbeline* 2.3.28–29 ("the voice of unpaved eunuch"). All references to Shakespeare cite *The Complete Works*, gen. ed. Stanley Wells and Gary Taylor (1986); our Oxford text is reproduced in *The Norton Shakespeare*, gen. ed. Stephen Greenblatt (1998).

41   **preserving their voices** Peter Holman, *Four and Twenty Fiddlers: The Violin at the English Court, 1540–1690* (1993), 128.

41   **Francis Rous**, *Thule, or Virtue's History* (1598), Book I, Canto 2.

42   **Ben Jonson**, *Every Man in His Humor* (Italian version, written and performed in 1598, printed in 1601), 1.2.58–59 ("Then will I be made an eunuch, and learn to sing ballads"); *Every Man in His Humor* (revised English version, published in 1616), 1.3.62–64 ("I'll be gelt, and troll ballads for Mr. John Trundle, yonder, the rest of my mortality"). Citations (modernized) from *Ben Jonson*, ed. C. H. Herford and Percy Simpson, 10 vols. (1925–1952).

42   **minikin voice"** John Marston et al., *The Insatiate Countess*, ed. Giorgio Melchiori (1984), 3.1.192–193 ("be gelded like a capon for the preserving of my voice"); Sharpham, *Cupid's Whirligig*, 5.1.74–76; Marston, *Antonio and Mellida*, ed. W. Reavley Gair (1991), 5.2.10–15 ("a servant with . . . such a high-stretched minikin voice . . . I should fear extremely that he were an eunuch").

42   **"squeaking"** John Marston, *The Malcontent*, ed. George K. Hunter (1975), 1.8.4–6: "O that I had been gelded! I should then have been a fat fool for a chamber, a squeaking fool for a tavern, and a private fool for all the ladies." (This is one of the added passages written by Webster.)

42   **Henry Glapthorne**, *The Hollander* (1640), 1.1.

42   *Duke of Milan* (printed 1623): "Command the eunuch / To sing the ditty that I last composed" (1.3.79–80), in *The Plays and Poems of Philip Massinger*,

ed. Philip Edwards and Colin Gibson, 5 vols. (1976).

42   **Marlowe . . . Shakespeare . . . Donne** Ovid, *Amores*, II.3, tr. Marlowe, *Ovid's Elegies*, ed. Fredson Bowers (1973); Shakespeare, *Love's Labour's Lost* 3.1.193–194; Donne, "The Anagram" (l. 35), in *The Elegies and The Songs and Sonnets*, ed. Helen Gardner (1965), 24.

42   **Joseph Hall**, *The Discovery of a New World*, tr. John Healey (1609), III, 8, 2. Healey freely adapts Hall in other places, but here follows closely the original Latin (first published in 1605): See *Another World and Yet the Same: Bishop Joseph Hall's 'Mundus Alter et Idem,'* ed. and tr. John Millar Wands (1981), 104.

42   **Thomas Heywood**, *Troia Britannica* (1609), Canto 16, marginal note.

42   **eunuch read it**" Charles Sonnibank, *The Eunuch's Conversion: A Sermon preached at Paul's Cross* (1617), 114, 32, 67.

42   **place and quality**" *The Sermons of John Donne*, ed. Evelyn M. Simpson and George R. Potter, 10 vols. (1953–1962), V, 36, 35.

43   **says Donne** *Sermons*, IX, 87, 86.

44   **most recent editors** Thomas Middleton, *A Game at Chess*, ed. T. H. Howard-Hill (1993); Howard-Hill emends the line, substituting "And" for the "I" of all the printed texts and manuscripts. He justifies his emendation by remarking that "The Black Knight's Pawn is not likely to have fitted his adversary to frustrate the Black Knight's plot" (128). Certainly, the Black Knight's Pawn did not deliberately do so; that is the irony (which he recognizes, but Howard-Hill does not). The emendation of "I" to "And" is not only paleographically and stemmatically implausible; it also requires emendation of the punctuation and a strained interpretation of "him" as "himself." Richard Dutton does not emend the phrase, but comments, "It makes no sense for the pawn to fit out a member of the opposing House, so presumably *made* means 'considered, reckoned'": See Thomas Middleton, *Women Beware Women and Other Plays* (1999), 436. But this strained interpretation of "made" does nothing to solve the alleged problem: *Why* should the Black Knight's Pawn *consider* the White Bishop's Pawn "fit and light"? And why should this alleged opinion of his be relevant?

44   **tendency toward obesity** See the passage already quoted from Marston's *Malcontent* ("O that I had been gelded! I should then have been a fat fool . . ."), and Thomas Nabbes, *Tottenham Court* (1638): "I thought he was gelt, he is so fat" (2.2).

44   **"flight" . . . "flock"** For this sense, see *The Oxford English Dictionary (Second Edition) on Compact Disc* (1994)—cited hereafter as *OED—n.*[1] 8.

44   **celibates to angels** Basil of Ancyra, *De Virginitate*, 51; Jerome, *Against Jovinian* I.36; Augustine, *On the Good of Marriage*, 8, tr. John T. Wilcox, and *Holy Virginity*, 4, 12, tr. John McQuade, both in *Treatises on Marriage and Other Subjects*, ed. Roy J. Deferrari (1955).

44   **images of angels** Debora Shuger, "Excerpts from a Panel Discussion," in *Renaissance Discourses of Desire*, ed. Claude J. Summers and Ted-Larry Pebworth (1993), 270; Mark Whittow, *The Making of Byzantium 600–1025* (1996), 130.

44   **testicle . . . stone** For this sense, see *OED n.* 11a, with examples from 1154–1713. For Middleton, compare *A Mad World, My Masters* 2.7.2, 29–30, 93, and *The Owl's Almanac* 1131 ("lib or geld cattle when you see

them grow stony–hearted"). Although the word *stones* does not appear in John Ford's *The Fancies, Chaste and Noble* (1638), the implicit weight of his lost testicles ("I am made a gelding, and, like a tame buck, have lost my dowsets") explains why the castrated character says, "I am not the heaviest in the company" (1.2.170). The pun is explicitly English, but descriptions of the testicles as a "weight" or "burden" also occur in Latin: See J. N. Adams, *The Latin Sexual Vocabulary* (1982), 71.

45   I can do her" Sharpham, *Cupid's Whirligig*, 2.4.82–91, 3.1.47–50.

45   to serve you" Massinger, *The Renegado*, 1.2.25–26 (performed a few months before *A Game at Chess*).

45   two stone presently" *The Dramatic Works of Richard Brome*, 3 vols. (1873), I, 243.

45   political "business" For Middleton's thematic use of the pun on *business* elsewhere, see Christopher Ricks, "Word-play in *Women Beware Women*," *Review of English Studies* 12 (1961), 238–250.

45   "one herd" Edward Topsell, *The History of Four-Footed Beasts* (1607), 324.

46   as I was" Thomas Heywood, *The Fair Maid of the West*, ed. Robert K. Turner, Jr. (1967), *Part II*, 2.1.51–52.

46   less than hanging" James Shirley, *Hyde Park* (1637), 5.1.

46   hernias Millant, *Eunuques*, 150; Tompkins, *Virgin and the Eunuch*, 21–22.

46   pluck out my tongue" Jonson, *The Devil Is an Ass* (1616), 2.5.1–2.

Contest of Organs

49   *David . . . in Caesar's Palace* Nicklas Sven Vollmer (director), *Roughly Cut: An Experimental Documentary on Circumcision* (1994).

50   *Gargantua and Pantagruel* Stephen Rawles, M. A. Screech, et al., *A New Rabelais Bibliography: Editions of Rabelais before 1626* (1987). For Middleton's use of Rabelais, see Paul Yachnin, "The Literary Contexts of Thomas Middleton's *A Game at Chess*," M.Litt. thesis (University of Edinburgh, 1978), 122, and "*A Game at Chess* and Chess Allegory," *Studies in English Literature 1500–1900* 22 (1982), 317–320. A passage at 2.1.222–224 is clearly indebted to *Gargantua and Pantagruel* II, 34.

50   "*enormement*" large François Rabelais, *Oeuvres*, ed. Abel Lefranc et al., 6 vols. (1912–1955), II, 1. (What is now Book II was published first.)

50   336 times J. E. G. Dixon and John L. Dawson, *Concordance des Oeuvres de François Rabelais* (1992). In the original editions, the lists in III, 26 and III, 28 abbreviate "couillon" to "c." after the first few instances.

51   *männliches Gleid* See Gutman et al., *Concordance to . . . Freud*. I have included figures for *penis, penises, phalli, phallic, phallus, member* (in a specifically penile sense) and *scrotum, testes, testi*. A similar emphasis can be found in more recent studies. For instance, in Bernie Zilbergeld's popular and respected *The New Male Sexuality* (1992), the testes are mentioned on only five scattered pages, testosterone on another six; by contrast, the penis warrants an entire chapter (89–119) and another fifteen pages elsewhere—in addition to two chapters on erection problems (477–520), one on ejaculatory control (443–476), and another thirty scattered references to ejaculation and erection.

51   the "penis" . . . the "phallus" See *OED* entries for *penis* and *phallus* 1b (first recorded in the "erect" sense in 1935). The usual word for the penis in early

modern English was *yard*: See *yard, n.²*, 11a (first citation 1379).

52   transcendental "signifier" Jacques Lacan, "The Signification of the Phallus" (1958), in *Écrits: A Selection*, tr. Alan Sheridan (1977), 285, 282.

52   illusions of authority" Jane Gallop, *Reading Lacan* (1985), 20–21.

52   refers to *penis*" Jane Gallop, *Thinking Through the Body* (1988), 126–128.

52   Dympna Callaghan, "The Castrator's Song: Female Impersonation on the Early Modern Stage," *Journal of Medieval and Early Modern Studies* 26 (1996), 344–366. Nevertheless, Callaghan accepts that "in psychoanalytic terms" all human beings are "symbolically castrated" and that "men enjoy patriarchal privilege only at a cost, namely the threat of castration." Such contradictions are characteristic of scholarship that accepts some psychoanalytic concepts while rejecting others, without recognizing their interdependence.

53   medical description *The Epitome of Medicine*, in *The Seven Books of Paulus Aegineta*, tr. F. Adams, 3 vols. (1844–1847), II, 379–380; for the original, see *Epitomate medicae libri septem*, ed. J. L. Heiberg, *Paulus Aegineta*, Corpus Medicorum Graecorum, vols. 9.1 (1921) and 9.2 (1924), VI, 68 (p. 111). Galen discusses the effects of removal of the testicles, in humans and pigs, but is less specific about the medical procedure itself: See *Opera Omnia*, ed. C. G. Kuhn, 20 vols. (1821–1833), 4:569, 8:40–41. Two Roman legal terms for eunuchs also make it clear that the testicles are involved: *thladiae* (crushed) and *thlibiae* (pressed) both refer to the method of compression described by Paulus Aegineta. See Walter Stevenson, "The Rise of Eunuchs in Greco-Roman Antiquity," *Journal of the History of Sexuality* 5 (1995), 497.

53   flesh rebel" Sharpham, *Cupid's Whirligig*, 2.4.95–96.

53   John Day, *The Isle of Gulls* (1606), sig. B1ᵛ.

53   fried in steaks" John Fletcher and William Rowley, *The Maid in the Mill* (1623), ed. Fredson Bowers, in *The Dramatic Works in the Beaumont and Fletcher Canon*, vol. IX (1994), 2.1.36–37.

53   *Merry Devil of Edmonton* 4.1.56–57, in *The Shakespeare Apocrypha*, ed. C. F. Tucker Brooke (1908).

53   o'th' stones" Middleton, *The Widow*, 2.1.44–45.

53   unpaved eunuch" Shakespeare, *Cymbeline*, 2.3.28–29.

53   purchase the place" Heywood, *Fair Maid, Part I*, 5.2.92–93, *Part II*, 5.4.133–134.

53   no stone" Augustine, *Of the City of God*, tr. Healey, 206.

54   "animals were everywhere" Keith Thomas, *Man and the Natural World: Changing Attitudes in England 1500–1800* (1983), 93–95.

54   Emmanuel Le Roy Ladurie, "The Aiguilette: Castration by Magic" (1974), in *The Mind and Method of the Historian*, tr. Siân Reynolds and Ben Reynolds (1981), 84–96.

54   an aphrodisiac Thomas, *Man and the Natural World*, 93; Middleton, *A Chaste Maid in Cheapside*, 2.2.66 ("lard their whores with lamb-stones").

54   pigs and sheep Topsell, *Four-Footed Beasts*, 67–70, 324, 673–674.

54   a spaniel" *Pericles* 19.150 (a Shakespeare scene).

54   George Chapman, *An Humorous Day's Mirth*, 5.2.14, in *The Plays of George Chapman: The Comedies*, ed. Allan Holaday (1970).

54   like a capon" Marston, *Insatiate Countess*, 3.1.192–193. Likewise, a castrated man in Sharpham's *Cupid's Whirligig* is called a "capon" (5.1.53).

54 like colts" John Fletcher, *Thierry and Theodoret*, 1.1.176–177 (repeated threats to geld men throughout the scene).

54 removing the testicles" According to the *OED*, the verb *castrate* means "to remove the testicles of," and the noun *castration* means "the removing of the testicles." However, this British definition comes from a fascicle of the *New English Dictionary* originally published in 1888; under the influence of psychoanalysis, current American popular usage is much looser.

54 Robert Burton, *The Anatomy of Melancholy* (1628), 3.2.3.

55 slash— My thanks to Carol Pierman for this anecdote.

56 such amputations In the Islamic empire contemporaneous with Middleton, three types of eunuchs were recognized: *sendelee* or *sandali* (penis and testicles removed), *ebter* (penis removed), and *ghezee* (testicles removed, damaged, or tied). But the first two categories were extremely rare, precisely because of the high mortality rates of the relevant operations. See Vern L. Bullough, *Sexual Variance in Society and History* (1976), 232, and Bon, *Seraglio*, 84 (not published in England until after *A Game at Chess*).

57 Surgery . . . syphilis Johannes Fabricius, *Syphilis in Shakespeare's England* (1994), 56, 67–75, 106, 173, 266.

57 Francis Bacon, in *Cobbett's Complete Collection of State Trails . . . From the Earliest Period to the Present Time*, volume II, *1603–1627* (1809), 187.

57 secret parts" Jean de Serres, *The Three Parts of Commentaries, containing the whole and perfect discourse of the Civil Wars of France* (1574), excerpted in Christopher Marlowe, *Dido Queen of Carthage and The Massacre of Paris*, ed. H. J. Oliver (1968), 175.

57 "shameful parts" Orest Ranum, "The French Ritual of Tyrannicide in the Late Sixteenth Century," *Sixteenth Century Journal* 11 (1980), 78.

57 revenge" Michel de Montaigne, *Essays*, tr. John Florio (1603), 3 vols. (1928), I, 223.

58 organ" Freud, "Anatomical Distinction," 19:252.

58 disdain for the penis Celia Daileader (privately circulated, Brandeis University, 1992). For another example see Kate Millett, *Sexual Politics* (1970), 181.

58 Carol Smart, "Collusion, Collaboration and Confession: On Moving beyond the Heterosexuality Debate," in *Theorising Heterosexuality*, ed. Diane Richardson (1996), 163.

60 "castrated" (females) Juliet Mitchell, *Psychoanalysis and Feminism* (1974), 87 (quoting and endorsing Freud).

61 obeisance to Freud As originally written, Keir Elam's 1996 essay on castration did not refer to Freud or Lacan, but the editors of *Shakespeare Quarterly* insisted that Elam incorporate them into his text. (Private conversation, October 1999.) As published, the essay cites both Freud and Lacan, and celebrates the "precocious psychoanalytical insight" in Shakespeare's portrayal of Viola "as an eunuch": See "The Fertile Eunuch: *Twelfth Night*, Early Modern Intercourse, and the Fruits of Castration," *Shakespeare Quarterly* 47 (1996), 1–36. Likewise, Stephen Orgel, in the same year, asserts that the same moment in the same play "acts out a classic Freudian fantasy, whereby gender difference is a function of castration": See *Impersonations: The Performance of Gender in Shakespeare's England* (1996), 55. But Orgel's book nowhere actually cites Freud or Lacan. Freud's interpretation of castra-

tion has become so much a part of a shared intellectual heritage that it does not need citation or justification; it has become common sense, a whole interpretive matrix suggested by the mere adjective *Freudian*. The work of Elam and Orgel is dense with the historical detail now required by major academic journals and university presses, but both accept Freud's claims about the transhistorical symbolic meaning of castration.

61   **fetishism** Gayle Rubin (interviewed by Judith Butler), "Sexual Traffic," *differences* VI, 2–3 (1994), 78–80.

61   **vaginal orgasm** See Thomas Laqueur, *Making Sex: Body and Gender from the Greeks to Freud* (1990), 326–343.

61   **John Varley,** *The Golden Globe* (1998), 11.

62   **statue of Priapus** Augustine, *City of God*, VI, 9 (p. 250); Freud, "The Taboo of Virginity," 11:204. Freud cites *The City of God* at second hand, as his footnote makes clear. He probably never read Augustine, who is only mentioned twice in his works: here, and once in recounting a conversation in which a companion mentions an Italian newspaper article on "What St. Augustine says about women" (6:10).

62   **Tori Amos,** "Father Lucifer," on *Boys for Pele* (1996).

Contest of Gods

64   **dream interpretation** George P. Murdock, "The Common Denominator of Cultures," in Ralph Linton, ed., *The Science of Man in the World Crisis* (1945), 124; Donald E. Brown, *Human Universals* (1991), 139.

65   **Freud . . . a train** *Interpretation of Dreams*, 5:608, 357 (added in 1919), 362 (added in 1911).

65   **J. Allan Hobson,** *The Chemistry of Conscious States: How the Brain Changes Its Mind* (1994), 90, 94, 33.

66   **of similarities"** *Artemidori Daldiani Oneirokritikon Libri V*, ed. R. A. Pack (1963), 2.25; translation from *The Interpretation of Dreams*, tr. R. J. White (1975), 105–106.

66   **personal experience** S. R. F. Price, "The Future of Dreams: From Freud to Artemidorus," in *Before Sexuality: The Construction of Erotic Experience in the Ancient Greek World*, ed. David M. Halperin, John J. Winkler, and Froma I. Zeitlin (1990), 365–387.

66   **allegorical dream-penis** Artemidorus, *Oneirokritikon*, 1.45 (my translation). White—citing A. H. Gardiner, *Hieratic Papyri in the British Museum, Third Series: Chester Beatty Gift I* (1935), 9–35—records two ancient Egyptian penis dreams from Chester Beatty Papyrus III (c. 2000–1790 B.C.E.): an enlarging penis signifies increasing possessions, but a stiff penis indicates "victory to his enemies" (*Interpretation of Dreams*, 75). This second significance perhaps derives from the Egyptian custom of cutting off the penises of captured or dead enemy soldiers.

67   **heaven's sake"** Augustine, *De sancta virginitate*, 23; *Holy Virginity*, tr. McQuade, 168.

68   **King's palace"** Augustine, *Reply to Faustus the Manichean*, 30:4, tr. Richard Stothert and Albert H. Newman, in *Nicene and Post-Nicene*, I, 4 (1887), 329.

68   **carnal relations"** Augustine, *De sancta virginitate*, 25; McQuade, 171. Augustine cites Matthew 19:12 in glossing this passage of Isaiah.

68   **of celibacy"** Augustine, *On Christian Doctrine*, III, 17, in *Patrologia Latina*,

34 (1887), 75.

68   Clement of Alexandria, *Paidagogus*, III, 4 (26); *Christ the Educator*, tr. Simon
      P. Wood (1954), 221.

68   man continent" Saint Ambrose, *Treatise Concerning Widows*, xiii.75, tr. H.
      de Romestin, *Nicene and Post-Nicene Fathers*, II, 10 (1896), 404.

68   but figuratively" Augustine, *On Christian Doctrine*, III, 17.

69   Ambrose, *Treatise Concerning Widows*, xiii.75.

69   Tertullian, *De monogamia*, 5, in *Treatises*, p. 79.

70   Christian polemicists Tertullian, *Ad Nationes*, II, vii, xii; Origen, *Against
      Celsus,* IV, xlvi; Theophilus of Antioch, *Theophilus to Autolycus*, III, viii;
      Athenagoras, *A Plea for the Christians,* xxvi, xxx; Augustine, *City of God*, II,
      7. For the related Christian turning-the-tables argument that it was "civi-
      lized" Romans who engaged in "barbaric" human sacrifice in the worship of
      "demons" who "hate mankind," see J. Rives, "Human Sacrifice among
      Pagans and Christians," *Journal of Roman Studies* 85 (1995), 65–85; he
      notes that at the end of the fourth century such arguments, originally used to
      distinguish Christians from pagans, were mobilized to distinguish orthodox
      from heretic. Castration clearly belongs to the same category of "barbaric"
      practices as human sacrifice and was similarly used rhetorically.

70   Origen According to his *Commentary on Matthew*, this is one of those "pas-
      sages of scripture, which have no literal meaning at all"; anyone who takes it
      literally "would make it seem as if Christ had taught men to be savage and
      barbaric, and only succeed in having men hate the very words of Jesus." See
      Gerard E. Caspary, *Politics and Exegesis: Origen and the Two Swords*
      (1979), 56–65; Caspary cites both the Greek and Latin versions. I have left
      an extended discussion of Origen out of the main text here because the appar-
      ent discrepancy between his alleged self-castration and his determinedly alle-
      gorical interpretation would introduce an ultimately irrelevant complication;
      so far as the meaning of this passage is concerned, Origen in his extant work
      simply belongs to the large roster of theologians who insist that the meaning
      must be figurative. However, Origen does worry about the consequences and
      procedures of such allegorizing much more systematically than other explica-
      tors. For instance, most allegorists seek a figurative meaning for only the last
      of the three categories of eunuchs; Origen objects that this wiggle offends
      against the most elementary rules of interpretation, which require that all the
      elements in a single rhetorical enumeration should be at the same level of
      meaning (Caspary, 57). Origen therefore, more logically, interprets all three
      categories of eunuch figuratively. But such logic leads him toward a whole-
      sale allegorizing of the Hebrew and Greek scriptures which the Church hier-
      archy eventually rejected. The escalating orthodox attacks on self-castration
      at the end of the fourth century overlap, perhaps not coincidentally, with a
      resurgence of interest in, and attacks on, Origen: See Elizabeth A. Clark, *The
      Origenist Controversy: The Cultural Construction of an Early Christian
      Debate* (1992), who concludes that "the critiques of Origenism levelled by its
      opponents" in the decades either side of 400 "increasingly focused on issues
      pertaining to 'the body'" (246).

70   or prisons" Clement of Alexandria, *Exhortation to the Heathen*, 10, in *The
      Ante-Nicene Fathers*, ed. Alexander Roberts and James Donaldson, rev. A.
      Clement Coxe, 10 vols. (1885–1887), 2 (1885), 197.

70   **be men"** Jerome, *Against Jovinianus,* I:49, tr. W. H. Fremantle, in *Nicene and Post-Nicene,* II, 6 (1893), 386.

70   **but tortures"** *The Octavius of Minucius Felix,* ed. Gerald H. Rendall (1931), 23.4.

70   **in none"** Augustine, *City of God,* VI, 10.

70   **"harlot goddess"** Augustine, *In Hoseam,* I, 4, 14.

71   **profertur"** *De Civitate Dei,* ed. Juan Luis Vives (1522), in *Aurelii Augustini Omnium Operum,* 10 vols. (1528–1529), V, 127 (sig. l4). Vives' text was the early modern standard, and the basis for the first English translation (Healey, 1610).

71   **religious tolerance** See Elizabeth DePalma Digeser, "Lactantius, Porphyry and the Debate over Religious Toleration," *Journal of Roman Studies* 88 (1998), 129–146.

71   *paganos* Peter Brown, *The Rise of Western Christendom: Triumph and Diversity* A.D. *200–1000* (1996), 35–36.

72   **closer to home** Augustine, *City of God,* ed. Green, II, xvi–xxxiv.

72   **hermaphrodite"** Hippolytus, *The Refutation of All Heresies,* V, ii, tr. J. H. Macmahon, in *Ante-Nicene Fathers,* V (1886), 49. Hippolytus is, of course, not an unbiased source. This heresy drew upon the Gospel of Thomas and the Gospel according to the Egyptians, which were ejected from the orthodox New Testament canon.

72   **Montanus** For ancient and modern sources on Montanism see Susanna Elm, "'Pierced by Bronze Needles': Anti-Montanist Charges of Ritual Stigmatization in Their Fourth-Century Context," *Journal of Early Christian Studies* 4 (1996), 409–439.

72   **Attis allegories** Julian, *Orationes,* V, 165b–168d, in *Works,* tr. Wilmer C. Wright, 3 vols. (1962–1980); Sallustius, *De diis et mundo,* ed. Arthur Darby Nock (1966), IV, 10, 10; Macrobius, *Saturnalia,* tr. Percival Vaughan Davies (1969), I, 21, 7–10 (p. 142).

72   **Attis and Christ** Maarten J. Vermaseren, *Cybele and Attis: The Myth and the Cult,* tr. A. M. H. Lemmers (1977), 101–103, 113–125, 180–182. See also G. Sfameni Gasparro, *Soteriology and Mystic Aspects in the Cult of Cybele and Attis* (1985).

72   **meant nothing** Firmicus Maternus, *De errore profanarum religionum,* ed. Konrat Ziegler (1987), III, 1–3; see *The Error of the Pagan Religion,* tr. Clarence A. Forbes (1970).

73   **condemnations of self-castration** Basil of Ancyra, *On the True Integrity of Virginity,* 62; Epiphanius, *De Fide* 13, 5; *Apostolic Constitutions,* canons 22–24; John Chrysostom, *Commentary on Galatians* 3, 717. All these texts are cited by Daniel F. Caner in "The Practice and Prohibition of Self-Castration in Early Christianity," *Vigiliae Christianae* 54 (1997), 396–415. On Leon I, see Cheney, *History of Castration,* 169. On the context and popularity of Basil's treatise, see Susanna Elm, *Virgins of God: The Making of Asceticism in Late Antiquity* (1994), 113–136.

74   **E. C. Morris,** "The Allegory in Middleton's *A Game at Chess," Englische Studien* xxxviii (1907), 48. According to Morris, "Ferdinand drove Frederick from the throne of Bohemia and so prevented the union of the Electorate of the Palatine and the Kingdom of Bohemia." This interpretation seems to have convinced almost nobody, but in the absence of rivals it has been recited by

every subsequent critic.

74   **Jane Sherman,** "The Pawns' Allegory in Middleton's *A Game at Chess*," *Review of English Studies* 29 (1978), 150, 153, 155. Sherman demonstrates that Middleton's text must be understood within the morality play tradition, where "social and political evils" are "presented as physical debility—a lame John the Commonweal, a spotted Truth, or a blind Commonalty." But she can provide no precedents for gelding in this allegorical tradition.

75   **his tongue** According to Sherman, the English Church has been "musled" to prevent it from "barking," and this "physical debility" renders it unable to "warn," as certain kinds of "preaching" have been banned. The English Church is muzzled, cannot bark, cannot warn, cannot preach; that is, it is speechless. If this is what Middleton meant, why didn't the Black Knight's Pawn cut out the tongue of the White Bishop's Pawn? Tongue amputation occurs in Thomas Kyd's persistently popular *The Spanish Tragedy* (1586?) and John Marston's *Antonio's Revenge* (1601); such an allegory would have been easy enough to understand.

75   **ministry"** Joseph Meade to Sir M. Stuteville, 5 September 1623, in British Library Harleian MS 389, f. 355. (This letter has not been cited in previous discussions of *Game at Chess*.)

75   **gossip and propaganda** On the explosion of "news" texts in the early 1620s, see Thomas Cogswell, *The Blessed Revolution: English Politics and the Coming of War, 1621–1624* (1989), 20–35; Richard Cust, "News and Politics in Early Seventeenth Century England," *Past and Present* 111 (1986), 60–90; Joseph Frank, *The Beginnings of the English Newspaper, 1620–1660* (1961).

76   **body modifications** John Bulwer, *Anthropometamorphosis: Man Transformed; or, The Artificial Changeling historically presented in . . . all the native and national monstrosities that have appeared to disfigure the human fabric* (1653). Callaghan makes much use of this text, as evidence of an emerging massive "castration anxiety," but she does not acknowledge that it is half a century later than the plays she interprets, or that her sixteen quotations from it are all taken from less than twenty pages of a book almost six hundred pages long, in which castration occupies a less significant place than many other body modifications.

77   **Barbary"** Burton, *Anatomy*, 3.3.2.

77   **orientalism** Although Edward W. Said's *Orientalism* (1978) has been the most influential analysis of such prejudices, Said has little to say about despotism or sexuality specifically; the more relevant work, in this context, is Alain Grosrichard's *The Sultan's Court: European Fantasies of the East* (1979), tr. Liz Heron (1998).

77   **Aristotle,** *Politics*, tr. T. A. Sinclair and Trevor J. Saunders (1992), I, 1252–1255.

77   **Barbary ambassadors** Bernard Harris, "A Portrait of a Moor," *Shakespeare Survey* 11 (1958), 89–97.

78   **clerical celibacy** Uta Ranke-Heinemann, *Eunuchs for the Kingdom of Heaven: Women, Sexuality and the Catholic Church*, tr. Peter Heinegg (1990), 5, 100–107.

78   **scoundrels"** Martin Luther, "The Babylonian Captivity of the Church" (1520), in *Luther's Works*, 55 vols. (1955–1986), 36:114; "The Schmalkald

Articles" (1537), ed. and tr. William R. Russell, in *Luther's Theological Testament: The Schmalkald Articles* (1995), III, 11 (p. 147). Russell also gives a full bibliography of Luther's writings on the marriage of priests (p. 173). The Rome/Babylon comparison became a trope of Protestant polemic.

78   **diabolical law"** Calvin, *Harmony of the Gospels*, Luke 1:21–25; *Commentary on the First Epistle of Timothy*, 1 Timothy 5:12, 5:15.

78   **a male"** Luther, *Schmalkald Articles*, 147.

78   **spurious celibacy"** "Babylonian Captivity," in *Luther's Works*, 36:114. Calvin specifically compared celibate priests (*caelibatum*) to the priests of great Cybele (*magnae Cybeles*) by punning on the word *Galli* (fusing the castrated priests of Cybele with the Roman province of Gaul, or France): See *Commentary on Acts*, 14:15.

79   **anathema"** Ranke-Heinemann, *Eunuchs*, 114.

80   **cruel"** William S. Malthy, *The Black Legend in England: The Development of Anti-Spanish Sentiment, 1558–1660* (1971).

82   **castrated"** "To the Reverend Joseph Mead" (30 November 1627), *The Court and Times of Charles I*, comp. Thomas Birch, ed. Robert Folkestone Williams, 2 vols. (1848), I, 295.

82   **expurgate"** OED geld v..2b, lib v.¹b.

82   **William Fulke,** *Two Treatises written against the papists* (1577), ii.250, *D. Heskins, D. Sanders, and M. Rastel, accounted three pillars of the popish synagogue, and overthrown* (1579), 338, and *A defence of the sincere and true translations of the holy scriptures into the English tong* (1583), xiii.358; all cited in *OED*. In the first of these, the author whose work was "gelded" was Origen himself: "In the latter end where he libbeth off the conclusion of Origen's words, he translateth . . . when he hath clipped, shaven, pared, gelded and falsified all that he can."

82   **William Crashaw** *Romish Forgeries and Falsifications* (1606), sig. E3ᵛ.

82   **John Donne,** *Ignatius His Conclave*, ed. T. S. Healy (1969), 67.3–24. (Since Middleton's play begins with Ignatius Loyola, he might well have read Donne's text.) Ben Jonson privately described an expurgated edition of Martial as "*Jesuitaru castratus*": *Ben Jonson*, I:216.

82   **John Gee,** *The Foot out of the Snare* (1624), sig. I4ᵛ–I5. Gee's pamphlet is a major source for Middleton's play.

82   **dictionaries** OED recognizes that *castrate* can mean "to mutilate (a book, etc.) by removing a sheet or portion of it; *esp.* to remove obscene or objectionable passages from; to expurgate" (*v.*, 4); but the first cited example of this, in 1627, actually concerns the censorship of a sermon and has nothing to do with obscenity. It gives the same definition for *geld v.*¹, 2.b, but again the earliest examples have nothing to do with obscenity, but are instead specifically related to religious controversy.

82   **Protestant opposition** Cogswell, *Blessed Revolution*, 20–50.

Contest of Reproductions

85   **stiff objects"** Freud, *Interpretation of Dreams*, 5:359.

85   **Pierre Charron,** *Of Wisdom*, tr. Samson Lennard (1608), I, iii (p. 12). Charron—whose book was more popular in England in the seventeenth century than Montaigne's *Essays*, which influenced it—presumably included the penis among the (later mentioned) "privy parts" that do "the work of gener-

ation," but that plural obviously includes the testicles, too.

86   **metaphorical penis"** Sandra M. Gilbert and Susan Gubar, *The Madwoman in the Attic: The Woman Writer and the Nineteenth-Century Literary Imagination* (1979), 3.

86   **cuckold"** For these idioms, which are common, see for instance Middleton's *Phoenix*, 2.102, and *Wit at Several Weapons*, 1.1.40.

86   **women authors** Maureen Bell, George Parfitt, and Simon Shepherd, ed., *A Biographical Dictionary of English Women Writers 1580–1720* (1990), 247.

86   **Germaine Greer**, *Slip-Shod Sibyls: Recognition, Rejection and the Woman Poet* (1995).

87   **maid"** Middleton, *Hengist, King of Kent*, 4.2.61 ("writ maid"), *Changeling* 3.4.145 ("writest maid"), *Ghost of Lucrece*, 506, 511, 532 (writing with her blood).

87   **Readers . . . texts** See, for instance, *Reader-Response: From Formalism to Post-Structuralism*, ed. Jane P. Tompkins (1980), and Umberto Eco, *The Role of the Reader: Explorations in the Semiotics of Texts* (1984).

88   **Cervantes**, Miguel de, *Don Quixote, Part I*, tr. Thomas Shelton (1612), preface.

88   **Sidney**, Philip, *The Countess of Pembroke's Arcadia*, preface.

88   **female reading** See David Cressy, "Literacy in Context: Meaning and Measurement in Early Modern England," in John Brewer and Roy Porter, ed., *Consumption and the World of Goods* (1993), 305; Nigel Wheale, *Writing and Society: Literacy, Print and Politics in Britain 1590–1660* (1999), 22, 105–131.

89   **dispense books** In the original version of the play, the Black Bishop attempted to rape the White Queen; in the revised version, that role is taken over by the Fat Bishop after he returns to the Black House. Although the books we see the Fat Bishop dispensing in 2.2 are anti-Catholic polemic, after he changes sides he promises to write anti-Protestant books that will be "printed at Douay, Brussels, or Spalatro" (3.1.293–294).

90   **roll . . . penis** Amy Richlin, *The Garden of Priapus: Sexuality and Aggression in Roman Humor*, rev. ed. (1992), 111, 162.

90   **Christian codex** Colin H. Roberts and T. C. Skeat, *The Birth of the Codex* (1983), 38–67; they suggest that the association of the codex with Christianity originated in Jerusalem and Antioch late in the first century, in conjunction with the composition and circulation of the Gospels.

91   **heavenly seed"** Sonnibank, *Eunuch's Conversion*, 4, 135; the entire sermon is organized around contrasts between the eunuch and a "pregnant" scripture or "fruitful" preaching. For the longer history of this religious sense of "seed," see *OED* n. 2a (and with the sense "semen," n. 4).

91   **fathers"** *OED, father, n.* 3b.

92   **condom** Norman E. Hines, *A Medical History of Contraception* (1936), 188–200.

92   **artifical insemination** F. N. L. Poynter, "Hunter, Spallanzani, and the History of Artificial Insemination," in *Medicine, Science, and Culture: Historical Essays in Honor of Owsei Temkin*, ed. Lloyd G. Stevenson and Robert P. Multhauf (1968), 97–114.

92   **injured penises** Callaghan devotes part of her essay to an interesting account of early modern surgery related to the male genitalia (325–334); but her sur-

gical examples and texts date from 1634–1696, clustering in the later decades of the century. These undoubtedly influenced Wycherley's *The Country Wife* (1675)—a work she never mentions—but they are very dubiously relevant to plays written before 1603 (to which she applies them), nor do they substantiate "a conceptual as well as a geographical proximity between the theater and the surgical procedure of castration" (325).

92 **military casualties** Lois N. Magner, *A History of Medicine* (1992), 279–304 (on anesthetics, antiseptics, and asepsis); Douglas Guthrie, *A History of Medicine* (1958), 337–362 (on military and naval surgery); Roy Porter, *The Greatest Benefit to Mankind: A Medical History of Humanity from Antiquity to the Present* (1997), 187–188, 279, 295, 361–362, 372–379, 399, 418–421, 443, 516–518 (on surgery and warfare from the sixteenth century).

92 **Ernest Hemingway,** *Selected Letters, 1917–1961,* ed. Carlos Baker (1981), 745. See also George Plimpton, "An Interview with Ernest Hemingway," in *Hemingway and His Critics: An International Anthology,* ed. Carlos Baker (1962): "his testicles were intact and not damaged. Thus he was capable of all normal feelings as a man but incapable of consummating them. . . . He was not emasculated" (29).

93 **operatic castrati** See Barbier, *Castrati,* 136–147; Beth Kowaleski-Wallace, "Shunning the Bearded Kiss: Castrati and the Definition of Female Sexuality," *Prose Studies* 25 (1992), 153–170.

93 **Charles Ancillon,** *Traité des Eunuques,* vii–viii. The title page of the 1718 English translation (with the more prurient title *Eunuchism Displayed*) highlights this circumstance: "Occasioned by a young Lady's falling in Love with *Nicolini,* who sung in the Opera at the Haymarket, and to whom she had like to have been married."

93 **Byron,** Lord George Gordon, *Letters and Journals,* ed. Leslie A. Marchand, vol. 7 (1977), 153 (8 August 1820).

93 **Tobias Smollett,** *The Expedition of Humfrey Clinker,* ed. O. M. Brack (1990), 91.

93 **primitive religion"** Giancarlo Carabelli, *In the Image of Priapus* (1996), 10, 112.

94 **James Frazer,** *The Golden Bough: A New Abridgement,* ed. Robert Fraser (1994), 347, 359–360 (II, 9–10).

94 **Western Christianity** Even the Eastern Christian church has been more tolerant: See Vern L. Bullough and James Brundage, *Sexual Practices and the Medieval Church* (1982), 16–21.

94 **unlawful intercourse"** Augustine, *Good of Marriage,* 16:18 (p. 32).

94 **not happen suddenly** For a critique of Foucault's model of radical epistemic shift and an alternative model of "graduated multidimensional proximities," see Gary Taylor, "The Renaissance and the End of Editing," in *Palimpsest: Editorial Theory in the Humanities,* ed. George Bornstein and Ralph G. Williams (1993), 125–129.

94 **Celia R. Daileader,** *Eroticism on the Early Modern Stage: Transcendence, Desire, and the Limits of the Visible* (1998), 20. Almost half of Daileader's book is devoted to Middleton.

94 **"Eloisa to Abelard"** ll. 17, 226, 268, in *The Poems of Alexander Pope,* ed. John Butt (1963), 252–261.

95 **sequels and replies** Edward Jerningham, *Abelard to Eloisa: A Poem* (1717),

sig. C1^V. There is also an anonymous *Abelard to Eloisa* published in 1725, James Delacour's *Abelard to Eloisa, in answer to Mr. Pope's Eloisa to Abelard* (1729), and five other sequels collected in the 1787 edition of John Hughes' *Letters of Abelard and Eloisa*.

95 **Marquis de Sade,** *Juliette*, tr. Austryn Wainhouse (1968), 67, 99.

95 **unifying economy"** Lucienne Frappier-Mazur, *Writing the Orgy: Power and Parody in Sade*, tr. Gillian C. Gill (1996), 1, ix.

95 **Clairwil** de Sade, *Juliette*, 492–493, 464.

96 **J. N. Katz,** *The Invention of Heterosexuality* (1995), 19.

96–97 **"an archaeology . . . reproduction"** Foucault, *History of Sexuality*, Volume I: *An Introduction*, 130, 106–107.

97 **"the bourgeoisie . . . censorship"** Ibid., 123–125 (on castration), 10, 12, 17, 34, 84 (on censorship). My italics, throughout this paragraph.

97 **Foucault as in Freud** One of the few specific Freudian texts to which Foucault alludes is the case study of "Little Hans" (the origin of the castration theory): ibid., 27.

98 **procreative couple"** Ibid., 3, 123.

98 **"symbolic"** Ibid., 124, 151.

98 **"repression"** Freud, *Studies in Hysteria* (1895), 2:269, 283; see also 3:182.

98 **"postal censorship"** Freud, *Interpretation of Dreams*, 5:529, 4:142 (footnote added in 1919); *Introductory Lectures*, 15:139.

99 **incitement"** Foucault, *Introduction*, 17–18, 33, 23.

99 **binary opposition** Foucault at times implicitly invokes Derrida in his dismissive references to the "binary" logic of positions he opposes—for instance, in asserting that there is "no binary and all-encompassing opposition between rulers and ruled" (ibid., 94)—but the rhetoric and structure of his *Introduction* is pervasively binary. See, for instance, his description of nineteenth-century society: "It did *not set boundaries* for sexuality; it *extended* the various forms of sexuality, pursuing them according to lines of indefinite penetration. It did *not exclude* sexuality, *but included* it in the body as a mode of specification of individuals. It did *not seek to avoid* it; it *attracted* its varieties by means of spirals in which pleasure and power reinforced one another. It did *not set up a barrier;* it *provided spaces* of maximum saturation. . . . Modern society *is* perverse, *not* in spite of its puritanism or as if from a backlash provoked by its hypocrisy; it *is in actual fact*, and directly, perverse" (p. 47). This "binary and all-encompassing opposition"—and similar examples that can be taken from every chapter, sometimes every page—is no more plausible than those Foucault sarcastically dismisses elsewhere.

99 **sodomy in Holland** Theo van der Meer, "Sodomy and the Pursuit of a Third Sex in the Early Modern Period," in *Third Sex, Third Gender: Beyond Sexual Dimorphism in Culture and History*, ed. Gilbert Herdt (1994), 137–212.

99 **history of the book** For overviews see—among many recent studies— Elizabeth L. Eisenstein, *The Printing Press as an Agent of Change: Communications and Cultural Transformations in Early Modern Europe*, 2 vols. (1979); Philip Gaskell, *A New Introduction to Bibliography* (1972, rev. 1985). Foucault cannot be excused on the grounds that such evidence was unavailable to him. The whole discipline now called "the history of the book" was inaugurated by two French historians, Lucien Febvre and Henri-Jean Martin, in 1958: See their *The Coming of the Book: The Impact of Printing*

1450–1800, tr. David Gerard (1976).

100 **empire of text** I specify "empire of text" rather than "empire of discourse" because there is no evidence that "talk" about sex increased between the seventeenth and nineteenth centuries. Although Foucault's concept of "discourse" includes "talk," surviving texts provide us with our only evidence of the latter; since there are more texts, there might appear to be more talk, but that may well be an illusion created by the increase in texts—especially since many texts describe prevailing inhibitions on public speech about sexuality. For a critique of Foucault's disregard of distinctions between oral and written discourse, see Gary Taylor, "Feeling Bodies," in *Shakespeare in the Twentieth Century*, ed. Jonathan Bate, Jill Levenson, and Roger Pringle (1998), 262–263.

100 **"real repression"** On Bowdler and other efforts to make literature a sex-free zone, see Taylor, *Reinventing Shakespeare*, 205–210. On the increasing prudery of translations, see for instance Felicity Nussbaum, *The Brink of All We Hate: English Satires on Women, 1660–1750* (1984), 77–93. On the bowdlerizing of Renaissance art, see Steinberg, *Sexuality of Christ*, 174–182. Foucault notes that attempts to contain the sexuality of children produced, in the eighteenth and subsequent centuries, an expanding pedagogic discourse about sex: thus, "an intensification of the interventions of power" led to "a multiplication of discourse" (*Introduction*, 30). The phenomenon Foucault here describes is, in part, simply a paradox of censorship, operative in all times and places, and not confined to early modern Europe. See Taylor, *Cultural Selection*: "A society can reduce unpredictable variation only by attempting to control more and more of the experience of all its members. But in order to do that, it has to enlist more and more of its members into the apparatus" for enforcement of repression (34). Foucault misrepresents the paradox, by (again) effectively ignoring the distinction between written and oral discourse: The discourse of the censors has survived (because it was codified in written texts), but the discourse of the much more numerous censored has usually disappeared (because it was primarily the speech of relatively disempowered persons). Foucault systematically fails to recognize the distinction between the experiences of a past society and the surviving written record of those experiences.

101 **new technology"** Foucault, *Introduction*, 116.

101 **"techno-determinism"** For a compelling critique of techno-determinist interpretations of the effect of the printing press, see Adrian Johns, *The Nature of the Book: Print and Knowledge in the Making* (1998).

102 **mobile relations"** Foucault, *Introduction*, 92, 94.

102 **authors . . . printers** Foucault, like Freud, had theorized censorship long before he got to castration. In 1969, he had already identified censorship not as a method of repression, but as a method of creation, in particular of the creation of "authorship" in the seventeenth and eighteenth centuries: See "What Is an Author?" in *Language, Counter-Memory, Practice*, tr. Donald F. Bouchard and Sherry Simon (1977), 113–138; originally published in *Bulletin de la Société française de Philosophie* 63 (1969), 73–104. But if censorship creates authorship, both have existed as long as there have been regimes trying to control the discourse of their subjects—that is, as long as there have been regimes. What changed, for censorship, in the period Foucault described

was the relationship with the reproducers of texts, not their originators.

102   *I Modi: The Sixteen Pleasures*, ed. and tr. Lynne Lawner (1988).

103   **paper money** V. H. Hewitt and J. M. Keyworth, *As Good as Gold: 300 Years of British Bank Note Design* (1987).

103   **printing businesses** D. C. Greetham, *Textual Scholarship: An Introduction* (1992), 88–89.

103   **Stationers' Company** Cyprian Blagden, *The Stationers' Company: A History, 1403–1959* (1960); *The Stationers' Company and the Book Trade 1550–1990*, ed. Robin Myers and Michael Harris (1997).

103   **East India Company** K. N. Chaudhuri, *The English East India Company: The Study of an Early Joint-Stock Company* (1965), 21–22, 55, 144, 150–167.

103–104 Joyce Oldham Appleby, *Economic Thought and Ideology in Seventeenth-Century England* (1978), 52.

104   **Fernand Braudel**, *The Structures of Everyday Life*, rev. tr. Siân Reynolds (1992), 31–103.

104   **Karl Marx** *The Communist Manifesto of Karl Marx and Friedrich Engels* (1848), ed. D. Ryazanoff (1963), 33.

104   **Thomas Malthus**, *An Essay on the Principle of Population* (1798), ed. Antony Flew (1970).

105   **paper money** Malthus calls paper money "specie"—a word that of course derives from the same Latin root as *species*. See *An Essay on the Principle of Population* (1826), ed. E. A. Wrigley and David Souden, in *The Works of Thomas Robert Malthus*, 8 vols. (1986), 3:360–361, 452–453; *Essays on Political Economy*, 7: 16, 43, 144.

105   **birth rate** On this revolutionary "fertility transition," see McLaren, *History of Contraception*, 178–214.

105   **bio-power"** Foucault, *Introduction*, 25, 140.

105   **statistical thinker** For a related critique of Foucault's misunderstanding of "numeric space," see Taylor, "The Renaissance and the End of Editing," 125–129.

109   **orgasms** Joan Cadden, *Meanings of Sex Difference in the Middle Ages: Medicine, Science, and Culture* (1993), 86; Gail Hawkes, *A Sociology of Sex and Sexuality* (1996), 70–71.

109   **"triumph of the dick"** Faludi, *Stiffed*, 543.

Contest of Genders

111   **Freud abandoned** *Fleiss*, ed. Masson, 264–267 (21 September 1897).

111   **moral cowardice** Marianne Krull, *Freud and His Father* (1979), tr. Arnold J. Pomerans (1986); Jeffrey Moussaieff Masson, *The Assault on Truth: Freud's Suppression of the Seduction Theory* (1984).

112   **assert that it did** Paul Robinson, *Freud and His Critics* (1993), 106–107.

112   **really abused** See *Fleiss*, ed. Masson, 286 (12 December 1897), 288 (22 December 1897); Freud, "My Views on the Part Played by Sexuality in the Aetiology of the Neuroses" (1905), 7:274; *Three Essays on Sexuality* (1905), 7:190; *Studies on Hysteria* (1895), 2:134 (footnote added in 1924); "Further Remarks on the Neuro-Psychoses of Defence" (1896), 3:168 (footnote added in 1924); *An Outline of Psycho-Analysis* (1938), 23:187.

112   **human condition"** William J. McGrath, *Freud's Discovery of Psychoanalysis: The Politics of Hysteria* (1986), 197. For another sympathetic narrative of

Freud's change of theory, see Peter Gay, *Freud: A Life for Our Time* (1988), 89–96.

112 **acts of abuse"** Gerald N. Izenberg, "Seduced and Abandoned: The Rise and Fall of Freud's Seduction Theory," in *The Cambridge Companion to Freud*, ed. Jerome Neu (1991), 42 (my italics).

112 **blame themselves** Alice Miller, *Thou Shalt Not Be Aware: Society's Betrayal of the Child*, tr. Hildegarde and Hunter Hannum (1984).

112 **"Very little"** Helene Cixous and Catherine Clément, *The Newly Born Woman*, tr. Betsy Wing (1986), 46.

113 **both genders"** Middleton, *Nice Valour* 5.3.177.

113 **sexual "thing"** See for instance Middleton's sexual innuendo at *Roaring Girl* 2.1.307: "'Tis a pleasure to me to join things together" (where *things* as often refers to both male and female sexual organs). In *Game*, the Black Bishop's Pawn insists that his daughters "must not hide from" him their "things" (1.1.112).

113 **Thomas Laqueur**, *Making Sex*; corrected by Winfried Schleiner, "Early Modern Controversies about the One-Sex Model," *Renaissance Quarterly* 53 (2000): 180–191.

113 **females "gelded"** *OED*, *geld v.*¹, 1a, 1b.

113 **castrating woman** Freud, "The Taboo of Virginity" (1917), 11: 191–208.

116 **Roland Barthes**, *S/Z: An Essay*, tr. Richard Miller (1974), 36.

116 **Virginia Woolf**, *A Room of One's One* (1929; rpt. 1989), 99, 101, 31–33. Woolf was demonstrably thinking of Freud when she described the imaginary Professor von X: "Had he been laughed at, to adopt the Freudian theory, in his cradle by a pretty girl? For even in his cradle the professor, I thought, could not have been an attractive child" (31).

117 **Harvey Mansfield** See Janet Tassel, "The Thirty Years' War: Cultural Conservatives Struggle with the Harvard They Love," *Harvard Magazine* 102 (1999), 66.

117 **Quinn Eli**, "A Liar in Love," in *Speak My Name: Black Men on Masculinity and the American Dream*, ed. Don Belton (1995), 141.

117 **feminist refutations** Freud, "Anatomical Distinction" (1925), 19:258. For feminist critiques, see the several early papers (1924–1933) collected in Karen Horney, *Feminine Psychology*, ed. Harold Kelman (1967), 37–70, 133–161; Simone de Beauvoir, *The Second Sex* (1949), tr. H. M. Parshley (1972), 69–84; Betty Freidan, *The Feminine Mystique* (1963), 103–125; Kate Millett, *Sexual Politics* (1970), 176–203; Mary Jane Sherfey, *The Nature and Evolution of Female Sexuality* (1972).

120 **male sexuality** Critiques of Freud's castration theory have begun to come from male analysts, too: See, for instance, Zilbergeld, *New Male Sexuality*, 92, and Arnold M. Cooper, "What Men Fear: The Facade of Castration Anxiety," in *The Psychology of Men: Psychoanalytic Perspectives*, ed. Gerald I. Fogel, Frederick M. Lane, and Robert S. Liebert (1996), 113–130.

121 **lecherous goat"** Day, *Isle of Gulls*, sig. F3.

121 **Robert Burton**, *Anatomy of Melancholy*, 3.3.3.

121 **capable of erections** Modern medical authorities have long recognized that castrated males can perform sexually. Jacobs cited C. H. Best and N. B. Taylor, *Physiological Basis of Medical Practice* (1961)—"Castration of male primates often produces no diminution in the capacity to mate"—and Bell,

Davidson, and Scarborough, *Physiology and Biochemistry* (1959): "The individual though potent is sterile" (Jacobs, *Keeper of the Bed*, 52). More evidence for continued sexual activity after castration is provided by A. P. Wilson and S. H. Vessey, "Behavior of Free-ranging Castrated Rhesus Monkeys," *Folia Primatologica* 9 (1968), 1–14, and C. H. Phoenix, A. K. Slob, and R. W. Goy, "Effects of Castration and Replacement Therapy on Sexual Behavior of Adult Male Rhesuses," *Journal of Comparative and Physiological Psychology* 84 (1973), 472–481.

122 **John Chrysostom**, *Homilies on the Epistle of St. Paul to Titus*, Homily V, tr. James Tweed, in *Nicene and Post-Nicene*, I, 13 (1889), 536.

122 **postpubertal operations** Peter Brown, *The Body and Society: Men, Women and Sexual Renunciation in Early Christianity* (1988), 19, 117, 140, 168–169; Aline Rousselle, *Porneia: On Desire and the Body in Antiquity*, tr. Felicia Pheasant (1988), 122–128. See also Theophylactus, tr. Cheney: "Those men who are castrated while still youths, with the intention of seducing women lost in iniquity, may assume that they can conquer them primarily because they have been castrated, and the dangers of pregnancy abated. These eunuchs are profligate in satisfying sexual desires" (121). Galen also recognized that eunuchs could be sexually aroused by women: See *Galen on the Usefulness of the Parts of the Body*, tr. Margaret T. May, 2 vols. (1968), II, 645.

122 **Juvenal**, *Satires*, VI, 366–78; *The Works of John Dryden*, vol. 4, *Poems, 1693–96*, ed. A. B. Chambers and William Frost (1974), 177–179 (printing the Latin and English texts in parallel). For an interesting discussion of translations of this and other passages, see Dror Wahrman, "Gender in Translation: How the English Wrote Their Juvenal, 1644–1815," *Representations* 65 (1999), 1–41. The Loeb edition of Juvenal, ed. G. G. Ramsey (1940), does not translate these lines at all, presumably considering them too obscene.

122 **Martial**, *Epigrammata*, VI, 67 (my translation): "Cur tantum eunuchos habeat tua Caelia, quaeris, Pannyche? vult futui Caelia, nec parere." Martial also has another epigram on eunuchs as adulterers (VI, 2).

122 **Semiramis** Athenaeus, *Deipnosophistae*, tr. C. B. Gulick (1951–1963), XII, 515e; *Ammianus Marcellinus*, tr. John C. Rolfe, 3 vols. (1935), XIV, 6.17. For the real Sammuramat (early ninth century B.C.E.), see Karen Rhea Nemet-Nejat, *Daily Life in Ancient Mesopotamia* (1998), 37. This myth presumably contributes to Shakespeare's "On purpose trimmed up for Semiramis" (*Taming of the Shrew*, Ind.2.39–40); although the verb technically means "arrayed" here, Shakespeare elsewhere associated it with lopping off body parts. An alternative Greek tradition, recorded by Hellanikos (a contemporary of Herodotus), even more absurdly attributes the invention to Atossa (daughter of Cyrus, wife of Darius, mother of Xerxes): See *Die Fragmente der griechischen Historiker*, ed. Felix Jacoby (1957), IV, F 178.

123 **Thomas Nashe**, "The Choice of Valentines," in *The Works of Thomas Nashe*, ed. R. B. McKerrow, rev. F. P. Wilson, 5 vols. (1966), III, 413.

123 **Pope Sixtus V** Ranke-Heinemann, *Eunuchs*, 250–251.

123 **Calvin**, *Harmony of the Gospels*, Matthew 19:10–12.

123 **William Perkins**, *Works*, 3 vols. (1609), III, 669, 678; William Gouge, *Of Domestical Duties* (1622), 181. See also Raphael Seligmann, "The Function

of Song in the Plays of Thomas Middleton," Ph.D. diss. (Brandeis University, 1997), 110.

124 **without orgasms** Augustine, *The Morality of the Manichaeans*, 18, 65, tr. Richard Stothert, in *Nicene and Post-Nicene*, I, 4 (1887), 86; *City of God*, XIV, 24.

124 **mimetic desire** René Girard, *Deceit, Desire, and the Novel: Self and Other in Literary Structure*, tr. Yvonne Freccero (1990), 2–47.

125 **Calvin,** *Commentary on the Gospel According to St. John,* John 8:11.

125 **Peter Abelard** Burton, *Anatomy*, 3.2.2.4. Middleton's plot divides the role of Abelard between two characters: the clerical teacher/seducer (Black Bishop's Pawn) and the castrated devotee (White Bishop's Pawn).

126 **seduction . . . incest** Of course, *incest* is not the word we would use to describe a carnal relationship between a priest and one of his female parishioners. But the incest taboos of one culture always look bizarre to another. For "spiritual incest," see *OED* 1b. This was a Catholic doctrine, not a Protestant one: The Black Bishop's Pawn is violating the taboos of his own religion.

126 **castration . . . incest** For a critique of Freud's reading of *Oidipous Tyrannos*, and of his Oedipal theory of incest, see Taylor, *Cultural Selection*, 199–236; I argue there that "A society that routinely leaves unwanted or defective children to die—as almost all early societies did—is haunted by dreams in which one of those abandoned children miraculously survives" (218). For the continuing historical practice I there describe, see John Boswell's *The Kindness of Strangers: The Abandonment of Children in Western Europe from Late Antiquity to the Renaissance* (1988); Boswell also links child abandonment to castration (113). Where Freud sees a universal fantasy of prohibited desire, Sophocles saw the consequences of primitive birth control. Freud thus reduplicates, in his account of incest, the same shift from reproduction to sexuality that underlies his redefinition of castration.

126 **"daughter"** Used, in this figurative sense, nineteen times in the play; "father," nine times. The only biologically literal father-daughter pair in the play is the incestuous "story of that monster" who "got his daughter, sister, and his wife of his own mother" (4.2.101–103)—an allusion completely extraneous to the plot, which follows an equally superfluous description of the financial penalty for a man's "lying with" his "daughter" (4.2.98).

126 **modern accounts** See, for instance, Herbert Maisch, *Incest*, tr. Colin Bearne (1972); Judith Herman, *Father-Daughter Incest* (1981); Mary de Young, *The Sexual Victimization of Children* (1982); Judith Lewis Herman, *Trauma and Recovery* (1992).

127 **ideology of obedience** Gary Taylor, "Forms of Opposition: Shakespeare and Middleton," *English Literary Renaissance* 24 (1994), 283–314.

127 **patriarchal absolutism** See Bruce Thomas Boehrer, *Monarchy and Incest in Renaissance England: Literature, Culture, Kinship, and Kingship* (1992): "The claustrophobic world of Renaissance English court politics . . . has bequeathed its values to modernity in the form of abusive patriarchalism" (148). Boehrer shows that incest in humble families received relatively casual treatment; it was only taken seriously when larger dynastic and political considerations were at stake (as they are in *Game at Chess*).

127 **"supposed to know"** Jacques Lacan, "Of the Subject Who Is Supposed to

Know, of the First Dyad, and of the Good," in *The Four Fundamental Concepts of Psycho-Analysis*, tr. Alan Sheridan (1981), 232: "What does an organization of psychoanalysts mean when it confers certificates of ability, if not that it indicates to whom one may apply to represent this subject who is supposed to know? . . . there can be only one such person. This *one* was Freud, while he was alive . . . he was not only the subject who was presumed to know. He did know."

128   **"transference"** Freud, "The Dynamics of Transference" (1912), 12:103, 105.

128   **affectionate ones"** Freud, *Introductory Lectures on Psycho-Analysis* (1915–1917), 16:443.

128   **unsatisfied"** Freud, "Dynamics of Transference," 12:100.

128   **repression"** Freud, *Introductory Lectures*, 16:437.

129   **politics of analysis** Freud likewise ignores the political content of *Oidipous Tyrannos*; on Freud's habit of "neutralizing politics," see Carl E. Schorske, *Fin-de-Siècle Vienna: Politics and Culture* (1980), 199.

129   **flesh"** Foucault, *Introduction*, 18–21.

129   **sexual site** Stephen Haliczer, *Sexuality in the Confessional: A Sacrament Profaned* (1996).

129   **ramifications"** Foucault, *Introduction*, 18–21.

129   **"impurity"** Henry Charles Lea, *A History of Auricular Confession and Indulgences in the Latin Church*, 2 vols. (1896), I, 374.

130   **Margaret Mead,** "Cultural Determinants of Sexual Behavior," in William C. Young, ed., *Sex and Internal Secretions* (1961), 1457.

130   **Xenophon,** *Memorabilia*, IV, 4, 21–23.

131   **postindustrial society** Boehrer, *Monarchy and Incest*, 151–152. Of the many sixteenth- and seventeenth-century English plays featuring incestuous relationships that Boehrer examines, Massinger's *The Unnatural Combat* (1626)—written two years after *Game at Chess*—is the only one that features father-daughter incest.

131   **pivot"** Foucault challenges the psychoanalytic claim that incest is universally "at the heart of" sexuality: "It may be that in societies where the mechanisms of alliance predominate, prohibition of incest is a functionally indispensable rule. But in a society such as ours, where the family is the most active site of sexuality, and where it is doubtless the exigencies of the latter which maintain and prolong its existence, incest—for different reasons altogether and in a completely different way—occupies a central place; it is constantly being solicited and refused; it is an object of obsession and attraction, a dreadful secret and an indispensable pivot" (*Introduction*, 109). Here again, however, while Foucault criticizes Freud he also adopts certain of his key suppositions; in particular, he takes for granted "children's sex" (27), especially as manifested in Freud's eroticized female child—not a victim of adult power, but a fully desiring sexual participant. Hence Foucault's naive or outrageous account of the "inconsequential bucolic pleasures" of an adult male farmhand who "obtained" sexual relief from "a little girl" (31–32), his references to "precocious little girls" (40) and "the hysterical or neurasthenic girl" (110), and his obvious disapproval of the late nineteenth century's "systematic campaign" against widespread rural "incestuous practices" (129–130).

131   **abuse of children** Freud's own theory—no doubt unintentionally—paradoxically legitimates the very sexual abuse he excoriated: By recognizing the erot-

ic psychological life of children, Freud scientifically eroticized children. Pedophiles now can and do justify the sexual abuse of children by citing Freud as evidence that powerless children actually desire what powerful adults want them to do.

132 **Andrea Dworkin**, *Intercourse* (1987), 194 (final paragraph of the book). Dworkin specifies that this is "becoming" true of incestuous rape "in our time," so her statement must be interpreted historically, as yet another indication of a shift in sexual attitudes between the early modern and postmodern West.

132 **bogus "fathers"** For Middleton's association of Spanish Catholicism with tutors *in loco parentis* sexually abusing children, compare *The Scourge of Villainy* (1598), which imagines a teacher at the Jesuit seminaries of Douai and St. Omers as "some pedant-tutor" who "in his bed Should use my fry, like Phrygian Ganymede" (3.77–78), and asks, "What though Iberia yield you liberty, To snort in source of Sodom villany? What though the blooms of young nobility, Committed to your Rodon's custody, Ye Nero-like abuse?" (3.58–62): See *The Poems of John Marston*, ed. Arnold Davenport (1961), 112–113.

132 **color line** W. E. B. Du Bois, *The Souls of Black Folk* (1903; rpt. 1982), 141: "The problem of the twentieth century is the problem of the color line."

Contest of Races

133 **Kim Hall**, *Things of Darkness: Economies of Race and Gender in Early Modern England* (1995), 62–122.

133 **Joseph Roach**, *Cities of the Dead: Circum-Atlantic Performance* (1996).

134 **"blackness"** OED, *black a.* 1c. In *Game*, "Indians and Moors" are compared to "blackbirds" (5.3.95); in Middleton's *More Dissemblers Besides Women*, gypsies have "black . . . faces" (4.2.199).

134 **Shakespeare** *Love's Labour's Lost* 1.1.175; *Antony and Cleopatra* 1.1.6, 1.5.28; *Titus Andronicus* 5.1.27.

134 **Edmund Spenser**, *A View of the Present State of Ireland*, ed. W. L. Renwick (1970), 43–44.

134 **Jews"** Peter Heylyn, *Microcosmus, or a Little Description of the Great World* (1621), sig. C4, p. 23. See also *The Estates, Empires and Principalities of the World*, tr. Edward Grimstone (1615): "The Spaniards are . . . of a tawny complexion" (p. 116).

134 **"fair"** occurs twenty times in *Game*; the physical sense is always available, but it is especially prominent in "fair eye" (3.3.37, 5.1.26) and "proportion . . . fair" (4.1.94).

135 **engraving . . . portrait** For the relationship between the two images, see R. A. Foakes, *Illustrations of the English Stage 1580–1642* (1985), 122–125.

135 **godless Jew"** Freud's Jewishness has generated an enormous literature, particularly in recent decades: See the four-page bibliographical note in Sander L. Gilman, *The Case of Sigmund Freud: Medicine and Identity at the Fin de Siècle* (1993), 229–232, and in particular Yosef Hayim Yerushalmi, *Freud's Moses: Judaism Terminable and Interminable* (1991).

135 **early modern Europe** James Shapiro, *Shakespeare and the Jews* (1996), 267–294.

135 **"swarthy"** Sander L. Gilman, *Freud, Race, and Gender* (1993), 20; for sev-

enteenth-century examples, see Shapiro, 170.

135 **African blacks"** Gilman, *Race*, 52, 58.

135 **castration"** Freud, *Outline*, 23:190.

135 **softened . . . circumcision"** Freud, "From the History of an Infantile Neurosis" (1914), 17:86; *Moses and Monotheism*, 23:122.

135 **despise Jews"** "Analysis of a Phobia," 10:36. See also *Leonardo*, 11:95–96: "Here we may also trace one of the roots of the anti-semitism which appears with such elemental force and finds such irrational expression among the nations of the West. Circumcision is unconsciously equated with castration. If we venture to carry our conjectures back to the primeval days of the human race we can surmise that originally circumcision must have been a milder substitute, designed to take the place of castration" (footnote added 1919).

136 **being lynched** W. Fitzhugh Brundage, *Lynching in the New South: Georgia and Virginia, 1880–1930* (1993), 7–8. See also National Association for the Advancement of Colored People, *Thirty Years of Lynching in the United States, 1889–1918* (1919); Trudier Harris, *Exorcising Blackness: Historical and Literary Lynching and Burning Rituals* (1984).

136 **rape . . . black man** Robin Wiegman, "The Anatomy of Lynching," *Journal of the History of Sexuality* 3 (1993), 445–467.

136 **William Faulkner** *Light in August* (1932), ed. Joseph Blotner and Noel Polk, in *William Faulkner Novels: 1930–1935*, Library of America (1985), 742.

136 **in 1908** Hugh M. Ruppersburg, *Reading Faulkner: Light in August: Glossary and Commentary* (1994), 264–265.

136 **communal affect** For a full account of one such episode, see James R. McGovern, *Anatomy of a Lynching: The Killing of Claude Neal* (1982); Neal's penis and then testicles were cut off while he was still alive (80).

137 **Spanish eunuch"** T. H. Howard-Hill, "The Unique Report of the Performance of Middleton's *A Game at Chess*," *Review of English Studies* 42 (1991), 168–178; A. R. Braunmuller, "'To the Globe I rowed': John Holles Sees *A Game at Chess*," *English Literary Renaissance* 20 (1990), 340–356. Holles reports that Olivares [Black Duke], Gondomar [Black Knight], Spalato [Fat Bishop], Jesuit [Black Bishop's Pawn], Spanish bishop [Black Bishop], "& a spannish euenuke ar . . . putt into the bagg" at the end of the play; in texts of the final scene, the Fat Bishop and Jesuit appear already in the bag, and the Black Duke and Knight are put there; so are the Black King and Black Queen (not mentioned by Holles). The bag also contains the Black Queen's Pawn and another pawn, identified as the Jesting Pawn in most texts, but just "Pawn" in others; I believe the Jesting Pawn scene (3.2) was cut in performance and that "Pawn" represents the version Holles witnessed.

137 **Freudian slip** Freud, *The Psychopathology of Everyday Life*, 6:53–133.

137 **medieval fabliaux** See, for instance, "Du Prestre crucefie," lines 71–73, in *The French Fabliau: B.N.MS. 837*, ed. Taymond Richmann and John DuVal, 2 vols. (1985), 64–65. See also the English *Knight de la Tour* (c. 1450): "They toke a knyff, and cutte awey the monkes stones" (71).

137 **castration of Jesuits** Elmer A. Beller, *Propaganda in Germany during the Thirty Years' War* (1940), 21–22, Plate III. At the end of the century, A. Baldwin published a pamphlet giving *Reasons most humbly offered for a law to enact the castration of Popish ecclesiasts, as the best way to prevent the growth of popery in England* (1700).

137 *Philaster* Francis Beaumont and John Fletcher, *Philaster*, ed. Andrew Gurr (1969), 5.4.54–55 ("Shall's geld him, Captain?—No, you shall spare his dowsets"). *OED* and Fletcher's editors have been confused by "I'll have you coddled" (5.4.26–27), but the verb probably derives from *cod* (testicle) and means "gelded."

137 **Abelard's castrators** *Abelard and Heloise*, 75.

138 **James Baldwin**, "The Black Boy Looks at the White Boy," in *Nobody Knows My Name: More Notes of a Native Son* (1962), 217.

138 **Andrew Young**, *An Easy Burden: The Civil Rights Movement and the Transformation of America* (1996), 471.

138 **Eldridge Cleaver**, *Soul on Ice* (1968), 164.

138 **Norman Mailer**, *The White Negro* (1959), 16.

138 **Luce Irigaray**, *This Sex Which Is Not One*, tr. Catherine Porter with Carolyn Burke (1985), 193.

138 **"The Rediscovery of the Clitoris"** Katharine Park, in *The Body in Paris*, ed. Hillman and Mazzio, 170–193.

138 **in a row"** de Sade, *Juliette*, 66, 72.

139 **these people"** Howard-Hill, ed., *A Game at Chess*, 197.

140 **racialized** Bernard Lewis, *Race and Slavery in the Middle East: An Historical Enquiry* (1990), 3–20.

140 **kill him"** Edward Gibbon, *The History of the Decline and Fall of the Roman Empire*, II, 29.

140 **whitened faces"** Augustine, *City of God*, VII, 26. Translations of the Latin here, unless otherwise specified, are my own.

140 **Julius Caesar**, *Commentaries on the Gallic War*, 2.30.4, 4.1.9; see also *The Oxford Companion to Classical Civilization*, ed. Simon Hornblower and Antony Spawforth (1998), 586.

140 **Claudian Claudianus**, "*In Eutropium*," in *Carmina*, ed. J. B. Hall (1985), 1.121 ("pallida"), 1.123 ("decolor"), 1.253 (a face unable "flagrare ruboris"). The most accessible English translation is in *Claudian*, tr. Maurice Platnauer, 2 vols. (1922), 1:138–229; but this is frequently imprecise in its treatment of words crucial to the interpretation of eunuchs, and I have supplied my own translations in the text. For Claudian as a stranger to Christianity, see Platnauer, 1:19, and Augustine, *De Civitate Dei*, 5.26.

140 **Ammianus Marcellinus**, XIV, 6.17; the Latin word is *obluridi*. For other nasty remarks about eunuchs, see *The Later Roman Empire (A.D. 354–378)*, tr. W. Hamilton (1986), 48, 95, 149, 232, 237–238. The *Historia Augusta* are similarly scathing: See Alan Cameron and Jacqueline Long, *Barbarians and Politics at the Court of Arcadius* (1993), 108, 138–139.

140 **clinical studies** Ralph I. Dorfman and Reginald A. Shipley, *Androgens: Biochemistry, Physiology and Clinical Significance* (1956), 208–210, 315–316; Johan Bremer, *Asexualization* (1959), 82–83, 109, 111, 307.

140 **minor differences"** Freud, "Taboo of Virginity," 11:199 (to the psychoanalyst, "nothing is too small to be a manifestation of hidden mental processes").

141 **Lucian** *Lucian*, tr. A. M. Harmon, 8 vols. (1936), 5:336–337.

141 **the species"** Maud W. Gleason, *Making Men: Sophists and Self-Presentation in Ancient Rome* (1995), 161, 46–47.

141 **law** William L. Westermann, *The Slave Systems of Greek and Roman Antiquity* (1955), 113; W. W. Buckland, *The Roman Law of Slavery* (1969),

37, 40–41, 80, 602–603.

141   **Eastern empire** Shaun F. Tougher, "Byzantine Eunuchs: An Overview, with Special Reference to Their Creation and Origin," in *Women, Men and Eunuchs: Gender in Byzantium,* ed. Liz James (1997), 177–180.

141   **resurrection** Caroline Walker Bynum, *The Resurrection of the Body in Western Christianity 200–1336* (1995), 1–114.

141   **Saint Basil,** *The Letters,* ed. Roy J. Deferrari, 4 vols. (1926), Letter CXV (p. 230); I have slightly modified his translation.

142   **Gregory Nazianzen,** *Orations,* XXXVII (on Matthew 19:1), 19; XXI (on Athanasius), 21, in *Nicene and Post-Nicene,* II, 7 (1894), 343, 275.

142   **Cyprian,** *Epistles,* I:8, tr. Ernest Wallis, in *Ante-Nicene Fathers,* V (1886), 277.

142   **Athanasius,** *Historia Arianorum,* V, 38, tr. Archibald Robertson, in *Nicene and Post-Nicene,* II, 4 (1892), 283.

143   **pacifist protest** W. H. C. Frend, *The Rise of Christianity* (1984), 491.

143   **women believed"** Chrysostom, *Homilies on the Acts of the Apostles,* Homily 36, tr. J. Walker et al., in *Nicene and Post-Nicene,* I, 9 (1889), 226.

143   **monstrosity"** Eusebius, *Life of Constantine,* 4.25.

143   **Eutropius** For the background of Claudian's poem, see Jacqueline Long, *Claudian's "In Eutropium": or, How, When, and Why to Slander a Eunuch* (1996). By contrast, John Julius Norwich, in *Byzantium: The Early Centuries* (1988), repeatedly cites Claudian's poem as though it were objective evidence (121–126).

143   **castrated consul"** *In Eutropium,* 1.296–297, 2:49.

143   **look at them"** John Matthews, *The Roman Empire of Ammianus* (1989), 274.

144   **John Chrysostom,** *Homilies on Eutropius,* I, 3–4, tr. W. R. W. Stephens, in *Nicene and Post-Nicene,* I, 9 (1889), 250–251. The Greek text of this first Homily is conveniently available in *Selections from St John Chrysostom,* ed. J. F. D'Alton (1940), 268–283.

146   **castration complex"** Freud, "Analysis of a Phobia," 10:36.

146   **the woman"** Gilman, *Race,* 87, 40. On the equation of woman and Jew, see also Gilman's discussion of "Jewish male menstruation" in *Doctor Freud,* 96–99.

146   **biographers** See Gay, *Life,* 501–522.

146   **psychology"** Freud, *The Question of Lay Analysis* (1926), 20:212.

146   **blindness** Paul de Man, *Blindness and Insight: Essays in the Rhetoric of Contemporary Criticism,* rev. ed. (1983), 109.

147   **"handmade"** Lucian, likewise, calls eunuchs "neither man nor woman . . . but something synthetic" (οὔτε ἄνδρα οὔτε γυναῖκα . . . ἀλλά τι σύνθετον): *Eunouxos,* 6.

147   **dead thing** This idea is not unique to Claudian. For further examples see Kathryn M. Ringrose, "Living in the Shadows: Eunuchs and Gender in Byzantium," in *Third Sex, Third Gender:* "Eustratius the Philosopher says that a eunuch, in his lack of fertility, is to a man as a dead man is to a living man" (89), and Psellus in his *Chronographia* describes the lives of eunuchs as a "half death" (96).

147   **Chrysostom,** *Homilies on Eutropius,* I, 2.

148   **human and animal** Compare Lactantius, *The Divine Institutes,* tr. Mary

Francis McDonald (1964): Eunuchs "are not all human" (cited in Cheney, 163).

148 **male and female** In insisting upon the importance of the binary male/female, I may seem to be ignoring Lacqueur's argument (in *Making Sex*) that the classical world had a "one-sex" model of human physiology. But "a bipolar model" was also available: See Ringrose, "Living in the Shadows," 89–90. In particular, Ringrose notes that the very structure of Greek (and Latin) categorizes individuals, grammatically, as masculine or feminine. In the poem by Catullus discussed below, at the moment of genital mutilation "he" becomes "she," and remains so consistently thereafter.

148 **Aristotle,** *Generation of Animals,* 4.1.766a, 20–35.

148 **Galen,** *Opera Omnia,* 8, 40–41.

148–149 *mas . . . semivir Concordantia in Claudianum,* ed. Peder S. Christiansen et al. (1988).

149 **forbids"** *Eutropius,* I:224–225: "*numquam mater eris, numquam pater; hoc tibi ferrum, hoc natura negat.*" Similar uncertainties about eunuch gender— "neither men nor women"—are expressed by Gregory Nazianzos, John of Damascus, and Saint Basil: See Ringrose, "Living in the Shadows," 89, 511.

149 **late antiquity** Michel Foucault, *The History of Sexuality,* volume III: *The Care of the Self,* tr. Robert Hurley (1986), 39.

149 **resurrection** Bynum, *Resurrection of the Body,* 86–99.

149 **sunlight** On the association of white soft skin with females (as well as eunuchs), see Ringrose, "Living in the Shadows," 94–95.

149 **Justin Martyr,** *Apologia,* 1:27, in *Saint Justin Martyr,* tr. Thomas B. Falls (1948): "For purposes of sodomy, some are publicly known to have been mutilated; and they impute these secret cults to the mother of the gods" (64).

152 **mutilate nature** Chrysostom, *Homilies on the Epistle of St. Paul to the Romans,* IV, tr. J. B. Morris et al., in *Nicene and Post-Nicene,* I, 11 (1889), 355–359.

152 **"Sodomy"** On the xenophobic projection of sodomy onto other cultures, see Daileader, "Gynosodomy," and Alan Bray, *Homosexuality in Renaissance England* (1982), 75.

153 **a species"** Foucault, *Introduction,* 43.

153 **lifestyle** Maud W. Gleason, "The Semiotics of Gender: Physiognomy and Self-Fashioning in the Second Century C.E.," in Halperin, ed., *Before Sexuality,* 389–415: See particularly Polemo's description of female physique, quoted by Gleason: "larger, fleshier hips . . . flabby, with soft limbs and slackened joints . . . weak voice, a hesitant gait" (392). Castration has similar effects on the male body.

153 **boy, or slave** Foucault, *The History of Sexuality,* volume II: *The Use of Pleasure,* tr. Robert Hurley (1990), 46–47. Foucault recognizes that certain males who engaged in sodomitical behaviors were stigmatized in ways which resemble modern stereotyping of homosexuals, but insists, "It would be completely incorrect to interpret this as a condemnation . . . of what we generally refer to as homosexual relations" (18–19). But there is indeed an issue of sexual identity involved here: What is being condemned is sexual behavior more appropriate to the *genus* "eunuch" than the *genus* "citizen." See Beert Verstraete, "Slavery and the Social Dynamics of Male Homosexual Relations in Ancient Rome," *Journal of Homosexuality* 5 (1980), 227–236.

153 *cinaedus* Gleason, "Semiotics of Gender," 411–412. Since 1990, more evidence for the *cinaedus* as a "sexual identity" has been collected and assessed by Amy Richlin, "Not before Homosexuality: The Materiality of the *Cinaedus* and the Roman Law against Love between Men," and Rabun Taylor, "Two Pathic Subcultures in Ancient Rome," in *Journal of the History of Sexuality* 3 (1993), 523–573, and 7 (1997), 319–371. Both note pallor, depilation, "fluting" voices and "softness" as stereotypical characterizations of the *cinaedus*, but neither relates these traits to the physiological condition of eunuchs (though both cite in passing cases where *cinaedi* were actual eunuchs or were compared to them). Taylor does recognize that the castrated priests of Cybele and Atargatis constituted a "religious subculture" of pathic transsexuals (328–337).

153 **Assyrian law** Roth, *Law Collections*, 160.

153 **Petronius**, *The Satyricon*, tr. William Arrowsmith (1959), 22 (chapter 23). In the notes to their translation (1996), R. Bracht Branham and Daniel Kinney note that "The joke consists of the comparison of *cinaedi* ('catamites') to capons" (20).

154 **empresses"** Suetonius, *The History of Twelve Caesars, Emperors of Rome*, tr. Philemon Holland (1606), 192. A generation earlier, Seneca the Elder had criticized wealthy Roman citizens for castrating their male slaves in order to prolong their availability as submissive sex objects (*Controversiae* 10.4.17).

154 **Foucault . . . ignorant** For a compelling critique of Foucault, see Richlin, *Garden of Priapus*, xiii–xvii.

154 **systematically stigmatized** This sexual typology continued long after Augustine and Claudian. In the twelfth century, the accuser of eunuchs charged that "It has also been said that most of them practice repugnant homosexual intercourse" (Theophylactus, tr. Cheney, 104). Similar prejudices are routinely expressed by such influential historians of eunuchs as Ancillon, *Traité des Eunuques* (1707), tr. Samber, 27, 75, and Penzer, *Harem* (1936), 134–150.

154 **"other sex"** Claudian's position here echoes Galen's: Eunuchs are "neither male nor female, but a third being different from both of the two" (*Opera Omnia*, vol. 4, pt. 5, p. 569).

154 **Tertullian**, *Ad Nationes*, I:20, in *Ante-Nicene Fathers*, III.

155 **Derrida**, "The Law of Genre," in *On Narrative*, ed. W. J. T. Mitchell (1981), 51–77.

155 **Theophylaktos**, *Orationes*, 289 (*Eun. Pro. 20–25*), using the same Greek word on all three occasions within these six lines.

157 **Terence**, *EVNVCHVS*, ed. John Barsby (1999), vii, 6–8, 15 (on the play's early performances and popularity), 13–19, 304–305 (on the lost Menander source play); Elam, "Fertile Eunuch" (on Terence's play's popularity through the sixteenth century, including its influence on Shakespeare's *Twelfth Night*); Vermaseren, *Cybele and Attis*, 124–125 (on performances at the Ludi Megalenses). On the familiarity of Menander's audience with eunuchs, see P. Guyot, *Eunuchen als Sklaven und Freigelassene in der griechisch-römischen Antike* (1980).

157 **plot from Terence** For Middleton's pervasive rewriting of the characters and plots of Plautus and Terence, see George E. Rowe Jr., *Thomas Middleton and the New Comedy Tradition* (1979). Rowe does not discuss *A Game at Chess*.

157 *Eunuchus velit* Terence in English (1598), 110–111. This is a dual-language edition, containing both the Latin text and an English translation; I have modified its rendition of the final line of the prologue, "that you may throughly know, what this *Eunuchus* meaneth." The Elizabethan text does not translate the key word *eunuchus*; instead, by italicizing and capitalizing the word, it insists that Terence is referring here to the title of his play (as do modern editions). But in spoken performance in its original language, the word would of course remain ambiguous.

Contest of Signs

159 **grammatological** Jacques Derrida, *Of Grammatology*, tr. Gayatri Spivak (1976). My argument is not particularly Derridean in its method, but it would hardly have been thinkable without Derrida's attack on the metaphysical assumption that writing is simply a derivative of originary speech. Moreover, I have chosen this Derridean emphasis upon the written sign in conscious opposition to Lacan's insistence upon castration as intrinsic to every "speaking being." Castration is a written mark, not a spoken phoneme.

160 **Michel Thévoz**, *The Painted Body* (1984). See also Robert Brain, *The Decorated Body* (1979); Victoria Ebin, *The Body Decorated* (1979).

160 **own species** Vicki Bruce and Andy Young, *In the Eye of the Beholder: The Science of Face Perception* (1998). See also Silvan Tomkins, *Affect, Imagery, Consciousness*, 4 vols. (1962–1992), 1:204 ("The Primary Site of the Affects: The Face"), and Alexandra M. Maryanski et al., "The Social and Biological Foundations of Human Communication," in *Human by Nature: Between Biology and the Social Sciences*, ed. Peter Weingart et al. (1997), 193.

160 **community** Freud, *Civilization and its Discontents* (1930), 21:114. Freud does not relate this phenomenon to the developmental structure of the perceptual system.

160 **Derrida**, "Racism's Last Word," tr. Peggy Kamuf, in *"Race," Writing, and Difference*, ed. Henry Louis Gates Jr. (1986), 331: "there's no racism without a language. . . . Racism writes, inscribes, prescribes"; it is "a system of marks."

160 **"cutting"** Jonathan Goldberg, *Writing Matter: From the Hands of the English Renaissance* (1990), 59–107.

161 **living vs. dead** Bynum, *Resurrection of the Body*, xviii.

161 **egg-maker** I may seem here to subscribe to the naive "sexual dimorphism" criticized by recent theorists of sexuality: See Gilbert Herdt, "Introduction," in *Third Sex, Third Gender*, 21–84. But my description of functional biological difference does not presuppose "a phylogenetically inherited structure of two types of human and sexual nature," but only a continuum of characteristics statistically distributed. For the purposes of this model, only the minimal difference of egg and sperm production is necessary.

162 **sexuality . . . markings** André Leroi-Gourhan—in *The Art of Prehistoric Man in Western Europe*, tr. Norbert Guterman (1968)—argues that sexual oppositions are fundamental even in the earliest cave paintings and carved objects in Western Europe (113–150). See also Thévoz, *Painted Body*, 12–13.

162 **Aboriginal Australia** Armando R. Favazza, *Bodies under Siege: Self-Mutilation and Body Modification in Culture and Psychiatry*, 2nd ed. (1996), 176–219.

162   **rites of initiation** Richard A Gould, *Yiwara: Foragers of the Australian Desert* (1969); John Cawte, *Medicine Is the Law: Studies in Psychiatric Anthropology of Australian Tribal Societies* (1974); Gilbert H. Herdt, ed., *Rituals of Manhood: Male Initiation in Papua New Guinea* (1982), 246–277, 330–340.

163   **genital mutilation** Rosemary Romberg, *Circumcision: The Painful Dilemma* (1985), 17–22.

163   **Darwin,** *The Descent of Man*, 215–268, 579–630.

163   **Ancient Egyptians** John F. Nunn, *Ancient Egyptian Medicine* (1996), 56.

163   **Aristotle** On Aristotle's ignorance of the ovaries, see *Galen on the Usefulness of the Parts of the Body*, I, 26, 57.

164   **circumcision** On the Jewish ritual and Christianity's long and complex relationship to it, see: Caroline Walker Bynum, *Fragmentation and Redemption: Essays on Gender and the Body in Medieval Religion* (1992), 79–117; Daniel Boyarin, *Carnal Israel: Reading Sex in Talmudic Culture* (1993), 1–10, 231–235; Augustine, *Tractatus adversus Judaeos*, vii, 9 (*Patrologia Latina*, 42, 57–58), *On Christian Doctrine* III, 34:49, and *The Spirit and the Letter*, 41; Uta-Heinemann, *Eunuchs*, 59–60; *The Policy of the Turkish Empire* (1597), 22; Shapiro, *Shakespeare and the Jews*, 115.

165   **ovariotomy** "The first ovariotomy" was performed in 1809 in Kentucky: See Harold Ellis, *Operations That Made History* (1996), 7–16. Although this is the first documented case in Western medicine, Athenaeus reports that ovariotomy was used by Adramytes, king of Lydia (sixth century B.C.E.), identified as "the first man who ever spayed women": *Deipnosophistae*, XII, 515e; if this has any basis in fact, it probably refers to clitorectomy or labiectomy. Even this legend, however, confirms the precedence of orchiectomy—and the association of genital mutilation with the eastern Mediterranean.

165   **"mark of the cut"** Adamantius Judaeus, *Physiognomonica*, ed. Richard Foerster, *Scriptores physiognomonici Graeci et Latini*, 2 vols. (1893), I, 352 (τομῆ σημεῖα). Lacan also uses the phrase "mark of the cut," but in a very different sense, in relation to the object of human sexual desire: See Lacan, *Écrits: A Selection*, 315, and Bice Benvenuto and Roger Kennedy, *The Works of Jacques Lacan: An Introduction* (1986), 177.

165   **marks a particular** In linguistic terms, the eunuch or not-man is the "marked form," as defined by R. L. Trask in *A Dictionary of Grammatical Terms in Linguistics* (1993): "A form or construction differing from another with which it stands in a paradigmatic relationship (the *unmarked form*) by the presence of additional morphological material" (167). For instance, *unman* (like *woman*) is the marked form, created by adding "additional morphological material" (*un-*, *wo-*) to the unmarked form *man*. This description of the historical and biological function of castration—as a way of marking a minority—obviously stands at the farthest possible remove from Lacan's insistence on the universality of castration, as an effect of the acquisition of language per se: See "The Meaning of the Phallus" (1958), in *Feminine Sexuality: Jacques Lacan and the École Freudienne*, ed. Juliet Mitchell and Jacqueline Rose, tr. Jacqueline Rose (1982), 74–85. Lacan justifies his revision of Freud's castration theory by reference to "modern linguistic analysis" (78), but he ignores the fundamental distinction between marked and unmarked forms.

165   punishment . . . sexual crimes In Middle Assyrian law, for sodomy: See Roth, *Law Collections*, 160. In Roman law, for adultery: See Ancillon, *Traité des Eunuches*, 44–45, citing Valerius Maximus (6, 1, 13) and Martial. In Arkansas, for alleged miscegnation and rape: See Guy Reel, *Unequal Justice: Wayne Dumond, Bill Clinton, and the Politics of Rape in Arkansas* (1993). In the mid-thirteenth century, a Castilian royal edict decreed that if two monks were caught performing homosexual acts together, both should "be castrated before the whole populace and on the third day after be hung by the legs until dead": See John Boswell, *Christianity, Social Tolerance, and Homosexuality* (1980), 288. As Boswell notes, what is remarkable about this law is not castration for homosexuality—also decreed by the Byzantine emperor Justinian in the sixth century, probably to cover a political purge—but the death penalty, and the claim that homosexual acts were "against nature."

165   **Shang dynasty** Kwang-chih Chang, *Shang Civilization* (1980), 201.

165   **Carib . . . strangers** Pietro Martire, *The Decades of the New World or West India*, tr. Richard Eden (1555), rpt. in *The First Three English Books on America*, ed. Edward Arber (1895), 159. Some Europhobe scholars have claimed that these and other such accounts of "native" cannibalism are slanderous propaganda; but for incontestable archaeological evidence of cannibalism, associated with ritual and/or warfare, in the New World and in pre-state tribal societies more generally, see Lawrence H. Keeley, *War before Civilization* (1996), 103–106.

165   **also eaten"** Gonzalo Fernandez de Oviedo, *Natural History of the West Indies* (1526), tr. Sterling A. Stoudemire (1959), 33. Oviedo continues: "The boys that they take from foreigners are castrated, fattened, and eaten."

166   **well fed"** Martire, *Decades*, 67.

166   **domesticated animals** For an overview on these issues, see Juliet Clutton-Brock, *A Natural History of Domesticated Mammals*, 2nd ed. (1999), and *The Oxford Companion to Archaeology*, ed. Brian M. Fagan et al. (1996), 178–183, 315–317.

166   **climate change** *The Origins and Spread of Agriculture and Pastoralism in Eurasia*, ed. David R. Harris (1996).

167   **Southwest Asia** John Troeng, *Worldwide Chronology of Fifty-three Prehistoric Innovations*, Acta Archaeologica Lundensia 21 (1993), 179–180. Clutton-Brock notes that the natural ranges of the progenitors of all four main species of domestic livestock—goat, sheep, pig, and ox—overlap in exactly this area (*Natural History*, 27).

167   **interglacial period"** Hans-Peter Uerpmann, "Animal Domestication—Accident or Intention?" in *Origins and Spread*, 227–237.

167   **mile per year** L. Luca Cavalli-Sforza, "The Spread of Agriculture and Nomadic Pastoralism: Insights from Genetics, Linguistics and Archaeology," in *Origins and Spread*, 51–69.

167   **preferential killing** M. L. Ryder, *Sheep and Man* (1983), 25, 30.

167   **harem-herd** Simon J. M. Davis, *The Archaeology of Animals* (1987), 39.

167   **cattle** Clutton-Brock, *Natural History*, 86–87; H. Epstein and Ian L. Mason, "Cattle," in *Evolution of Domesticated Animals*, ed. Ian L. Mason (1984), 6–27.

167   **cultivation and pastoralism** On the importance of this complementarity for

the development of sustained civilizations in an unpredictable environment, see Robert M. Adams, *Heartland of Cities* (1981).

167 **two technologies** See Frank Hole, "A Two-Part, Two-Stage Model of Domestication," in Juliet Clutton-Brock, ed., *The Walking Larder: Patterns of Domestication, Pastoralism, and Predation* (1989), 97–107, and J. Carr, "Why Didn't American Indians Domesticate Sheep?" in *Origins of Agriculture*, ed. C. A. Reed (1977), 637–693.

167 **secondary-products revolution** Andrew Sherratt, "Plough and Pastoralism: Aspects of the Secondary Products Revolution," in *Pattern of the Past: Studies in Honor of David Clarke*, ed. Ian Hodder, Glynn Isaac, and Norman Hammond (1981), 261–305—and many studies since.

168 **remains of . . . cattle** Susan Alling Gregg, *Foragers and Farmers: Population Interaction and Agricultural Expansion in Prehistoric Europe* (1988), 103.

168 **traction transport** The first bovine-drawn wheeled carts and wagons had been developed in Mesopotamia by c. 3200 B.C.E.: See Mary A. Littauer and Joost Crouwel, *Wheeled Vehicles and Ridden Animals in the Ancient Near East* (1979) and Stuart Piggott, *The Earliest Wheeled Transport from the Atlantic Coast to the Caspian Sea* (1983).

168 **castrated cattle** Peter Bogucki, *Forest Farmers and Stockholders: Early Agriculture and Its Consequences in North-Central Europe* (1988), 85–89. I think it is unlikely that the innovation originated in Europe, but Brian Hesse informs me that although cattle castration in southwestern Asia "must have been pre-3000 B.C.E.," comparable studies of bovine remains from the ancient Near East have yet to be undertaken; the emphasis on wool production that shows up c. 6000 B.C.E. in Iran suggests the presence of castrated sheep, but again hard evidence has not yet been found (personal communication, 14 February 2000). Until zooarchaeologists do the work, we can only speculate. Sumerian written texts from c. 2300 B.C.E. refer to a—certainly castrated—"yoked bull": See Marten Stol, "Old Babylonian Cattle," *Bulletin of Sumerian Agriculture* 8 (1998), 173–213. Likewise, by about 2000 B.C.E. castrated bullocks are mentioned in Hindu records (Ryder, *Sheep and Man*, 31). But written evidence of course cannot occur until the invention of writing, and even when texts survive we often cannot interpret them; as Stol notes, we do not know the Akkadian or Sumerian words for castration (205).

168 **precedent for horses** D. F. Walker and J. T. Vaughan, *Bovine and Equine Urogenital Surgery* (1980), 52–54 (bovine), 145–156 (equine). The earliest domesticated horses date from c. 4000 B.C.E., in the Ukraine, making them the last of the major domesticated species; stallion mating, territorial, and hierarchical behaviors make them even more recalcitrant than bulls. See Juliet Clutton-Brock, *Horse Power: A History of the Horse and the Donkey in Human Societies* (1992), 11–12, 22, 80; she gives no dating of the introduction of geldings, but in any case they postdated oxen.

168 **Old Testament** Hayim Tadmor, "Was the Biblical *Sarîs* a Eunuch?" in *Solving Riddles and Untying Knots: Biblical, Epigraphic, and Semitic Studies in Honor of Jonas C. Greenfield*, ed. Ziony Zevit, Seymour Gitin, and Michael Sokoloff (1995), 317–325.

168 **castration in Egypt** G. E. Kadish, "Eunuchs in Ancient Egypt," in *Studies in Honor of John A. Wilson* (1969), 55–62; "Eunuchen," in W. Helik and E. Otto, *Lexikon der Ägyptologie*, II (1977), 46–47. On Egypt's late domestica-

tion of cattle, see Epstein and Mason, "Cattle," 9.

169 **Stone Age origin** Walter Burkert, *Structure and History in Greek Mythology and Ritual* (1979), 105, 191 (citing Plutarch, Catullus, Ovid, Pliny, Juvenal, and Martial). Lotte Motz, in *The Faces of the Goddess* (1997), convincingly refutes claims for a widespread "mother goddess" religion in prehistoric cultures; as part of that necessary agenda, she insists upon the specifically Phrygian origins of the Cybele cult (99–120). Although we have no written evidence of ritual castration in her cult until 415 B.C.E., a goddess who in many ways resembles Cybele was worshiped in nearby areas from c. 6000 B.C.E.; by 800 or 900 B.C.E. at the latest, devotees in Mesopotamia would "delight the heart of Ishtar" by using a "flint knife" ("Erra" 4.56, in Dalley, *Myths*, 305)—sixteen centuries after the invention of bronze.

169 **"palace punishment"** Anderson, *Palace Eunuchs*, 29.

169 **Uruk** See Robert Adams and Hans J. Nissen, *The Uruk Countryside* (1972); Hans J. Nissen, *The Early History of the Ancient Near East, 9000–2000 B.C.*, tr. Elizabeth Lutzeier with Kenneth J. Northcott (1988), 100, 105; *Oxford Companion*, 454, 735. Domesticated cattle have been identified in Uruk by the beginning of the fourth millennium B.C.E. (Epstein and Mason, "Cattle," 9). The primacy of Uruk and its association with Inanna are uncontested; my suggestion that castration originated there in the fourth millennium B.C.E. is necessarily speculative. But visual images from the late fourth millennium do include three types of human figures: men, women, and what anthropologist Susan Pollock calls "genderless figures," lacking hair and genitals, who may represent "a third gender category with which we are unfamiliar" and who engage in tasks elsewhere assigned to men or elsewhere assigned to women— and are also sometimes portrayed as captives: See *Ancient Mesopotamia: The Eden That Never Was* (1999), 102–103. Human remains might settle the issue, but in the Uruk period burials were extremely rare (204–205); in the third millennium, some individuals were buried "with markers of both genders" (213), but scholars have attempted few "sex determinations on skeletons" (214).

169 **writing** Albertine Gaur, *A History of Writing* (1992), 42, 60, 65–67; Nissen, *Ancient Near East*, 14, 85–92. Martin A. Powell specifically proposed that writing was invented by a Sumerian-speaking citizen of Uruk: See "Three Problems in the History of Cuneiform Writing: Origins, Direction of Script, Literacy," *Visible Language* 15 (1981), 422. According to Marc Van De Mieroop, "the first evidence of writing on clay tablets" has been found not only in Uruk but specifically in the Inanna temple complex there: See *The Ancient Mesopotamian City* (1997), 38.

170 **home range"** Clutton-Brock, *Natural History*, 31, 212.

170 **mortality ratios** Keeley, *War before Civilization*, 83–97.

170 **professional armies** Trevor Watkins, "The Beginnings of Warfare," in *Warfare in the Ancient World*, ed. John Hackett (1989), 15–35.

170 **hierarchical continuum** Marvin A. Powell, *Labor in the Ancient Near East* (1987).

171 **foreign country"** Isaac Mendelsohn, *Slavery in the Ancient Near East* (1949), 1.

171 **amputated genitals as trophies** Millant quotes the cenotaph from Karnak recording a victory of King Menephta (1300 B.C.E.), itemizing a total of more than thirteen thousand phalli trophies, most of them explicitly from dead

bodies; other cenotaphs record "three thousand" and "2525" (*Eunuques*, 83–84). The Hebrew David brought Saul two hundred foreskins of conquered Philistines (1 Samuel 18:27). For more recent examples see Tompkins, *Eunuch and the Virgin*, 14–15, 20–21, and Jacobs, *Keeper of the Bed*, 20–21.

171   Herodotus *Histories*, tr. Robin Waterfield (1998), 6.32.

171   Edouard Benveniste, *Le Vocabulaire des institutions indo-européennes*, 2 vols. (1969), I, 323–324.

171   Claude Meillassoux, *Anthropology of Slavery*, 23–26, 78–84, 99.

172   Tennessee Williams, *Sweet Bird of Youth* (1959), 90, 103, 122.

173   foreign dynasties Jack Martin Balcer, *Sparda by the Bitter Sea: Imperial Interaction in Western Anatolia* (1984), 51.

174   al-Djāhiz, *K. al-Hayawān*, I, 108–137.

174   hermaphrodite The hermaphrodite has been much championed by social constructivist theorists: See, for instance, *Herculine Barbin: Being the Recently Discovered Memoirs of a Nineteenth-Century French Hermaphrodite*, intro. Michel Foucault, tr. Richard McDougall (1980); Ann Rosalind Jones and Peter Stallybrass, "Fetishizing Gender: Constructing the Hermaphrodite in Renaissance Europe," in *Body Guards: The Cultural Politics of Gender Ambiguity*, ed. Julia Epstein and Kristina Straub (1991).

174   berdache See Will Roscoe, *The Zuni Man-Woman* (1991).

174   *semivir* Hermaphroditus, in Ovid's account, is "biformis . . . semivir neutrumque et utrumque" (*Metamorphosis* 4:284–289). This vocabulary closely resembles that used in descriptions of the eunuch by Claudian, Augustine, etc.

175   nature and accident In Middleton, castration is both "a crime of that unmanning nature" and "an inhuman accident"; in either case, not-human, un-manning, but somehow both simultaneously "accident" and "nature."

175   Judith Butler, *Gender Trouble: Feminism and the Subversion of Identity* (1990), and *Bodies that Matter: On the Discursive Limits of "Sex"* (1993).

175   variety of social identities See, for instance, Zia Jaffrey, *The Invisibles: A Tale of the Eunuchs of India* (1996); Serena Nanda, "Hijras: An Alternative Sex and Gender Role in India," in Herdt, ed., *Third Sex, Third Gender*, 373–418; Shih-shan Henry Tsai, *The Eunuchs in the Ming Dynasty* (1996); Alev Lytle Croutier, *Harem: The World behind the Veil* (1989); Taj Al-Saltana, *Crowning Anguish: Memoirs of a Persian Princess from the Harem to Modernity, 1884–1914*, ed. Abbas Amanat (1993), 121–122, 134, 141, 206–207, 214–215; Ehud R. Toledano, *Slavery and Abolition in the Ottoman Middle East* (1998), 40–53.

175   social environment" James Loy, Kent Loy, Geoffrey Keifer, Clinton Conaway, *The Behavior of Gonadectomized Rhesus Monkeys* (1984), 124.

175   biochemically determined Eugene Pittard, *La Castration chez l'homme et les modifications morphologiques qu'elle entrain. Recherches sur les adeptes d'une secte d'eunuques mystiques. Les Skoptzy* (1934). See also Dorfman and Shipley, *Androgens*, and Bremer, *Asexualization*.

176   gonadectomized Loy et al., *Gonadectomized Rhesus Monkeys*: "Compared to intact controls, the castrated males were lighter, shorter from crown-to-rump, and had smaller glans penis widths and shorter adult canines" (24). As this study demonstrates, the biological effects of castration are clearly related to its life-cycle timing and to the species-specific differences between infant and adult males. For similar qualifications in relation to other mammals, see

L. E. McDonald and M. H. Pineda, *Veterinary Endocrinology and Reproduction*, 4th ed. (1989), 269–272, 288.

176 **eggite lifespans** Cheney, *Castration*, 198–202; Martin Daly and Margo Wilson, "Darwinism and the Roots of Machismo," in *Men: The Scientific Truth about Their Work, Play, Health and Passions*, ed. Scientific American (1999), 8–14; T. J. Crow, "Sexual Selection, Machiavellian Intelligence, and the Origins of Psychosis," *Lancet* 342 (1993), 594–598.

176 **unprecedented** Howard-Hill (ed. *A Game at Chess*) argues that Jesuits did not recognize gelding as a sin because they practiced it themselves (note to 4.2.128). But this argument is undermined by the fact that Jesuits clearly do practice other sins—murder, lechery, sodomy—that are recognized by the *Taxa Poenitentiaria*. Howard-Hill does not relate this passage to the larger allegory of castration in the play.

176 **un-man** This repetition of negative prefixes (*in-*, *un-*) parallels the Byzantine description of eunuchs by a sequence of negatives: See Ringrose, "Living in the Shadows," 93.

177 **Dea Syria** See Lucian, *De Dea Syria*, and H. W. Attridge and R. Oden, *The Syrian Goddess* (1976).

177 **Babel . . . Babylon** Middleton explicitly refers to Babel at *Hengist* 4.3.155 and to Babylon at *The Triumphs of Integrity* 40; he was clearly thinking of the Whore of Babylon when, in *A Trick to Catch the Old One*, one of his characters says "Out, you *babl*iaminy, you unfeathered, cremitoried *quean*" (4.5.53–54, my italics). *Quean* was a synonym for "whore."

177 **no way our own"** Jean Bottéro, *Mesopotamia: Writing, Reasoning, and the Gods* (1987), tr. Zainab Bahrani and Marc Van De Meiroop (1992), 140. Bottéro is criticizing the tendency of "good-natured" Assyriologists to deny aspects of Mesopotamian culture they find bizarre, sadistic, or revolting.

177 **first castration cult** In *Sex and Eroticism in Mesopotamian Literature* (1994), Gwendolyn Leick claims that "the concept of a castrating goddess . . . is alien to the Mesopotamian religious sytem and was probably an import from western Syria and the Levant, where, at least in Hellenistic times, the cult of the Dea Syria involved the self-inflicted removal of genitals in ecstatic rituals" (225). But who is to say what is alien to the Mesopotamian religious system? The cult of Inanna is the one place where that system articulated issues of sexual transformation; no a priori claims about the system as a whole can arbitrate interpretation of the details of that particular cult.

177 **temple household** See I. M. Diakonoff, "The City-States of Sumer," in *Early Antiquity*, ed. I. M. Diakonoff and Philip L. Kopl, tr. Alexander Kirjanov (1991), 72–73.

177 **war goddess** Thorkild Jacobsen, *The Treasures of Darkness: A History of Mesopotamian Religion* (1976), 140–141.

177 ***assinnu* ("eunuchs")** For a recent full survey of the evidence, which comprehensively refutes earlier doubts on this subject, see A. Kirk Grayson, "Eunuchs in Power: Their Role in the Assyrian Bureaucracy," in *Vom Alten Orient Zum Alten Testament*, ed. Manfried Dietrich and Oswald Loretz (1995), 85–98.

178 **no goddess of fertility** See Jerrold S. Cooper, "Sacred Marriage and Popular Cult in Early Mesopotamia," in *Official Cult and Popular Religion in the Ancient Near East*, ed. Eiko Matsushima (1993), 81–96. This article con-

vincingly disposes of a good deal of nonsense in earlier scholarship about the sacred marriage.

178   **holy vulva** Inanna's vulva as ubiquitous in Sumerian literature as Enki's penis: See Jerrold S. Cooper, "Gendered Sexuality in Sumerian Love Poetry," in I. L. Finkel and M. J. Geller, ed., *Sumerian Gods and Their Representations* (1997), 85–97, and "Enki's Member: Eros and Irrigation in Sumerian Literature," *DUMU-e²-dub.ba.a: Studies in Honor of Ake W. Sjöberg*, ed. H. Behrens et al. (1989), 87–89: "The tender, sensuous sexuality of the Inana-Dumuzi poetry does not lead to conception, and privileges the female organ over the male"—in contrast to the male god Enki's "raw, often violent, phallocentric and . . . reproductive" sexuality. Leick devotes a chapter to Inanna's vulva: *Sex and Eroticism*, 90–96.

178   **never a mother** See Tikva Frymer-Kensky, *In the Wake of the Goddesses: Women, Culture, and the Biblical Transformation of Pagan Myth* (1992), 26–27: When Inanna marries, "she never takes on the jobs of wives . . . Inanna does not turn into a maternal figure. . . . She is not 'mother': having neither maternal nor domestic economic duties, Inanna remains without any of the usual roles and functions of the ordinary married woman."

178   **prostitution . . . bread and beer** Wilfried G. Lambert, "Prostitution," in *Außenseiter und Randgruppen: Beiträge zu einer Sozialgeschichte des Alten Orients*, ed. Volkert Haas (1991), 127–128. Several of Lambert's (traditional) assumptions about Mesopotamian "holy prostitution" have been recently challenged in Gonzalo Rubio's "¿Virgenes o meretrices? La prostitución sagrada en el Oriente antiguo," *Gerión* 17 (1999), 129–148; Rubio argues that the classical accounts are "a misconstruction of a religious and cultural otherness" which belonged to the "progressive demonization" of Mesopotamian cult by Graeco-Roman civilization. However, Rubio does not deny the early association of prostitution with civilization and Inanna.

178   **no-male-and-no-female-organ** "The Birth of Man," in *The Harps that Once . . . Sumerian Poetry in Translation*, tr. Thorkild Jacobsen (1987), 161. The extant texts of this myth are Old Babylonian (Lambert, "Prostitution," 148).

178   **royal harems** Harems were an important part of Old Babylonian culture. For a detailed account of one, see N. Ziegler, *Le Harem de Zimri-Lim* (1999).

178   **naturally occurring eunuchs** In the United States, chances of a baby being born with undescended testes are one in three hundred; chances of being born without a penis, no more than one in a million (Grayson, "Eunuchs in Power," 95).

178–179   **sexual transformation** See A. W. Sjöberg, "in-nin-sà-gur₄-ra. A Hymn to the goddess Inanna by the en-Priestess Enheduanna," *Zeitschrift für Assyriologie* 65 (1976), 163–253: "She [changes] the right side into the left side, She [changes] the left side into the right side, She [turns] a man into a woman, She [turns] a woman into a man" (225). Some of the devotees who approach the goddess "walk before the holy Inanna, Their right side they cover with men's clothes, They walk before the holy Inanna, Their left side they cover with women's clothes" (224).

179   **"abhominations"** Bottéro, *Mesopotamia*, 191 (citing "Erra," 4.55). Bottéro complains that "prudish lexicographers" have denied or obscured the sexual activities of Inanna's male devotees; Assyriologists continue to dispute the exact meanings of *kur-gar-ru* and *sag-ur-sag* (although the latter was subse-

quently equated with *assinnu*, which most scholars now finally agree means "eunuch"). In part, the lexical difficulty arises from attempting to interpret a dead language unrelated to any known language group, but it also reflects the category confusion always created by eunuchs. Thus, by different Assyriologists the disputed words are variously interpreted to mean "homosexual" or "transvestite" or "hermaphrodite" or "courtier" or "official" or "temple functionary." But as we have seen, the eunuch historically fits all these categories, and these mixed signals seem to me good evidence that such passages do refer to eunuchs.

179 **temple singers** Diakanoff, "General Outline," in *Early Antiquity*, 42–43; Lambert, "Prostitution," 150–151.

179 **"makes eunuchs"** See D. J. Wiseman, *The Alalakh Tablets* (1953), 25: "may ISTAR deliver him into the hand of his conquerors, may ISTAR who makes eunuchs . . . bind (?) (him) in his privates" (Tablet 1). Nadav Na'aman translates the tablet slightly differently—"may Ishtar deliver him into the hands of those who pursue him; may Ishtar . . . impress feminine parts into his male parts"—but agrees that the passage identifies Ishtar as a "castrating goddess": See "The Ishtar Temple at Alalakh," *Journal of Near Eastern Studies* 39 (1980), 209–214. The historical references in this tablet date it to the reign of Hammurapi or his son (Wiseman, 2–3); Hammurapi reigned from 1848 to 1808 B.C.E. (I adopt here the "long chronology," which places dates 56 years earlier than the traditional "middle" chronology: See Dalley, ed., *Myths from Mesopotamia*, xvi.)

179 **tribute in eunuchs** Herodotus, *Histories*, 3.92 (500 child eunuchs per year).

179 **galli . . . hijra** See Taylor, "Two Pathic Subcultures," 328–337. Taylor does not discuss Inanna, and seems to assume some (historically improbable) direct link between the Phrygian Cybele and India. Leick much more plausibly connects the Inanna cult directly to India, but she also notes that sexually dysfunctional spermites "were more fully integrated into the Mesopotamian public ritual by virtue of Inanna's inclusive sexual competence" (*Sex and Eroticism*, 158–159).

179 **worshipped by shepherds** According to F. A. M. Wiggermann, Inanna of Uruk began as one of the "central grasslands shepherd's gods": "Transtigridian Snake Gods," in *Sumerian Gods*, 33.

179 **called "holy"** See E. Jan Wilson, *"Holiness" and "Purity" in Mesopotamia* (1994). "Although one might expect the gods to be called holy, that does not occur with any great frequency. The divinity with whom that epithet is most commonly associated is Inanna" (30). Inanna's vulva is called holy" (31). KU_3 means "pertaining to the world of the gods" (holy), but does not appear to indicate purity, or "free of pollutants" (93); Akkadian *ellu* means "pure, free from pollutants," but there is no Akkadian equivalent of "holy"/KU (94).

180 **confounding of categories** See Herman Vanstiphout, "Inannan/Ishtar as a Figure of Controversy," in H. Kippeberg, ed., *Struggles of Gods: Papers of the Groningen Work Group for the Study of the History of Religions* (1984), 225–238. Among other things, Vanstiphout refutes the traditional scholarly assumption that Inanna/Ishtar is a "syncretic" figure, who absorbed elements originally separate; there is no evidence known to us that at any date she lacked any of her central attributes. In any case, the syncretic hypothesis would still leave unexplained why these separate attributes were combined in

one figure; postponing the problem does not solve it.

180   **withhold sex** See S. N. Kramer, "The Woman in Ancient Sumer: Gleanings from Sumerian Literature," in *La Femme dans le Proche-Orient antique*, ed. Jean-Marie Durand (1987), 107–122. In the Enheduanna composition "The Exaltation of Inanna" (c. 2300 B.C.E.), to punish a rebellious, disrespectful city Inanna "kept her distance from the womb," so that "its woman no longer speaks of love to her husband; in the deep of the night she does not have intercourse with him; she does not reveal that which is 'holy' in her heart" (lines 51–57).

180   **mixes female and male** Leick has an admirable discussion of Inanna's "ambiguous feminity" (*Sex and Eroticism*, 55–63).

180   **revere her"** *Erra* 4.56 (eighth or ninth century B.C.E), in Dalley, *Myths*, 305. See the discussion by Walter Burkhert, *Creation of the Sacred: Tracks of Biology in Early Religions* (1996), 48, 168–169.

181   **Sander Gilman**, *Freud, Race and Gender*, 84.

181   **envied** "In the eyes of an impartial judge, those who attack eunuchs make reckless and inconsiderate statements because of their envy" (Theophylactus, tr. Cheney, 119).

181   **imitated . . . uniforms** Ringrose, "Living in the Shadows," 95, 513–514.

181   **"passing"** See Erving Goffman's analysis of "the natural cycle of passing" in *Stigma* (1963) and Harold Garfinkel's concept of "cultural genitals" in *Studies in Ethnomethodology* (1967), 122–136.

182   **tomb of the Prophet** Shaun Marmon, *Eunuchs and Sacred Boundaries in Islamic Society* (1995).

182   **"betwixt and between"** On the importance of liminal positions, see Arnold van Gennep, *The Rites of Passage*, tr. Monika K. Vizedom and Gabrielle L. Caffee (1960). On eunuchs (and angels) as go–betweens, see Ringrose, "Living in the Shadows," 97; on eunuchs as pimps, see Claudian, *Eutropius*, 1.77–100, and Clement, *Paidogogus*, III, 4(26): "scores of eunuchs who are little more than panderers."

182   **immolation of children** Shelby Brown, *Late Carthaginian Child Sacrifice and Sacrificial Monuments in Their Mediterranean Context* (1991).

182   **finger sacrifice** Burkhert, *Creation of the Sacred*, 34–40. On the extraordinary proportion of missing fingers on the human hands represented in early art, see André Leroi-Gourhan, *The Dawn of European Art: An Introduction to Palaeolithic Cave Painting*, tr. Sara Champion (1982).

182   **proximity to the divine** Arthur Darby Nock, "Eunuchs in Ancient Religion" (1925), in *Essays on Religion and the Ancient World*, 2 vols. (1972), I, 7–15. A more recent survey is provided by Ranke-Heinemann, *Eunuchs*, 99, citing Karlheinz Descher, *Das Kreuz mit der Kirche: Eine Sexualgeschichte des Christentums* (1974).

183   **cultic castrations** Browe, *Zur Geschichte der Entmannung*, 13ff.; Ranke-Heinemann, *Eunuchs*, 99.

183   **androgynous"** Hippolytus, *Refutation of all Heresies*, V, 2.

Contest of Times

185   **Bethlehem"** Tori Amos, "Muhammad My Friend," on *Boys for Pele* (1996), and "Crucify," on *Little Earthquakes* (1991).

186   **Salome**, Thomas, 61; Salome is mentioned briefly at Mark 15:40 and 16:1, but not recognized as a disciple; she appears frequently, and is regarded as a

disciple, in the Gospel according to the Egyptians. For translations of and commentaries on the Gospel according to Thomas, see *The Nag Hammadi Library in English*, ed. James M. Robinson, 3rd ed. (1988); *The Gnostic Scriptures*, tr. Bentley Layton (1987); *Nag Hammadi Texts and the Bible: A Synopsis and Index*, ed. Craig A. Evans, Robert L. Webb, and Richard A. Wiebe (1993).

186   **to men** For the presumed male audience of the Gospel according to Matthew in particular, see Antoinette Clark Wire, "Gender Roles in a Scribal Community," in *Social History of the Matthean Community: Cross-Disciplinary Approaches*, ed. David L. Balch (1991), 87–121.

186   **ὁ δὲ . . . χωρείτω** *The Greek New Testament*, ed. Kurt Aland et al. (1966), 73. Neither this nor other editions I have consulted records any significant textual variants for this passage. Randomly recovered manuscript fragments preserve early texts of about two-thirds of the New Testament, but no such fragments have yet been found for Matthew 14:6–20:23: See *The Complete Text of the Earliest New Testament Manuscripts*, ed. Philip W. Comfort and David P. Barrett (1999).

187   **more widely read** Édouard Massaux, *The Influence of the Gospel of Saint Matthew on Christian Literature before Saint Irenaeus*, tr. Norman J. Belval and Suzanne Hect, ed. Arthur J. Bellinzoni, 3 vols. (1990–1993).

187   **revisionist minority** See, for instance, William Farmer, *The Synoptic Problem: A Critical Analysis* (1976), and Arthur Bellinzoni, *The Two-Source Hypothesis: A Critical Reappraisal* (1985).

187   **earliest Gospel** *Matthew*, ed. and tr. W. F. Albright and C. S. Mann, *The Anchor Bible* (1971), clx–clxxxv. For further evidence of an origin in Antioch or Palestine, see the essays in *Matthean Community*, ed. Balch. Given the Roman antipathy to eunuchs, Mark's deliberate omission of this "saying" would hardly be surprising.

187   **Ignatius of Antioch** Massaux, *Influence of Matthew*, I, 94; III, 14. On Ignatius, see also the essays by William R. Schoedel and John P. Meier in *Matthean Community*, ed. Balch, 129–186. For a survey of early Christian interpretations of this passage in particular, see Walter Bauer, "Matth. 19,12 und die alten Christen," in *Neutestamentiliche Studien*, ed. H. Windisch (1914), 235–244.

187   **"absurd"** Jerry H. Bentley, "Erasmus, Jean le Clerc, and the principle of the harder reading," *Renaissance Quarterly* 31 (1978), 309–321. For the continued currency of this principle, see, for instance, *New Testament Textual Criticism: Its Significance for Exegesis*, ed. Eldon Jay Epp and Gordon D. Fee (1981), 26, 64, 114, 125–126, 247, 316.

187   **"rare"** On the principle *praestat insolitior lectio*, see Gary Taylor, "'Praestat difficilior lectio': *All's Well that Ends Well* and *Richard III*," *Renaissance Studies* 2 (1988), 27–46.

188   **"unique"** Stephenson H. Brooks, *Matthew's Community: The Evidence of His Special Sayings Material* (1987), 107–109.

188   **Greek verbs** Liddell and Scott, *Greek-English Lexicon*, 724.

188   **Hebrew or Aramaic** For Hebrew, see Menahem Moreshet, *A Lexicon of the New Verbs in Tannaitic Hebrew* (1980), 256–257. (This work is in modern Hebrew.) For Aramaic, see Michael Sokoloff, *A Dictionary of Jewish Palestinian Aramaic of the Byzantine Period* (1990), 389. The Aramaic verb occurs in the *Targum Neofiti*, an Aramaic translation of the Torah, at

Deuteronomy 23:2. (I do not read either language myself; these references were supplied to me by Gary A. Rendsburg, confirming my hunch about Semitic influence on the Greek text.)

188   **semitic usage** According to Eusebius (*Ecclesiastical History*, III, 39, 16), in a lost work Papias of Hierapolis (c. 130) testified that "Matthew compiled the *Sayings* in the Aramaic language, and everyone translated them as well as he could." This may be a reference to the lost "Q" that most New Testament scholars believe lies behind the original "sayings" material in the Gospels of Matthew and Luke (and Thomas). Some scholars contend that Matthew was written in Aramaic, and later translated into Greek; but what Papias says is compatible with Greek composition of the Gospels as a whole, drawing upon an Aramaic collection of sayings. Although the Gospel according to Matthew includes much narrative material, 19:12 clearly constitutes a "saying," which probably came from an early Aramaic anthology of the λογοι of Jesus.

188   **Palestine"** Harvey Cox, "Jesus and Generation," in Marcus Borg, ed., *Jesus at 2000* (1997), 101.

188   **Jesus spoke"** Herschel Shanks, *The Mystery and Meaning of the Dead Sea Scrolls* (1998), 64, 198.

189   **striking similarities** "Introduction," *The Complete Dead Sea Scrolls in English*, tr. Geza Vermes (1997), 22.

189   **Hebrew Bible at Qumram** Shanks, *Scrolls*, 160–161.

189   **Qumram . . . celibate** Vermes, *Scrolls in English*, 34–35, 44, 83; Shanks, *Scrolls*, 104.

189   **men's children"** *The Jewish War*, in *Josephus*, ed. H. St. J. Thackeray (1926), II.120. "Another order of Essenes" did marry, according to Josephus, but "their motive in marrying is not self-indulgence but the procreation of children" (II.161). Likewise, the Qumram regulations demand that "whoever has intercourse with his wife for lust, which is against the rule, he shall depart and never return" (Shanks, *Scrolls*, 86). These attitudes of course anticipate later Christian orthodoxy. In *Jewish Antiquities*, Josephus transformed the Deuteronomic ban on eunuchs into a ban specifically on *"Galli"*—presumably because the eunuchs he found most objectionable, and pertinent, were men who castrated themselves for religious reasons: See IV, 8:40 (translated as "eunuchs," but Γάλλους in the Greek). See also *Against Apion*, II.270–271: "Apollonius actually imitated all the Persian practices, outraging his neighbours' wives and castrating their children. With us such maltreatment even of a brute beast is made a capital crime."

189   **is born"** *Hypothetica*, 11.14, in *Philo*, tr. F. H. Colson (1961); Pliny, *Natural History*, ed. H. Rackham (1969), 5.15.73.

189   **polluted"** Clement of Alexandria, *Stromateis: Books I–III*, tr. John Ferguson (1991), III, 1.1, 1.4, 46.5.

190   **lifelong virginity** Brown, *Body and Society*; Rouselle, *Porneia*; Elm, *"Virgins of God."*

190   **intercourse"** Philo, *The Worse Is Accustomed to Attack the Better*, quoted by Origen in his *Commentary on Matthew XV*, 3 (GCS 40, 354–355), using the rare verb ἐξευνουχισθῆναι. Origen is quoted and translated by Caner in "Self-Castration in Early Christianity," 396–415.

190   **peril"** *The Sentences of Sextus*, ed. Henry Chadwyck (1959), maxims 13 and 273; Chadwyck believes these refer to physical castration (99–100).

190 **Acts of John** 53–54, tr. G. Stead, in *New Testament Apocrypha*, ed. E. Hennecke, W. Schneemelcher and R. Wilson (1965), 2:241.

190 **Justin Martyr,** *Apologia*, 1:29: "Recently, one of us Christians, to convince you that promiscuous intercourse is not one of our practices, presented a petition to Felix, the Prefect of Alexandria, asking that a surgeon be allowed to make him a eunuch" (tr. Falls, 65).

190 **gelded themselves** Eusebius, *Ecclesiastical History*, VI, 8, 2 (Origen); Socrates, *Ecclesiastical History*, II, 26.

190 **Valesius** *The Panarion of Epiphanius*, tr. Philip R. Amidon (1990), 58.1.4–7 ("all of them are castrated except for a few. . . . Once they have persuaded or forced him to be castrated . . . often they do the same to strangers who pass through and stay with them as guests, as is frequently reported. They snatch them inside, tie them to the furniture behind them, and force upon them the operation of castration"). They cite in justification Matthew 5:29, 18:8, and 19:12 (58.2.1–58.4.5)

191 **stay a child"** Ovid, *Fasti*, 4:221–233 (account of the foundation of the cult of Attis).

192 **pursuit of chastity** Theophylactus, tr. Cheney, 105; Engelstein, *Russian Folktale*, 19.

192 **euphemism** See J. Enoch Powell's idiosyncratic *The Evolution of the Gospel: A New Translation of the First Gospel with Commentary and Introductory Essay* (1994), 82; for the euphemism *hand*/penis in "several Semitic languages," he cites Edward Ullendorff, "The Bawdy Bible," *Bulletin of the School of Oriental and African Studies* 42 (1979), 427–456.

192 **Xenophon,** *Cyropaideia*, VII.v.61; *School of Cyrus*, 179.

192 **passions"** Clement of Alexandria, *Paidagogus*, III, 4 (26); *Christ the Educator*, tr. Simon P. Wood (1954), 221.

192 **merit"** Tertullian, *The Five Books against Marcion*, I, 29.

193 **continent"** Saint Ambrose, *Treatise Concerning Widows*, xiii.75.

193 **Basil of Ancyra,** *On the True Integrity of Virginity*, 61 (Patrologia Graeca 30, 793).

193 **disguises incontinence** Cyril of Alexandria, "Against Eunuchs," *Hom.* 19, ed. C. de Boor in *Georgii Monachi Chronicon* 2 (1904), 652–654; Chrysostom, *In cap. V. Ep. ad Galatians comm.* 3717 (Patrologia Graeca 61, 668); both translated by Caner, "Self-Castration," 407–412. See also Chrysostom, *Homilies on the Epistle of St. Paul to Titus*, Homily V.

195 **necessities"** Clement, *Stromateis*, III.1.1.

195 **"praised eunuchs"** See the discussion of this passage in Massaux, *Influence of Matthew*, II, 200–201.

196 **Tertullian,** *On Monogamy,* 7.

196 **Hippolytus,** *Treatise on Christ and Antichrist*, 3, in *Ante-Nicene Fathers*, 5 (1886), 205.

196 **Jerome,** *Select Letters*, ed. F. A. Wright (1933), XXII, 21.

196 **Daniel and Nehemiah** According to Josephus (*Antiquities*, 10, 16), Nebuchadnezzar caused all the Jews, and all other prisoners of war, to be gelt or cut, that he might have none to attend his private service but eunuchs.

197 **cut off"** For the dating and interpretation of this passage, see *Second Isaiah*, tr. and ed. John L. McKenzie, The Anchor Bible (1968), xv–xxx, 149–151.

197 **influenced by Isaiah** Reginald H. Fuller, "Jesus Christ," in *The Oxford*

Companion to the Bible, ed. Bruce M. Metzger and Michael D. Coogan (1993), 357.

197 **Wisdom of Solomon** For the authorship and dating of this text, see *The Wisdom of Solomon*, ed. and tr. David Winston, *The Anchor Bible* (1979), 20–25.

197 **Gospel according to the Egyptians** Clement, *Stromateis*, III, 45.3, 63.2, 92–93.

198 **The Book of Thomas the Contender**, 139:6–11, in *Gnostic Scriptures*, tr. Layton, 404; see also *Nag Hammadi Library in English*, 202.

198 **traditional saying"** Helmut Koester, "Introduction," *The Gospel of Thomas*, in *Nag Hammadi Library in English*, 125.

200 **sacred slavery** See Elm, "Pierced by Bronze Needles." She does not cite Matthew 20:27–28, which I quote from the Revised Standard Version; all earlier translations—of this passage, and parallels in Romans 1:1, Philippians 1:1, 1 Corinthians 9:19–23, Galatians 1:10, 1 Corinthians 7:22, Titus 1:1, James 1:1, Revelations 1:1, 7:3, 15:3, etc.—euphemize "slave" to "servant" or "minister."

201 **tattoos** See Elm, "Pierced by Bronze Needles," and C. P. Jones, "*Stigma*: Tattooing and Branding in Graeco-Roman Antiquity," *Journal of Roman Studies* 77 (1987), 139–155.

201 **aristocratic families** Meillassoux, *Anthropology of Slavery*, 138–140, 185–191.

201 **E. R. Leach,** *Rethinking Anthropology* (1961), 124–136.

201 **Claude Lévi-Strauss,** *La Pensée sauvage* (1962).

202 **Maurice Bloch,** *From Blessing to Violence: History and Ideology in the Circumcision Ritual of the Merina of Madagascar* (1986), 184, 168.

202 **end of the world** David C. Sim, *Apocalyptic Eschatology in the Gospel of Matthew* (1996).

204 **Rodney Stark,** *The Rise of Christianity: How the Obscure, Marginal Jesus Movement Became the Dominant Religious Force in the Western World in a Few Centuries* (1996), 3–28, 95–128.

204 **cultural memory** Taylor, *Cultural Selection*, 3–20, 74–81, 121–142.

205 **Sociobiologists** For this emphasis on the breeding imperative, often at the expense of the individual organism, see especially Edward O. Wilson, *Sociobiology: The New Synthesis* (1975), and Richard Hawkins, *The Selfish Gene*, rev. ed. (1989) and *The Extended Phenotype* (1989).

205 **"voluntary celibacy"** William Hendriksen, *New Testament Commentary: Exposition of the Gospel According to Matthew* (1973), 718; Douglas R. A. Hare, *Matthew* (1993), 222; Donald Senior, *Matthew*, Abingdon New Testament Commentaries (1998), 215. Even the Anchor Bible avoids the literal sense here, translating *eunuchs* as "those incapable of marriage," and glossing it in relation to celibacy: See *Matthew*, tr. Albright and Mann, 224, 227.

205 **"chaste"** The Tyndale, Geneva, and Bishops' Bibles had all put a figurative *chaste* in place of the literal *eunuchs*. See *The New Testament Octapla: Eight English Versions of the New Testament in the Tyndale-King James Tradition*, ed. Luther A. Weigle (1962), 112–113. Only the (Catholic) Rheims translation has the verb *geld*.

205 **castrate the text** That castrating exegesis may itself have been preceded by a much earlier act of textual expurgation—for although the other Gospels

record versions of what Jesus said about marriage immediately before this passage and what he said about children immediately after this passage, only Matthew preserves this disturbing central remark about eunuchs, which links the one to the other. However, there are many other examples of sayings preserved in only one Gospel, so willful omission from the other Gospels is impossible to prove.

206 **"recessive memes"** Taylor, *Cultural Selection*, 212–235.

206 **apocalyptic sects** See, for instance, C. R. Patrides and Joseph Wittreich, eds., *The Apocalypse in English Renaissance Thought and Literature* (1984); Walter Klaassen, *Living at the End of the Ages: Apocalyptic Expectation in the Radical Reformation* (1992); Katharine R. Firth, *The Apocalyptic Tradition in Reformation Britain, 1530–1645: Politics of Revelation in the English Renaissance* (1998).

206 **"beyond nature"** Ringrose, "Living in the Shadows," 99–109; Cheney gives a much fuller enumeration of high-ranking eunuchs in Byzantium (61–98).

206 **Skoptsy** Engelstein argues that the sect began very shortly before the authorities discovered it (*Russian Folktale*, 24–30), but the accounts she cites, if accurate, could push the founding self-castration back to the 1750s.

207 **Harmony Society** Favazza, *Bodies under Siege*, 180–181.

207 **Faulkner,** *Light in August*, 588, 742–743; Ruppersburg, *Reading Faulkner*, 265–266.

207 **whitest of the white** Middleton could have read of the unnatural pallor of eunuchs in Augustine or Claudian. Although *In Eutropium* had not yet been translated into English, Claudian was widely read in early modern Europe: His works, edited by Taddeo Ugoleto da Parma, were published in Venice in 1500, and subsequent Latin editions were published in Venice (1523), Florence (1519), London (1535), Antwerp (1571, 1585, 1596), Paris (1602), and Germany (1612).

208 **"spiritual marriage"** For the Christian valorization of conjugal unions without sexual union, see Dyan Elliott, *Spiritual Marriage: Sexual Abstinence in Medieval Wedlock* (1993). Middleton depicts such a marriage in *Hengist, King of Kent*; in *A Game at Chess*, the White Bishop's Pawn claims in his very first speech to "marry" the White Queen's Pawn through "religious joys" (rather than carnal ones).

209 **pawn his life** Middleton's adolescent praise of sterility uncannily anticipates even the language of a game at chess: *game* (4.36) and *pawns* (4.18)— although the latter is a verb.

The Future of Man

213 **vasectomy** David and Helen Wolfers, *Vasectomy and Vasectomania* (1974), 12–17; Stephen Trombley, *The Right to Reproduce: A History of Coercive Sterilization* (1988), 218–222; McLaren, *History of Contraception*, 252–253.

215 **sterilization of the unfit** F. B. Smith, *The People's Health, 1830–1910* (1979), 120.

216 **sterilization laws** J. H. Landman, *Human Sterilization: The History of the Sexual Sterilization Movement* (1932).

216 **70,000** Daniel Kevles, *In the Name of Eugenics: Genetics and the Uses of Human Heredity* (1985), 111–116.

216 **racism** Stefan Kuhl, *The Nazi Connection: Eugenics, American Racism, and German National Socialism* (1994); Edward Larson, *Sex, Race, and Hygiene:*

Eugenics in the Deep South (1995).

216 **"unfit" Danes** Trombley, *Right to Reproduce*, 159.

216 **Veracruz** Nancy Leys Stepan, *"The Hour of Eugenics": Race, Gender, and Nation in Latin America* (1991), 131–132.

216 **British Columbia** Angus McLaren, *Our Own Master Race: Eugenics in Canada, 1885–1945* (1990), 105.

216 **"removal of the gonads"** Michael Burleigh and Wolfgang Wippermann, *The Racial State: Germany 1933–1945* (1991), 48, 136–141.

216 **homosexuals** Richard Plant, *The Pink Triangle: The Nazi War against Homosexuals* (1986); Benno Muller-Hill, *Murderous Science: Elimination of Jews, Gypsies and Others, Germany 1933–1945* (1988).

216 **German population** Robert N. Proctor, *Racial Hygiene: Medicine under the Nazis* (1988).

216 **progressives** Atina Grossmann, *Reforming Sex: The German Movement for Birth Control and Abortion Reform, 1920–1950* (1995).

216 **Romania** Gail Kligman, *The Politics of Duplicity: Controlling Reproduction in Ceaucesceu's Romania* (1998).

217 **ethnic cleansing** Taylor, *Cultural Selection*, 249–252.

217 **improvements of livestock** Barbara A. Kimmelman, "The American Breeders' Association: Genetics and Eugenics in an Agricultural Context, 1903–1913," *Social Studies of Science* 13 (1983), 163–204.

217 **biological prostheses** Nissen, *Ancient Near East*, 15–38.

217 **Hegel** G. W. F. Hegel, *The Phenomonology of Mind*, tr. J. B. Baillie, rev. ed. (1949), 228–240.

217 **Nietzsche** *The Anti-Christ*, tr. Hollingdale, 3–4.

218 **scientific establishment** Catrine Clay and Michael Leapman, *Master Race: The Lebensborn Experiment in Nazi Germany* (1995), 181–196.

218 **artificial miscarriages** For the ancient pharmacological tradition (apparently confirmed by recent medical research) that recognized the juniper tree as an abortifacient, see John M. Riddle, *Contraception and Abortion from the Ancient World to the Renaissance* (1992).

219 **women . . . welcome** Castration among Europeans "consecrated to the Church"—according to a cynical Islamic observer—"was intended simply to prevent the monks from impregnating the nuns" (al-Djāḥiz, *Hayawan*, I, 12).

220 **Arthur C. Clarke,** *Imperial Earth* (1976), 47.

220 **Harvey Danger,** "Flagpole Sitta," on *Where Have All the Merrymakers Gone?* (1998).

221 **E. O. Wilson** *On Human Nature* (1978), 157.

221 **human genome** Pauline M. H. Mazumdar, *Eugenics, Human Genetics and Human Failings: The Eugenics Society, Its Sources and Its Critics in Britain* (1992), 256–268.

221 **Huntington's chorea** Ray L. White and Jean-Marc Lalouel, "Chromosome Mapping with DNA Markers," *Scientific American* 258 (1988), 40–48.

221 **E. O. Wilson,** *Consilience*, 273–278.

222 **kinky body sculpting** On this subculture see Robert Draper, "Farewell, My Lovelies," *Gentlemen's Quarterly* (April 2000), 245–252.

222 **Steve Mann,** "Humanistic Computing: 'Wearcomp' as a New Framework and Application for Intelligent Signal Processing," *Proceedings of the Institute of Electrical and Electronics Engineers* 86 (November 1998), 2123–2151.

222 **"body constructs"** Arthur Korker and Michael A. Weinstein, *Data Trash: The*

Theory of the Virtual Class (1994), 132–135.

223 **"humanity, mankind"** James Tiptree Jr., "Houston, Houston, Do You Read?" in *The 1977 Annual World's Best Science Fiction*, ed. Donald Wollheim (1977), 213–266.

223 **Suzy McKee Charnas**, *Motherlines* (1978), 79.

224 **Octavia E. Butler**, *Xenogenesis* (1989), 2, 3, 36, 189, 90.

224 **Iain M. Banks**, *Consider Phlebas* (1987), 201.

224 **Jesus and Buddha** Charles Pellegrino and George Zebrowski, *The Killing Star* (1995), 163–193.

224 **John Varley**, *Golden Globe*, 81, 3–11.

225 **R.E.M.**, "It's the End of the World as We Know It (and I Feel Fine)," on *Document* (1987).

225 **medieval art** Bynum, *Fragmentation and Redemption*, 93–117.

225 **immune rejection"** Nicholas Wade, "Human Cells Revert to Embryo State, Scientists Assert," *New York Times* 12 November 1998, A1, A24.

225 **Sudjai Panitphan** The on-line *Bangkok Post* (3 December 1999) reported that Sudjai Panitphan, a former hospital nurse, severed her relationship with her philandering husband in this way; "by the time it was found, too many cells had died and doctors could not re-unite it with its owner."

226 **Diderot, Denis**, *Le Rêve de d'Alembert*, ed. Jean Varloot et al. (1987), 153 (*Rêve*), 424–426 (*Éléments de Physiologie*); my translation.

227 **sexual constitutions"** Freud, *Three Essays on Sexuality*, 7:235.

227–28 **chimpanzees . . . in Europe"** Álvares, *Ethiopia Minor*, tr. Hair, chap. 1 (folios 50–51).

228 **pet monkeys** George Chapman, Ben Jonson, and John Marston, *Eastward Ho* (1605), sig. A4 (*"Beatrice leading a monkey after her"*). Monkeys or apes are called for in some other dramatic texts, but elsewhere were certainly or probably played by actors: See Berger, *Index of Characters*, under "monkey" and "ape(s)". Here, however, the monkey is a prop, and its dramatic function would only be served by the genuine article.

228 **page or monkey"** Middleton, *Michaelmas Term*, 1.2.320.

228 **play an o'ergrown ape"** Massinger, *The Bondman*, 3.3.83–85.

228 **Middleton . . . monkeys"** *A Mad World, My Masters* 3.3.141; *Wit at Several Weapons* 4.1.363.

229 **Edmund Spenser**, *The Faerie Queene* (1590), I, i, xiv–xxv.

229 **like an animal"** Nine Inch Nails, "Closer," on *The Downward Spiral* (1994).

229 **monster to man"** Diderot, *d'Alembert*, 152.

231 **Celia R. Daileader**, "The Uses of Ambivalence: Pornography and Female Heterosexual Identity," *Women's Studies* 26 (1997), 73–88.

232 **Peter Singer**, *Animal Liberation* (1975; rev. ed. 1990), and *Practical Ethics* (1979; rev. ed. 1993).

232 **"monster holiness"** Middleton, *Game at Chess*, 5.3.197 (of the Jesuit Black Bishop's Pawn).

Appendix

236 **excess of affect** For the "commodification of affect" by commercial theaters in early modern London, see Taylor, "Feeling Bodies," in *Shakespeare in the Twentieth Century*, 258–276. *A Game at Chess* produced more recorded affect, and was at the same time the most immediately lucrative commodity produced by that system.

236 Teresa de Lauretis, "The Stubborn Drive," *Critical Inquiry* 24 (1998), 864–867.

236 Harold Bloom, *Shakespeare: The Invention of the Human* (1998).

236 **cultural evolution** See Taylor, *Cultural Selection*, 43–68.

237 *Henry the Fourth, Part One* For the original political controversy over Shakespeare's play, see Gary Taylor, "The Fortunes of Oldcastle," *Shakespeare Survey* 38 (1985), 85–100.

238 **Aristophanes"** Sara Jayne Steen, *Ambrosia in an Earthern Vessel: Three Centuries of Audience and Reader Response to the Works of Thomas Middleton* (1993), 138.

238 **T. S. Eliot,** "Thomas Middleton" (1927), in *Selected Essays* (1951), 166.

238 **micro-politics** See the critical introduction and commentary to "*A Game at Chesse*: An Early Form" in Middleton, *Collected Works*.

238 **later additions** T. H. Howard-Hill was the first scholar to recognize the centrality and precedence of the pawn plot: See *Middleton's "Vulgar Pasquin": Essays on "A Game at Chess"* (1995), 25–76.

238 **pawn plot dominates** Scenes or parts of scenes entirely given over to the pawns: 838 lines. Scenes or parts of scenes entirely given over to the politicos: 709 lines (including material dealing with the White King's Pawn, who is not connected to the castration plot, but is linked to the other political impersonations). Scenes or parts of scenes mixing the pawn plot and the political plot (i.e. 1.1.244–294, 2.1.164–194, 2.2.100–266, 3.1.45–244, 4.2.1–134, 5.1.1–19, 5.3.185–196): 539 lines. In most of this third category, the action is initiated by the pawn plot, to which the politicos are responding. These statistics would be even more lopsided for the early form of the play, which does not contain the Fat Bishop and some other political material: pawn plot, 828; politicos, 466; mixed, 519.

242 **weapon** For the sexual pun, see Middleton's *The Phoenix* 2.3.181–182, 4.1.218. The pun is used visually, at a similarly climactic moment of the penultimate scene of Middleton's *The Lady's Tragedy* (a.k.a. *The Second Maiden's Tragedy*), when the adulterous wife "dies" on the "weapons" of two men.

242 **prefatory poem** In *Collected Works*, I include "The Picture Plainly Explained" among "Occasional Poems," and argue that it is Middleton's work.

243 **"Cock"** For the slang meaning "penis," see *OED*, *n.*[1], 20 (first example Nathan Field's play *Amends for Ladies*, printed in 1618). But Field's play was performed in 1610–1611, and the sexual sense was clearly used in 1609 in John Healey's *The Discovery of a New World*: "if her husband's cockship be any way declining" (III, 1; p. 138). Middleton supplies several examples: Compare "The cocks of age are dry" (*Phoenix* 6.95, 1603), the character "Cockstone" in *Michaelmas Term* (1605), and the Ward's speech in *Women Beware Women* (1621), which complains about eating aphrodisiacs: "Ne'er a one I eat but turns into a cock In four and twenty hours; if my hot blood Be not took down in time, sure 'twill crow shortly" (1.2.123–125).